I1029785

Milton and Scriptural Tradition

Milton and Scriptural Tradition
The Bible into Poetry

Edited by James H. Sims
and Leland Ryken

University of Missouri Press
Columbia, 1984

Library of Congress Cataloging in Publication Data

Main entry under title:

Milton and scriptural tradition.

   Contents: Introduction / Leland Ryken—Scriptural formula
and prophetic utterance in Lycidas / Michael Lieb—Paradise lost
and its biblical epic models / Leland Ryken—The council scenes
in Paradise lost / Sister M. Christopher Pecheux—[etc.]
   Includes index.
   1. Milton, John, 1608–1674—Religion and ethics—Addresses,
essays, lectures.   2. Bible in literature—Addresses, essays, lectures.   3. Bible—Influence—Addresses, essays, lectures.   4. Christian poetry, English—History and criticism—
Addresses, essays, lectures.   I. Sims, James H.   II. Ryken,
Leland.
PR3592.B5M54   1984   821'.4   83–16781
ISBN 0–8262–0427–9

In Memory of
KESTER SVENDSEN and ANTS ORAS
Hic Charis, atque Lepos

Preface

The essays gathered in this volume approach from various perspectives and with differing emphases the question of how Milton responded as an artist to Scripture and to scriptural tradition—of how he transformed the Bible into poetry. Yet, except for Leland Ryken in his Introduction, the essayists do not define the phrase *scriptural tradition*; they do not describe the particular aspect of the many-sided Milton coupled with that phrase by the noncommittal *and*. These scholars imply by their discussions, however, an understanding of "scriptural tradition" very much like Milton's own: "scriptural" excludes the apocryphal, the noncanonical, and "tradition" is limited to the interrelationships and literal meanings of the texts that comprise Scripture and to what can be reasonably inferred from those texts, taking into account the principle of the analogy of faith—that is, treating the Bible as one inspired book without internal contradictions and, therefore, interpreting particular passages in the light of the clear tenor of the whole of scriptural teaching. Certainly much that appears in Milton's works and some of the material in these essays will not fit within such a narrow definition; but tradition from pagan, parascriptural, or speculative sources, even that tradition which results from the theological systems of individual Christian thinkers (Saint Augustine, John Calvin, Martin Luther), is always distinguished by Milton from that tradition which his Spirit-led reason convinces him is firmly rooted in the text of Scripture, correctly understood. For instance, for his epic voice, the biblical description of Eden and the list of four rivers that flow from it (Gen. 2:8–14) locate the Garden as "*Assyrian*," not Ethiopian, though Mount Amara has been "by som suppos'd / True Paradise" (*PL*, 4.281–82). The Ethiopian hypothesis yields the striking image of the "shining Rock / A whole day's journy high" (283–84), but Milton's narrator cannot admit unchallenged error into his account, no matter how scenic an effect he could achieve. Mount Amara can be admired and can lend its aura of secluded security to the Mount of Eden, but the believer-poet must finally reject it as unscriptural for the truth's sake.

But the epic voice is not properly the subject of the following essays, except for the very last. For just as *scriptural tradition* indicates tradition growing out of and unmistakably grounded in Scripture, *Milton*, in the title of this collection and throughout most of the essays, indicates the historical poet, John Milton, who believed in Scripture as the Word of God, shaped his poetry according to his understanding of that Scripture, and filled in with scriptural features the forms he constructed from their surface adornment to the deepest level of their divine and human characters and actions. When in the Afterword special attention is given to Milton's persona, the mask is seen as fundamentally identical, on one score at least, with Milton the seventeenth-century poet: both are concerned constantly to clarify and proclaim Truth, insofar as that is possible in a world so full of contradictory claims on one's imagination and belief. The Scripture and its interpreter, the Spirit, can reveal the truth and expose falsehood; but if they, responded to with the full use of God's gift of Right Reason, do not set truth and falsehood in clear contrast, then one may hold two or more reasonable alternatives in suspension, assuming that to believe only one and reject the others is unjustified by the evidence and unnecessary to one's spiritual development; though one may prefer a particular alternative, one cannot declare it as absolute truth—it is matter of opinion, not of knowledge or faith. For instance, which is the center of our universe, the sun or the earth? Adam never receives an answer to this question, and he really does not need to know during his lifetime; either hypothesis, within his present situation, explains appearances satisfactorily. As Raphael tells him, he must learn (and, we are aware, demonstrate to many generations of readers) that "to know / That which before us lies in daily life, / Is the prime Wisdom" (*PL*, 8.192–93).

Within the evolving critical context described in the Introduction, the following essays move from Milton's use of scriptural formula in *Lycidas* through a few ramifications of scriptural principles in Milton's epics: for *Paradise Lost*, the basic epic form, the supernatural councils, the demonic counterpart to divine creation, God's name as the key to his character and to his desired relationship with his creatures; and for *Paradise Regained*, the peculiarly Johannine character of Jesus. Then Milton's concept of the nature of God's covenant with men is shown to be essential to a full understanding of much of his poetry. Finally, an Afterword examines the tension felt by Milton's epic voice in *Paradise Lost* and *Paradise Regained* between loyalty to scriptural tradition and fascination with wide-ranging lore from many sources, a tension eased by an awareness of areas of thought where a doctrinaire stance is inappropriate, where alternatives may be freely entertained.

James H. Sims
Hattiesburg, Mississippi
November 1983

Acknowledgments

For their generous support in many ways, the editors are especially grateful to Wheaton College and to the University of Southern Mississippi.

For the initial capitals heading each essay in this book, the editors wish to thank the Henry E. Huntington Library and the Ellis Library, University of Missouri—Columbia. The capitals are reproduced from the same edition of the King James Version of the Bible as was owned by John Milton, an edition printed in London in 1612 by Robert Barker. The frontispiece is from the same Bible, courtesy of the Henry E. Huntington Library.

The editors wish to acknowledge with thanks for their always considerate and efficient assistance with correspondence and manuscript preparation the invaluable help of Emma Lou Roberts, Catherine Rhodes Adams, and Jane Massengale.

For Mary Ryken and Elizabeth Sims, the editors record here in inadequate words their gratitude; such encouragement as these dear companions provide makes scholarly effort possible.

J. H. S.
L. R.

Contents

Note on Texts and Abbreviations

Unless otherwise indicated, all biblical citations are to the King James Version, known also as the Authorized Version (AV). The Revised Standard Version is abbreviated parenthetically as RSV.

Unless otherwise indicated, the following editions have been used for quotations from the works of Milton: *The Complete Prose Works of John Milton*, gen. ed. Don M. Wolfe (New Haven: Yale University Press, 1953–1982), 8 vols., cited throughout as *CPW*. *The Works of John Milton*, gen. ed. Frank Allen Patterson (New York: Columbia University Press, 1931–1938), 18 vols., cited throughout as *Works*.

In parenthetical references, Milton's works have been abbreviated as follows: *CD*, *Christian Doctrine*; *PL*, *Paradise Lost*; *PR*, *Paradise Regained*.

Milton and Scriptural Tradition

Introduction

Leland Ryken

he topic of this book is paradoxically both old and new. The roots reach back three centuries, to the time when editors of Milton began commenting on the poet's indebtedness to the Bible. Yet the present collection of essays is also a contribution to a critical approach that is just beginning to emerge. What is new is the way in which critics view the Bible, which in turn determines how they view the relationship between it and Milton's poetry.

If we are willing to simplify for the sake of clarity, we can contrast the old and new approaches to the subject in terms of the following dichotomies.

1. Instead of viewing the Bible as a source for Milton's poetry, critics now consider it as an influence and model.

2. Instead of emphasizing biblical content, critics are interested in biblical genres.

3. Instead of using the Bible to identify the origin of Milton's poetry, critics use the Bible as an interpretive context for examining the poetry.

4. Instead of finding biblical allusions in Milton's poetry, critics conduct intertextual readings in which the important thing is the interaction between the Bible and Milton's poetry.

5. Instead of viewing the Bible as primarily doctrinal, critics look upon it as a work of imagination.

The two halves of these pairs are not mutually exclusive, nor do I wish to sever new approaches from more traditional ones. But in each case the center of gravity has shifted.

The new approaches to the topic of Milton's relationship to the Bible have resulted chiefly from different ways of looking at the Bible. As I survey the field in this introduction, therefore, my focus will be on the nature of the Bible itself as a literary text,

3

since this is the starting point for any discussion of how the Bible enters Milton's poetry. My purpose in the introduction is to provide an overview of the current critical climate on the subject, noting how the essays in this volume fit into the landscape and suggesting directions that future discovery might take in this ever-expanding scholarly universe.

The Bible as an Influence and Model

It was C. S. Lewis who established the important distinction between the Bible as a literary source and as a literary influence. In his words, "A source gives us things to write about; an influence prompts us to write in a certain way."[1] That the Bible gave Milton material about which to write is a self-evident and somewhat exhausted topic. But the impact of the Bible on *how* Milton wrote is very much on the cutting edge of criticism. It is a topic, moreover, that is broader than Lewis's term *influence* suggests, since it includes the idea of literary models that Milton studied and followed.

Milton's use of the Bible as a model or influence encompasses an immense range of techniques. A good starting point is the style of the Bible as a whole. Its most notable feature is its combination of two distinct stylistic tendencies. One is the elemental simplicity that is particularly characteristic of the Hebrew language and mind, whether in the Old Testament or in the New. This strand in the Bible is characterized by a reliance on simple, concrete, elemental images. Such simplicity is complemented by a grand style in which the keynotes are sublimity, grandeur, stateliness, and abstraction. These two tendencies are even more prevalent in the King James Bible than in the Hebrew and Greek originals.[2] Milton's poetry is built out of a similar mixture of the simple and the grand, the concrete and the abstract. This has

1. *The Literary Influence of the Authorized Version* (1950; rpt. Philadelphia: Fortress Press, 1967), p. 15.
2. Some excellent material on the style of the English Bible has been brought together by D. G. Kehl, ed., *Literary Style of the Old Bible and the New* (Indianapolis: Bobbs-Merrill, 1970). See also J. C. Gardiner, *The Bible as English Literature* (New York: Charles Scribner's Sons, 1906).

been noted, but its indebtedness to the influence of the Bible
has not.[3]
  The Bible has its own descriptive technique. Erich Auerbach
pioneered in delineating the unembellished nature of the biblical style, a style that gives only minimal information and requires the reader to fill in the details.[4] Milton's descriptive technique shows a similar tendency, though its sources have been
incorrectly identified (usually as a result of his blindness or the
influence of classicism). In discussing Milton's portrayal of Paradise, C. S. Lewis correctly analyzed how Milton, "while seeming
to describe his own imagination . . . must actually arouse ours,"[5]
and it is a commonplace of Milton criticism that Milton's visual
imagination aims at general rather than particularized effects.[6]
Philip Hobsbaum uses the word *indeterminacy* to describe this
style, a style in which descriptions are "left to be filled in by the
imagination," as Raleigh long ago noted. It is a style that demands the "answering imagination" of the reader.[7]
  Consider, for example, the following two descriptions of
Paradise:

> And higher than that wall a circling row
> Of goodliest trees loaden with fairest fruit. (*PL*, 4.146–47)

> And out of the ground made the Lord God to grow every tree that
> is pleasant to the sight, and good for food. (Gen. 2:9)

  3. W. B. C. Watkins, for example, notes the presence of these two styles in Milton's account of Creation but does not link them to the Bible, even though Genesis 1 and 2 themselves are built on these complementary styles. See *An Anatomy of
Milton's Verse* (Baton Rouge: Louisiana State University Press, 1955), pp. 62–64.
  4. *Mimesis: The Representation of Reality in Western Literature* (Princeton: Princeton University Press, 1953), esp. chap. 1. Robert Alter has also recently demonstrated "the Bible's highly laconic mode of narration" in *The Art of Biblical Narrative* (New York: Basic Books, 1981), p. 184.
  5. *A Preface to Paradise Lost* (New York: Oxford University Press, 1942), p. 49.
  6. For a representative treatment, see Phyllis MacKenzie, "Milton's Visual
Imagination: An Answer to T. S. Eliot," *University of Toronto Quarterly* 16 (1946):
17–26.
  7. Hobsbaum, *A Theory of Communication* (London: Macmillan, 1970), p. 39;
Walter Raleigh, *Milton* (London: Edward Arnold, 1922), p. 223. I have taken the
phrase *answering imagination* from Ray L. Hart, *Unfinished Man and the Imagination* (New York: Herder and Herder, 1968), p. 260.

5

The descriptive strategy in both passages is identical: a reliance on general descriptive terms that activate readers to fill the words with a particular content from their own memories and imaginations. What Hobsbaum says of Milton's style is equally true of the biblical account: "Each imagination . . . is likely to fill in something different; the reader will get very little out of this passage unless he has a gift for fiction."[8] Milton's adherence to the biblical model on this score may be one reason his poetry has proved such a ready point of illustration for recent critical theories of the active participation of readers in the literary process.

Biblical style also relies heavily on repetition as a rhetorical and rhythmic principle. The best illustration is the parallelism of thought that is the basic element in biblical poetry, but patterns of repetition are also characteristic of biblical narrative, lyric, and oratory.[9] Repetition is equally a staple of Milton's poetry. *Lycidas* provides an obvious illustration,[10] but Milton's major poems also reveal examples of repetition, many of them rooted in a similar technique in the Bible. In the present volume, Michael Lieb traces how the biblical formula *once more—no more* forms a central iterative pattern in *Lycidas*, and Michael Fixler does something similar with the words *all* and *love* as names for God in *Paradise Lost*.

Especially noteworthy is the Bible's use of incremental repetition, which takes many forms. It can occur in a narrative genre

8. Hobsbaum, *Theory of Communication*, p. 38. For documentation that the Bible also partakes of the same tendency that Milton displays toward general rather than specific visual effects, see Dom Aelred Baker, "Visual Imagination and the Bible," *Downside Review* 84 (1966): 349–60.

9. Studies of Hebrew parallelism in poetry include James L. Kugel, *The Idea of Biblical Poetry: Parallelism and Its History* (New Haven: Yale University Press, 1981); Stephen A. Geller, *Parallelism in Early Biblical Poetry* (Missoula: Scholars Press, 1979); and George Buchanan Gray, *The Forms of Hebrew Poetry* (1915; rpt. n.p.: KTAV Publishing House, 1972). For repetition, see James Muilenburg, "A Study of Hebrew Rhetoric: Repetition and Style," *Vetus Testamentum Supplements* 1 (1953): 97–111; P. C. Sands, *Literary Genius of the New Testament* (1932; rpt. Westport, Conn.: Greenwood Press, 1970), pp. 50–55, 142–45; Robert C. Culley, *Studies in the Structure of Hebrew Narrative* (Philadelphia: Fortress Press, 1976); and Alter, *Art of Biblical Narrative*, pp. 88–113.

10. As shown by the analysis of Josephine Miles, "The Primary Language of *Lycidas*," in *Milton's "Lycidas": The Tradition and the Poem*, rev. ed., ed. C. A. Patrides (Columbia: University of Missouri Press, 1983), pp. 86–91.

such as the annunciation story, which can be traced from Sarah through the mother of Samson through Hannah through Zechariah/Elizabeth to its climax in the story of Mary. The same principle of incremental repetition can involve as small a unit as the phrase *yet once more* (as discussed in Lieb's essay). Milton's longer works are replete with such incremental repetition. To cite a single instance, Eve's love song in *Paradise Lost* (4.139–56) is built on the rhetorical contrast "with thee/without thee." Once introduced into the poem, the same formula reappears with ever richer nuances at several key points in the story: when Eve tempts Adam to share her sin (9.877–80), when Adam chooses to fall with Eve (9.906–10), when the human couple leaves the garden forgiven by God and each other (12.615–17). What is Milton's model for such an effective use of incremental repetition in a long story? The most crucial influence may well prove to be the Bible. G. K. Hunter has claimed that reading the Bible is "an accumulative experience, as the same ideas, images, phrases, echo and re-echo and move towards clarification and total coherence," and he has noted further that *Paradise Lost* imitates this tendency "in a way that separates it from its classical models."[11]

There are other stylistic traits of Milton's poetry that can profitably be viewed in the light of biblical style. Milton's use of personification has never received the attention it deserves.[12] From "the meek-eyed Peace" of the *Nativity Ode*, to the personified abstractions of the twin poems, to the evocative personifications of Time and Patience in Sonnets 7 and 19, to "Camus, reverend sire" in *Lycidas*, to the grand personifications of *Paradise Lost*, personification was a Miltonic staple. Some of his great personifications become leading actors in the poems.

The only other place that I know of where personification has a similar prominence and vitality is the Bible: "sin is couching at the door" (Gen. 4:7, RSV). "Lift up your heads, O ye gates" (Ps. 24:7). "O send out thy light and thy truth: let them lead me; let them bring me to thy holy hill" (Ps. 43:3). "Mercy and truth are met together; righteousness and peace have kissed each other"

11. *Paradise Lost* (London: George Allen and Unwin, 1980), pp. 46–47.
12. The only study that I can recall is that by A. L. Keith, "Personification in Milton's *Paradise Lost*," *The English Journal* 17 (1928): 399–409.

↑ descriptive adjective, noun, or phrase with or in...

(Ps. 85:10). "Then when lust hath conceived, it bringeth forth sin: and sin, when it is finished, bringeth forth death" (James 1:15). I would suggest that Milton developed the ability to give such vivid and palpable form to abstractions by intuitively appropriating it from passages such as these in the Bible.

√ Milton was as much a master of epithets as he was of personification. Epithets were essential to his exalted style in general and his epic genre in particular. A study of the correspondence between his specific epithets and those in Scripture will show the degree to which Milton's epithets were influenced by the Bible.[13]

Milton's religious subject matter generated a need for models of specific modes of discourse. Perhaps the best example is his choice of heavenly characters, scenes, and events, which necessitated a rhetoric of transcendence. In describing such spiritual reality, "Milton's debt to Scripture extended to method as well as images and scenes."[14]

The examples I have cited are only specimens. The stylistic traits in Milton that have been influenced by the Bible are still being discovered, partly because we are still on the edge of discovering the literary nature of the Bible itself. I can only say that, having been alerted to the possibility, I find much that critics say about Milton's style and rhetoric capable of being linked to the Bible. Scott Elledge, for example, has noted that some common rhetorical features in *Paradise Lost* are the narrator's involvement of his reader by the use of the pronoun *our*, the interjection *O*, and apostrophe.[15] All three happen to be common
√ rhetorical features in various parts of the Bible.

√ The influence of the biblical style on Milton's versification is

13. To cite just one example, S. Vernon McCasland, in "Some New Testament Metonyms for God," *Journal of Biblical Literature* 68 (1949): 99–113, discusses fifteen New Testament metonyms for God ("Power," "The Most High," "Creator," and so on). One is struck at once by how many of these are also common in Milton.

14. Michael Murrin, "The Language of Milton's Heaven," in *The Allegorical Epic* (Chicago: University of Chicago Press, 1980), p. 158. Murrin's essay shows that Milton used biblical models in describing transcendental reality. See also Michael Lieb, *Poetics of the Holy: A Reading of "Paradise Lost"* (Chapel Hill: University of North Carolina Press, 1981).

15. Scott Elledge, ed., *Paradise Lost* (New York: W. W. Norton, 1975), pp. xxiii–xxiv.

8

another study that calls for exploration. The time is ripe for a volume on biblical style comparable to F. T. Prince's book *The Italian Element in Milton's Verse*. Such a volume will show that the impulse toward parallelism in its variety of specific forms (repetition, antithesis, balance, completion) and the sense of onward momentum in the verse paragraph are characteristic of both biblical poetry and Milton's prosody. Reading an Old Testament psalm produces an effect very similar to what happens when we read one of Milton's verse paragraphs, and analysis is capable of showing how the one has influenced the other. Among other things, such an analysis would partly explain Milton's typical strategies of parallel construction, apposition, and catalog. Prince ascribes to Italian influence the frequency with which Milton's sonnets employ parallel constructions joined by the coordinates *and* or *or*.[16] Yet the same tendency toward doublets exists in biblical poetry, where the need to restate the same content in different words even led to a system of fixed pairs of words that conventionally appear together.[17]

If Milton's style is influenced by the Bible, so are the events and characters in his stories. In saying this I again do not primarily mean the obvious fact that the Bible was a *source* for Milton's characters and events, but that the Bible influenced them in more subtle ways. Milton got the basic story for *Samson Agonistes* from Judges, but the actual characterization of Samson as a hero of repentance who learns wisdom by adversity is modeled partly on the biblical characterization of David (and Puritan interpretations of the scriptural data).[18] The Harapha episode is Milton's invention, but it is colored throughout by the biblical story of David and Goliath. Sometimes it is even a specific version of

16. *The Italian Element in Milton's Verse* (Oxford: Oxford University Press, 1954), pp. 94–97.

17. The best studies are by William Whallon, "Formulaic Poetry in the Old Testament," *Comparative Literature* 15 (1963): 1–14, and "Old Testament Poetry and Homeric Epic," *Comparative Literature* 18 (1966): 113–31; and Stanley Gevirtz, *Patterns in the Early Poetry of Israel* (Chicago: University of Chicago Press, 1963, 1973).

18. See Miriam Muskin, "'Wisdom by Adversity': Davidic Traits in Milton's *Samson*," *Milton Studies XIV*, ed. James D. Simmonds (Pittsburgh: University of Pittsburgh Press, 1980), 233–55.

the Bible that influenced Milton's handling of characters and events.[19] In the present volume, John Shawcross's essay explores how Milton's understanding of the biblical idea of covenant influenced characters and events in his poetry, Fixler shows how the preoccupation with the names of God in the Bible influenced such specific scenes in *Paradise Lost* as the angelic hymn in book 3 and Adam's emerging consciousness in book 8, and Stella Revard demonstrates how the Gospel of John left its imprint on the characterization of Jesus and the dialectic between divine truth and Satanic falsehood in *Paradise Regained*.

Milton's transformation of classical genres such as elegy, epic, and tragedy has been one of the most prominent themes of recent Milton criticism. In a variety of ways, Milton's poems themselves insist on the reader's paying attention to what Milton has done with his classical models. In general, critics have attributed Milton's transformation of classical genres to his Christian world view. What needs to be demonstrated, however, is how often Milton's strategy has been influenced by the literary forms found in the Bible. Two essays in the present volume make exactly that attempt: Sister Christopher Pecheux's discussion of the demonic and celestial councils in *Paradise Lost* in the light of biblical precedents, and my own analysis of *Paradise Lost* as an anti-epic based on biblical models.

To speak of the influence of the Bible on Milton's poetic style and narrative technique is to open up a topic so broad that it can easily dissipate into vagueness and unsupported impressionism. One way to guard against that tendency is to take a single book of the Bible and show how it has influenced a specific Miltonic poem or strategy. Examples in this book are Revard's analysis of how the Gospel of John influenced *Paradise Regained*, Harold Fisch's exploration of links between Milton's portrayal of evil and the book of Job, and my suggestion that three epic books in the Bible (Genesis, Exodus, and Revelation) offered Milton a model for writing the particular type of epic that we find in *Paradise Lost*.

19. See George Wesley Whiting, *Milton and This Pendant World* (1958; rpt. New York: Octagon Books, 1969), pp. 129–68, 201–22.

To sum up, William Riley Parker, after noting that Milton's own copy of the English Bible was a 1612 edition of the King James Version (perhaps given to him by his parents on his fourth birthday), makes the claim that "its diction, its imagery, its rhythms, early became a part of him."[20] My remarks on biblical influence have suggested some avenues by which the truth of Parker's claim can be demonstrated.

Biblical Genres

Milton's own theory that the Bible is a repository of literary genres is capsulized in a passage in *The Reason of Church Government* in which he lists pastoral drama, tragedy, odes, hymns, and songs as biblical genres.[21] That he is thinking in terms of generic construction is evident from his comment that biblical songs are incomparable "over all the kinds of lyric poesy," not in "their divine argument alone, but in the very critical art of composition" (p. 816).

Modern scholarship is only beginning to catch up with Milton's thinking about the Bible as a source of literary genres emulated by Christian poets of the Renaissance. These genres partly parallel classical ones, a fact that functions as a curb on the claims that can be made for Milton's indebtedness to biblical models. But the Bible is also filled with genres unique to itself and that need to be related to Milton's poetry.

The genres of the Bible extend from the very large to the very specific. The Bible as a whole is a sacred book, encyclopedic in scope and comprising a compendium of smaller genres. The chief genres are narrative, lyric, drama, vision, discourse, and epistle. All of these except the last figure prominently in Milton's canon.[22] As a sacred book, the Bible as a whole is built around a single organizing pattern whose key points are creation, fall, re-

20. *Milton: A Biography* (Oxford: Oxford University Press, 1968), 1:10.
21. *CPW*, 1:813, 815–17.
22. In excluding the New Testament epistle from Milton's canon I have in view only the generic features of this biblical form. That the imagery and motifs of the New Testament epistles are present in Milton's poetry has been demonstrated by Timothy J. O'Keefe, *Milton and the Pauline Tradition: A Study of Theme and Symbolism* (Washington, D.C.: University Press of America, 1982).

demption, and apocalypse.[23] The extent to which Milton's imagination gravitated toward this pattern in nearly everything that he wrote has been partly but not fully explored.[24]

A host of smaller biblical genres can be identified and used to explain Milton's poetry and his modifications of classical genres. Within the genus *lyric*, for example, the Bible contains a number of species: praise psalm (with its constituent divisions of call to praise, motivation for praise, catalog, and resolution), psalm of lament (with its predictable five-part structure of invocation, complaint, petition, statement of confidence, and vow to praise God), encomium, doxology, prayer, confession, and thanksgiving. Barbara Lewalski has identified the lyric subgenres that Milton's Protestant tradition saw in the Bible.[25] It remains now for critics to explore how extensively and to what effect those enter Milton's poetry. The model for such explication is Mary Ann Radzinowicz's discussion of how the Old Testament psalms of lament, wisdom, trust, and thanksgiving permeate *Samson Agonistes*.[26] In the present volume, Fixler does something similar with selected psalms and the devotional mode of *Paradise Lost*.

Some of the most pervasive of all biblical forms are so small that we might call them formulas rather than genres. Milton's fellow Puritans tended to classify the whole Bible in terms of several of these formulas, including divine promises, commands, and threats. We can extend that list to include praise, curse, beatitude, taunt, doom song, prayer, confession, thanks, and adoration. Within the Bible, each of these tends to have its distinctive

23. For further comment on the unified structure of the Bible, see Northrop Frye, *The Great Code: The Bible and Literature* (New York: Harcourt Brace Jovanovich, 1982).

24. A good starting point is C. A. Patrides, *The Grand Design of God: The Literary Form of the Christian View of History* (London: Routledge and Kegan Paul, 1972). A good overview also exists in chap. 2 of Isabel MacCaffrey's *"Paradise Lost" as "Myth"* (Cambridge: Harvard University Press, 1959).

25. *Protestant Poetics and the Seventeenth-Century Religious Lyric* (Princeton: Princeton University Press, 1979).

26. *Toward "Samson Agonistes": The Growth of Milton's Mind* (Princeton: Princeton University Press, 1978), pp. 208–26. Also excellent is the essay by John N. Wall, Jr., "The Contrarious Hand of God: *Samson Agonistes* and the Biblical Lament," *Milton Studies, XIV*, ed. James D. Simmonds, 117–39.

content, rhetoric, and tone, and when they appear in Milton's
poetry, they tend to retain the qualities of the biblical original.

Consider, for example, Raphael's solemn commands to Adam
near the end of book 8 of *Paradise Lost*:

> Be strong, live happie, and love, but first of all
> Him whom to love is to obey, and keep
> His great command; take heed least Passion sway
> Thy Judgement. . . ;
> > beware. . . .
> I in thy persevering shall rejoyce,
> And all the Blest: stand fast. (633–40)

The solemnity of the moment—indeed, its very nature—
emerges with its full imaginative power only if a reader can hear
the commands in a context of the command genre as it appears
in the Bible. This is especially true when we have in mind the
specific commands that Milton echoes in the passage: "Finally,
my brethren, be strong in the Lord" (Eph. 6:10); "If ye love me,
keep my commandments" (John 14:15); "let him that thinketh
he standeth take heed lest he fall" (1 Cor. 10:12); "Watch ye,
stand fast in the faith, . . . be strong" (1 Cor. 16:13).

If the command seems almost too small to rate as a biblical
genre, visionary literature seems almost too big and amorphous.
Its two main subtypes in the Bible are prophecy and apocalypse.
Visionary poetry is a notoriously elusive form, and a great deal
more descriptive work remains to be done on the biblical texts
(especially their characteristic imagery and rhetoric). As the pio-
neering work of Joseph Wittreich has shown,[27] the more we learn
about the poetic strategies of visionary poetry in the Bible, the
better we will understand some of the most striking effects in
Milton's major poems.

One of the most notable advances of recent criticism of Milton
in the light of biblical genres has been to show that many fea-

27. *Angel of Apocalypse: Blake's Idea of Milton* (Madison: University of Wisconsin
Press, 1975); "'A Poet Amongst Poets': Milton and the Tradition of Prophecy," in
Milton and the Line of Vision (Madison: University of Wisconsin Press, 1975), pp.
97–142; *Visionary Poetics: Milton's Tradition and His Legacy* (San Marino, Calif.:
Henry E. Huntington Library, 1979).

tures of Milton's poetry that were previously thought to be wholly classical are also biblical. More often than not, Milton's handling of a given motif has been deeply influenced by the biblical version. Epic is an obvious case in point. The Bible is filled with epic motifs; indeed, it contains whole epics within it, as my essay later in this volume demonstrates. Equally important are the specific epic patterns within the Bible: the divine council, celestial battle, the vision of the future, epic epithets, invocation, supernatural agents and settings. Milton's version of such motifs is not necessarily more biblical than classical, but the biblical influence has traditionally been obscured and is what now needs to be established. Sister Christopher Pecheux's study of the supernatural council in the Bible and *Paradise Lost* does so for one of these epic motifs.

It has become a commonplace of biblical criticism that the generic and rhetorical forms derived from classical literature fail to describe accurately or fully the literature of the Bible. Amos Wilder has said in regard to the Bible that "when we bring such basic categories into play as those of Aristotle we are moving in a different world."[28] Milton's poetry has traditionally been discussed in terms of classical genres. Biblical scholarship has now provided a lexicon of biblical genres and subtypes that only partially overlap with classical genres. Milton criticism is ready to make the application to the poetry of Milton.

The Bible as Interpretive Context

My comments about the Bible as an influence and a source of genres have anticipated the concept that the Bible consistently provides a context within which Milton's poetry reveals its fullest meanings to a reader. The theoretic principle underlying my remarks is Northrop Frye's premise that "the central activity of criticism . . . is essentially one of establishing a context for the works of literature being studied. This means relating them to other things."[29]

28. *Early Christian Rhetoric: The Language of the Gospel* (Cambridge, Mass.: Harvard University Press, 1971), p. 35.
29. *The Stubborn Structure* (Ithaca: Cornell University Press, 1970), p. 88.

To look upon the Bible as the assumed interpretive framework for Milton's poetry is an outgrowth of two venerable branches of Milton criticism: the scholarly practice of finding biblical allusions or background for specific passages, and the history of ideas criticism. Here, too, there is a new slant in recent criticism. Contextual criticism of the new type has shifted the focus from the author to the reader, from origin to meaning. The governing question now is not where Milton got his material but how an awareness of the biblical context helps a reader to understand Milton's poetry. And whereas history of ideas criticism has traditionally been preoccupied with ideas, contextual criticism now is more likely to be concerned with specifically literary dimensions of the Bible—a biblical event or characterization or image, for example, rather than a doctrine.

Once alerted to the principle of interpreting Milton's poetry in a biblical framework, we can find the principle operating at both minute and large levels. An example of the former occurs in *Samson Agonistes* when Dalila claims to Samson that she was assured by the Philistine lords who tempted her "that nothing was design'd / Against thee but safe custody, and hold" (lines 801–2). Milton here depends on the reader's placing Dalila's claim in the context of the biblical account; Judges 16:5 makes it clear that in their first overture to Dalila the lords had already told her their intention to bind Samson "to afflict him."

The Bible also provides a context for understanding some of Milton's most striking effects. Although Judges is the source for the story in *Samson Agonistes*, the essential character of Milton's Samson is illuminated more when placed into a context of the story of Job (whose suffering leads to illumination and union with God) and the encomium to faith in Hebrews 11 (where faith is defined and celebrated by its effects on various Old Testament believers). Or, to cite another case, none of Milton's epic characters taken from the Bible exists only in Milton's epics; these characters exist fully only in a context that includes the Bible's portrayal of them and commentary on them.

The critical procedure that I am describing builds on the older practice of identifying allusions. But it then proceeds to show how the reader's response and/or interpretation is affected by an awareness of the biblical context. The test of such criticism is not the proof of a parallel between two texts but the degree of illumination that results when a passage from Milton is put into a biblical framework (which is also implicitly assumed to be a source). For example, the effect of God's calling the garden into which he places Adam a "Mansion" (*PL*, 8.296) and a "seat prepar'd" (8.299) depends on a reader's ability to assimilate the description in terms of one of the most evocative of all Gospel passages: "In my Father's house are many mansions. . . . I go to prepare a place for you" (John 14:2).

Or, to cite another local effect in *Paradise Lost*, when Satan rises from the burning lake in book 1, the physical action is compared to that of a volcanic eruption. The narrator's comment, "Such resting found the sole / Of unblest feet" (1.237–38), is no more than a description embellished by irony and pun until it is received as a fulfillment of the series of curses uttered in Deuteronomy 28, one of which is, "neither shall the sole of thy foot have rest" (28:65).

The interpretive potential of the Bible is particularly active in Milton's longer works, where Milton faced "the problem of expanding Scripture without distorting the Word of God."[30] Milton was especially adept at using single brief comments from the Bible as his guiding principle for building whole scenes in his epics. Much of the dynamics of the Fall in *Paradise Lost*, for example, is explained by the comment in 1 Timothy 2:14 that "Adam was not deceived, but the woman being deceived was in the transgression." This New Testament comment is an interpretation of an Old Testament story and is only one of many examples of how the Bible itself gave Milton suggestions for how to elaborate a brief biblical episode into an extended epic or dramatic scene, in keeping with clues contained in the Bible. An awareness of this, in turn, can help a reader put Milton's passage into focus. A passage in Romans 3 says regarding the wicked that their "mouth is full of cursing and bitterness" and that they will ultimately be judged by God, "that every mouth may be

30. It is expressed thus by Harold Bloom, *A Map of Misreading* (New York: Oxford University Press, 1975), p. 125.

stopped" (3:13, 19); Milton expands the situation into the vivid scene of the demons' punishment in book 10 of *Paradise Lost*.[31] Milton constructs his "primal scene" of God's exaltation of the Son from a few brief statements in Psalm 2:5–7 and Hebrews 1:5–6. In all of these instances, a reader's awareness of the biblical skeleton upon which Milton has fleshed out the episode provides an interpretive framework that helps to explain exactly what Milton is doing with the scene.

The Bible thus becomes a storehouse of interpretive statements, images, and stories that will enhance a reader's understanding of what is happening in Milton's poetry. It is not a question of proving a source but of illuminating a text. Lieb's essay, for example, shows how our interpretation of *Lycidas* is enhanced when we put the poem's formulas *once more* and *no more* into a biblical context. Revard's essay demonstrates that if a reader is familiar with the Gospel of John, numerous features of *Paradise Regained* fall into place and assume richer meanings. Sister Christopher's essay only asks us as readers to observe what happens when we read certain aspects of *Paradise Lost* in the light of the scriptural tradition of the supernatural council.

A knowledge of the biblical background of Milton's poetry will sometimes be decisive in our choosing from among interpretive options. Consider, for example, the endlessly fascinating and controversial conversation between Adam and Eve prior to the Fall about working separately. Who has the more accurate arguments in the discussion? Eve's adventuresome spirit tends to win modern readers, but a crucial echo in Adam's last speech suggests something else. When Adam states, "Seek not temptation then, which to avoide / Were better" (*PL*, 9.364–65), we are much more likely to conclude that he is right if we recall that he is stating as a command a petition from the Lord's Prayer: "Lead us not into temptation, but deliver us from evil" (Matt. 6:13). How many examples of the same thing exist in Milton's poetry I do not know, but criticism is in an advantageous position to make interpretive use of the multitude of biblical allusions that editors

31. See Ernest W. Sullivan, "The Bible and Satanic Deceit: *Paradise Lost* X. 460–572," *English Studies* 61 (1980): 127–29.

have through an incremental process bequeathed to us. James Sims's *The Bible in Milton's Epics* remains the model for reading Milton's poetic effects in terms of a biblical context.

Contextual criticism provides content for Milton's poetry. It does so even for specific words and images. Consider the last line of Milton's most famous sonnet: "They also serve who only stand and wait." Kept within the context of the poem, the key words *serve, stand,* and *wait* are relatively bland. They cease to be so if one consults a biblical concordance and begins to catalog the relevant scriptural verses that provide a context of feeling and meaning for the words. A word like *new,* the last word in *Lycidas,* reverberates with meaning in the New Testament, where it possesses meaning and overtones lacking in ordinary contexts.[32] Or what is at stake when Milton speaks of God's eye or arm? If we trace such images through a series of biblical examples, we will find that the images suddenly take on a rich and specific content. A concordance to the Bible will reveal meanings in Milton's poetry that have remained only latent.

It is in connection with this matter of context that the idea of scriptural tradition becomes crucial. The Bible itself is a book that calls for interpretation. Writing in the milieu of Reformation controversy, Milton was well aware that what he or anyone else regarded as biblical truth was only what a given interpretive community had agreed upon as the right interpretation. For Milton, therefore, *scriptural tradition* meant the plain meanings of the biblical text and what can reasonably be inferred from that text. Milton's inferences are overwhelmingly those of Puritanism, broadly defined to mean non-Anglican Protestantism (though we must at the same time realize that on many issues of biblical interpretation Anglicans and Puritans represented a united Protestant tradition).[33]

32. R. A. Harrisville, "The Concept of Newness in the New Testament," *Journal of Biblical Literature* 74 (1955): 69–79, shows that the word implies "a qualitative as well as a temporal significance" and that "four distinctive features are found to be inherent in the concept of newness: the elements of contrast, continuity, dynamic, and finality."

33. The latest study to document Milton's adherence to the Protestant tradition of scriptural exegesis is by Georgia B. Christopher, *Milton and the Science of the Saints* (Princeton: Princeton University Press, 1982).

Puritan exegesis of Scripture, and on occasion the exegesis of other traditions (including the Hebrew), thus provides an important interpretive framework for Milton's poetry. This has long been recognized. Often, however, the exegetical tradition has been treated as an independent source, and the resulting criticism has been history of ideas criticism rather than what is in view in the present volume. The essay in this book by Shawcross shows how the Renaissance Protestant milieu represented an interpretation of biblical data that is active in Milton's poetry.

Milton criticism has been greatly enriched by studies that show how Protestant traditions of biblical exegesis found their way into Milton's poetry. Not much has been done, however, in the analysis of *Milton's* exegesis of a given book of the Bible as an interpretive framework for the poetry. What this will involve is an inquiry into the peculiarly Miltonic way of reading the Bible, in its individual parts or more generically. Such an analysis will surely prove fruitful when used as a context for illuminating how Milton used various parts of the Bible in his poetry. We already know how he used such exegetical principles as typology and accommodation, but the way is now open to see how his actual way of reading specific parts of the Bible also opens windows onto his poetry.

Intertextual Criticism

This book is a study of the reliance of texts upon texts. That study has developed into a highly sophisticated critical procedure. It bears hardly any resemblance to the older practice of finding sources for a work, though it is, of course, deeply indebted to source criticism. It does not even duplicate the analysis of allusions in works of literature.

The new procedure is built around the concepts of a pre-text and an intertext. The pre-text is any previous work that a writer assumes as a necessary framework for his work. The real meaning of the new work is not self-contained but consists of what lies *between* the texts. In such instances, the object of critical attention is the interaction that takes place between the two texts.

This critical procedure is closely tied to current literary theory, which stresses the continuity and interrelatedness of literary works. It shares the antipathy of formalist criticism to a preoccupation with "background material" that, once assembled, lies like a lifeless corpse beside the critic's attention to a literary work. Like formalist criticism, too, intertextual criticism is interested in close reading of the subtle nuances of a text. But the "text" is no longer single; it is bifocal, engaging two texts at the same time. Critics now read "interpoems," not simply poems, and the action considered worthy of critical comment is the dynamics of what happens between two works. In the words of Harold Bloom, the leading theorist of the movement, "there are *no* texts, but only relationships *between* texts."[34]

Intertextual criticism also implies a theory of composition. It shares with twentieth-century poetics the view that poets learn their art mainly from other poets. To use Milton's famous metaphor, books are not dead things; in fact, in the imaginations of great writers they reproduce themselves in the form of new poems. Intertextual criticism thus becomes a study of the ways of the creative imagination, an exploration of the creative uses that great writers make of their own reading experiences.

Because of Milton's vast assimilative abilities, his poetry has been prominent in the intertextual movement. The focus, however, has usually been on Milton's relation to classical texts or to English predecessors such as Spenser. The present volume seeks to correct that imbalance by suggesting that the Bible was Milton's single most important pre-text and that the majority of what he wrote can be read as an interpoem in which the Bible figures as one of the active ingredients. It is the presence of the Bible *in* Milton's poetry that is the crucial factor in this regard.

We should note at the outset that the Bible itself provided Milton with the classic example of intertextual literature. The Bible, a single book, is divided into two parts, significantly called the Old Testament and the New Testament. The second builds upon the first. There are several thousand allusions to the Old Testament in the New Testament,[35] and the majority of them involve

34. Bloom, *Map of Misreading*, p. 3.
35. See Henry M. Shires, *Finding the Old Testament in the New* (Philadelphia: Westminster Press, 1974).

some type of reinterpretation, whether large or small, of the earlier source. The result is a book, the New Testament, in which the Old Testament is a continuous presence—so continuous that Northrop Frye believes that references to the Old Testament "extend over every book—not impossibly every passage—in the New Testament."[36] The crucial principle is that the New Testament does not refute but rather fulfills the Old Testament. There is both continuity and change, both reverence for the pre-text and a radical reorientation of it, sometimes a replacement of it. The essay by Shawcross on the biblical idea of the covenant shows this principle in microcosm.

The relationship between Milton's poetry and the Bible follows the same pattern that Milton found within Scripture itself. Milton's poetry is consistently rooted in the Bible, not by way of static allusion but in such a way as to involve interaction or carryover between the two texts, with the second text often pushing the earlier one in a new direction. Perhaps we can say that Milton's poetry is engaged in an ongoing dialogue with the Bible as its pre-text, applying it to a new situation, as the New Testament applies the Old. Certainly Milton's poetry does not exist apart from the reader's awareness of the active presence of the Bible in it.

The precise ways in which the Bible enters Milton's poetry in this manner are varied. The possibilities include allusion, echo, parallel, antithesis or reversal (resulting in irony or parody), and the interpolation of a detail from the Bible into a new context. The biblical pre-text can provide imagery, scene, characterization, or action for Milton's poetry. Intertextual reading takes place whenever a person assimilates the poetry of Milton with a simultaneous awareness of something in the Bible. Intertextual reading is bifocal in nature. The interplay of the old and the new is crucial.

The model for intertextual criticism of Milton's poetry is, once again, Sims's *The Bible in Milton's Epics,* which reveals the range and specific ways in which the effects of Milton's poetry depend on the reader's awareness of something that existed in the Bible before Milton's poetry. All of the essays in the present volume

36. *The Great Code,* p. 79.

employ, in a variety of ways, a process of looking simultaneously at the biblical text and the poetry of Milton, and all of them are variations on the theme of how Milton made creative use of his reading of the Bible.

Robert Alter has popularized the idea of type-scenes in biblical narrative—a "grid of conventions upon which, and against which, the individual work operates." These scenes are based on "an elaborate set of tacit agreements between artist and audience about the ordering of the art work," agreements that are "at all times the enabling context in which the complex communication of art occurs." [37] With the grid of expectations as an implied context, what is often most crucial are the omissions and additions and transformations that a specific instance of the type contains.

Milton critics have historically been preoccupied with the presence of type-scenes from classical sources in Milton's poetry. But those from the Bible are equally important. Sister Christopher's essay explores the supernatural council as a biblical type-scene present in *Paradise Lost*, noting how Milton includes, omits, or changes the motif in various council scenes in *Paradise Lost*. Revard's essay in effect treats the challenge to Jesus' mission and the test by adversaries as type-scenes in the Gospel of John and then observes how they are present in *Paradise Regained*. In a variation on that procedure, my essay discusses how biblical epic models influenced Milton's treatment of various type-scenes from the classical epic tradition.

The Bible and the Literary Imagination

The Bible is today increasingly seen as it was during the Renaissance, as a work of imagination. This means, first of all, that it is a book in which the image, broadly defined, is dominant. The starting point for such a study is Northrop Frye's theory of literary archetypes and his treatment of the Bible as a grammar of those archetypes.[38] Among other things, Frye's list of archetypes shows a basic feature of the human imagination much in

37. *The Art of Biblical Narrative*, p. 47.

38. See especially *Anatomy of Criticism* (Princeton: Princeton University Press, 1957), pp. 141–50; and *The Great Code*, pp. 139–98.

evidence in the Bible, its tendency to divide reality into a dialectical pattern of opposites.

There is a remarkable paucity of literary analysis of biblical imagery.[39] An adequate study of the subject will need to take at least two forms. One is to identify in depth the master images of the Bible. A single major image like light turns out to be a complex biblical symbol.[40] It stands for God and, by extension, his heavenly dwelling. It implies moral goodness or holiness, and is contrasted to darkness. It pictures salvation and is linked especially with the redemptive activity of Christ. It symbolizes truth and understanding, as opposed to error or ignorance. And it represents joy, God's favor, and life, in contrast to sorrow and death. The fact that Merritt Hughes could conduct a comprehensive survey of criticism on Milton's light imagery without touching upon these complex biblical meanings is an index to how much remains to be done on the biblical imagination in Milton's poetry.[41]

In addition to an analysis of individual images, a study of biblical imagery should identify the images that characteristically cluster around key biblical themes, such as creation, judgment, heaven, hell, salvation, and the end. Such clusters are an index to how the imagination of biblical writers experienced and expressed reality.

Imagination, in short, is a way of perceiving reality, moral and spiritual as well as physical. It includes the habitual furniture of one's mind, a person's characteristic way of organizing and ex-

39. Such scholarship as exists is rudimentary. A cursory introduction to the topic is Stephen J. Brown, *Image and Truth: Studies in the Imagery of the Bible* (Rome: Officium Libri Catholici, 1955). Northrop Frye's discussion in *The Great Code*, pp. 139–98, does not trace any archetype through the Bible systematically, but it does indicate directions to follow. Another helpful source is Othmar Keel, *The Symbolism of the Biblical World: Ancient Near Eastern Iconography and the Book of Psalms*, trans. Timothy J. Hallett (New York: Seabury Press, 1978). In the final analysis, it may be best to use a biblical concordance and Bible dictionaries to build one's repertoire of master images of the Bible.

40. A good but cursory study is that by Elizabeth R. Achtemeier, "Jesus Christ, the Light of the World: The Biblical Understanding of Light and Darkness," *Interpretation* 17 (1963): 439–49.

41. "Milton and the Symbol of Light," in *Ten Perspectives on Milton* (New Haven: Yale University Press, 1965), pp. 63–103.

plaining experience. It includes the valuing mechanism by which a person attaches approval or aversion to the phenomena of existence.

No one's imagination develops in a vacuum. It is always influenced and nurtured from outside sources, chiefly written ones. Literary scholarship has long been aware of how a writer's intellectual milieu affects his or her thinking, but biblical scholarship provides a better model for viewing a writer's *literary* milieu as an influence on the writer's *imagination* and characteristic forms of expression. As long ago as 1942, Nils Wilhelm Lund approached the New Testament on the premise that the New Testament writers had had their imaginations nurtured on the "Hebrew literary models" of the Old Testament. These models, argued Lund, "were used in the liturgy of the temple and the synagogue, and soon came to be used for a similar purpose in the church. Under such circumstances, not only the religious and ethical conceptions, but also the vocabulary and literary style of the community as well, came to be influenced by its liturgical writings. . . . Among writers the forms of the Old Testament would be the literary models nearest at hand."[42] Lund rested his case on the presence of chiastic structures in the New Testament. Not everyone has found his illustrations convincing, but what strikes me about his theory is the thoroughness with which he believes that *literary* models (and not simply ideas) in a culture form a deep structure within a writer's imagination.

From Lund's early attempts we can turn to an example of the current state of the art. In his *Literary Patterns, Theological Themes, and the Genre of Luke-Acts*,[43] Charles H. Talbert theorizes and illustrates that "Luke's cultural context presented him with a suitable mode of expression" (p. 142). This concern to delineate the deep structure of a writer's "formal patterns, rhythms, architectonic designs, or architecture" on the basis of "a document's content and its roots in a cultural *Zeitgeist*" (p. 7) strikes me as different from the more ideational approach of traditional literary criticism, and more like the main thrust of the present book.

---

42. *Chiasmus in the New Testament: A Study in Formgeschichte* (Chapel Hill: University of North Carolina Press, 1942), pp. 24–28.

43. (Missoula: Scholars Press, 1974).

Milton's imagination was fostered to a significant degree by the Bible. A thorough study of the biblical imagination, either en masse or as it is exemplified in a given book, is a window to the salient features of Milton's imagination and poetry. Milton's poetry is often cut from the same fabric as the Bible, displaying the same modes of perception and feeling. Common to both is a way of seeing and a language of expressive symbols.

As a specimen case, consider the strongly ingrained tendency in the Bible toward antithesis or dualism. The Bible as a whole is a vast system of contrasts: good/evil, divine/human, God/Satan, angels/demons, history/eternity, light/darkness, before/after, now/then. A biblical scholar has identified ten types of dualism in the Bible, all of which permeate Milton's poetry.[44] It is a commonplace that for the New Testament writer Paul, antithesis was both a stylistic staple and a view of reality—the deep structure of his thinking. The habitual furniture of Milton's imagination includes exactly the same tendency toward antithesis. What Johannes Weiss says of Saint Paul can equally well be said of Milton: antithesis is a "deeply rooted habit and tendency of thought and speech, firmly imbedded in the very soul of a personality."[45] From the beginning of his poetic career to the end, the same contrasts that make up the individual and communal imagination of the biblical writers pervade the work of Milton.

If the dualistic tendency is a hallmark of Milton's imagination, so is its aphoristic bent. Aphorism is both a mode of thought and a literary form.[46] Milton's skill at aphorism is truly impressive. "They also serve who only stand and wait." "License they mean when they cry liberty." "I may oftener think on what He has bestowed than on what He has withheld." For what other author besides Milton do the titles for scholarly books and articles con-

44. John B. Gammie, "Spatial and Ethical Dualism in Jewish Wisdom and Apocalyptic Literature," *Journal of Biblical Literature* 93 (1974): 356–85.

45. Johannes Weiss, *Earliest Christianity* (1937; rpt. New York: Harper and Brothers, 1959), 2:413; see also 2:411–16, and Leonard L. Thompson, *Introducing Biblical Literature: A More Fantastic Country* (Englewood Cliffs: Prentice-Hall, 1978), pp. 285–86.

46. For the current state of proverb scholarship, see *The Wisdom of Many: Essays on the Proverb*, ed. Wolfgang Mieder and Alan Dundes (New York: Garland Publishers, 1981).

tain such frequent aphoristic quotations from the poet's works? People are not born with an aphoristic imagination; it is a mode of thought and expression that is developed and nurtured.

The Bible is the most aphoristic book in the world.[47] The Victorian poet Francis Thompson, in talking about how the Bible influenced his poetry, seized upon the fact that it is "a treasury of *gnomic* wisdom. I mean its richness in utterances of which one could, as it were, chew the cud. . . . Upon this single quality, I think, I finally would elect to take my stand in regard to the Bible; and by this it has firmest hold of me."[48] Its influence upon Milton, I would suggest, was similar.

To draw a connection between a pervasive tendency of the biblical and Miltonic imaginations as I have done with contrast and aphorism is one possible approach to the topic. An alternate procedure is to begin with a specific biblical text and then ask what passages in Milton's poetry are cut from the same imaginative fabric. G. Wilson Knight has written a provocative essay on the master symbols in the New Testament Gospels.[49] These archetypal images include vine, harvest, water, bread, sight, light, dark, orchard, hill, coins, garments, sheep, fruit, banquet, marriage, and women. If we turn from that imaginative matrix to specific Miltonic texts like the sonnets or *Lycidas*, the connections begin to appear all over the place. In Milton's imagination, moreover, the images tend to have specifically biblical content and associations, in a way that would not be true if we used Homer or Virgil for a subtext. What this shows, in my view, is that Milton's imagination was influenced more by the Bible than by any other source.

Once the imaginative links between Milton's poetry and the Bible come into focus, a host of questions have ready answers. Why did Milton write with such frequency and intensity about

47. The findings of modern biblical scholarship are well summarized in James G. Williams, *Those Who Ponder Proverbs: Aphoristic Thinking in Biblical Literature* (Sheffield: Almond Press, 1981). The book has full bibliographic apparatus.
48. "Books that Have Influenced Me," in *Literary Criticisms of Francis Thompson*, ed. Terence L. Connolly (New York: E. P. Dutton and Co., 1948), pp. 543–44.
49. "The Pioneer of Life: An Essay on the Gospels," in *The Christian Renaissance* (London: Methuen and Co., 1962), pp. 145–72.

light? Why is his mind so strongly binary (tending even to reduce the Trinity to a duality)? Why is heaven one of Milton's
most important poetic subjects, and why does he portray it as he
does? Why is Milton's God portrayed so anthropomorphically?
The essay in this book that explores the nature of the biblical
imagination and its counterpart in Milton's poetry is Fisch's study
of how Milton's pattern of imagery in his portrayal of Satan and
Hell in the early books of *Paradise Lost* is an extension of the
imaginative vision of the writer of Job.

As with the Bible itself, so with biblical traditions. The English
Puritan imagination possessed its own framework of expressive
symbols in terms of which it defined the world, expressed its feel-
ings, and made its judgments. There has been a rich tradition of
scholarship on the American Puritan imagination.[50] What the
criticism shows is how American Puritans assimilated the Bible
and transformed it into a distinctive imaginative vision of the
world. Comparable studies of the English Puritan imagination
have lagged behind. To redress the situation, Miltonists, especially, will need to follow the critical procedures laid down by
criticism of American Puritanism.

The Primacy of the Bible in Milton's Poetry

This collection of essays is an implicit challenge to the consensus of Milton criticism of the last century. According to that
consensus, Milton's genres and literary genealogy are mainly
classical; his dependence on the Bible is secondary and largely
nonliterary, the Bible being a source of ideas and allusions and
plots. The contributors to this volume believe that the Bible is a
literary presence in Milton's poetry. Analysis of the poetry itself is
the final court of appeal.

There are, however, several external factors that should pre-
dispose us to accept this verdict. One is Milton's own literary

50. The best introduction to the field is the books of Sacvan Bercovitch and
the sources listed in them: *The American Puritan Imagination* (Cambridge: Cambridge University Press, 1974); *The Puritan Origins of the American Self* (New
Haven: Yale University Press, 1975); *The American Jeremiad* (Madison: University
of Wisconsin Press, 1978).

comments about the Bible, combined with his translation of selected Psalms as a literary exercise on three different occasions in his life. A second is that both Aubrey and the anonymous biographer inform us that when the blind Milton composed *Paradise Lost* he listened everyday to someone read from the Bible as a stimulus to his creative imagination. The anonymous biographer adds in this context that "David's Psalms were in esteem with him above all poetry."[51]

A third factor is the growth away from classical literature and toward biblical literature that we can trace in Milton over the course of his lifetime. This can be seen, for example, in the changes that occurred in Milton's thinking about the subject for his epic. As a Cambridge student, Milton assumed axiomatically that the subject of his epic would be classical mythology. Fifteen years later, he was undecided whether he would follow classical or biblical epic as his model.[52] By the time he wrote *Paradise Lost*, he had resolved the question of epic subject in favor of the Bible. In his early poems, Milton calls Christ "the mighty Pan" and God "Jove," but in *Paradise Lost* he introduces pagan analogues to biblical literature only to repudiate them. Milton's progress over a lifetime was away from classical models to biblical ones.

We should note, too, the claims that Milton makes in his invocations in *Lycidas* and *Paradise Lost*. Milton's invocations to the classical muses are metaphoric; he does not really believe that the muses can hear his prayer. Instead he uses them to declare metaphorically his indebtedness to the classical tradition for his genre. But having invoked the muses, he lets the reader know that his use of classical forms has been surpassed by his use of biblical or Christian ones. Each of the invocations in *Lycidas* contains a hint that Milton has consciously overshot his classical model for pastoral elegy: "somwhat loudly sweep the string" (17); "The strain I heard was of a higher mood" (87); "Return *Alpheus*, the dred voice is past / That shrunk thy streams" (132–

51. Quoted from James Holly Hanford, *A Milton Handbook*, 4th ed. (New York: Appleton-Century-Crofts, 1954), p. 61.
52. "At a Vacation Exercise"; *The Reason of Church Government*, CPW, 1:813–14.

33). And in *Paradise Lost*, in the invocation to book 3, having pictured himself as haunting "where the Muses haunt" (27), Milton conspicuously adds, "but chief / Thee *Sion* . . . / Nightly I visit" (29–32). Douglas Bush's comment on the lines can serve as an epigraph to this entire volume: "Milton turns from the pagan classics to the higher visions of the Bible and Christian truth."[53]

None of the contributors to this volume wishes to overstate the case for the biblical influence on Milton's poetry. There is an indisputable need, however, to correct some traditional imbalances in Milton scholarship. Many of the effects in Milton's poetry may be as dependent on the classical literary tradition as on the biblical tradition, yet the former has been the focus of attention to date. A sensitive reader can discern many of the facets of Milton's poetry discussed in this book without relating them to a biblical context, yet it is a fact that many of these poetic effects have emerged only when critics have looked at Milton's poetry in the light of the Bible.

We are indebted to recent reader-response criticism for making us aware that the meanings that readers find in works of literature depend heavily on what they bring to the text, including even the individual words that make up the text. In the words of Paul Ricouer, "every reading of a text always takes place within a community, a tradition, or a living current of thought, all of which display presuppositions and exigencies."[54] Milton criticism has long applied this principle to Milton as writer, as though this is all that needs to be done. But the essays in this volume also aim to place *readers* within a biblical tradition that will allow them to discover more in Milton's poetry than would otherwise be possible. The essays that follow repeatedly enhance the content that readers can bring to the words and images and motifs of Milton's poetry, and in that sense the claim can be made that an awareness of the Bible and scriptural tradition is indispensable to a full understanding and enjoyment of Milton's poetry.

53. *The Complete Poetical Works of John Milton* (Boston: Houghton Mifflin Co., 1965), p. 257, n. to lines 30–32 of *Paradise Lost*, book 3.
54. *The Conflict of Interpretations: Essays in Hermeneutics*, ed. Don Ihde (Evanston: Northwestern University Press, 1974), p. 3.

Ralph Waldo Emerson once said that the purpose of a principle is that it gives us eyes with which to see something. This book is based on the principle that Milton's poetry exists in a biblical context. The value of placing Milton's poetry into that biblical framework is in the final analysis simple to prove: it gives us eyes to see what we would otherwise miss.

Scriptural Formula and Prophetic Utterance in *Lycidas*

Michael Lieb

lthough no reader of *Lycidas* can fail to recognize something of its indebtedness to scriptural tradition, the full extent of that indebtedness is only now receiving the attention it deserves. A case in point is the significance of the phrase "Yet once more" with which the poem opens.[1] As recently as 1972, the ongoing *Variorum Commentary on the Poems of John Milton* made almost nothing of the scriptural underpinnings of this phrase.[2] Since that time, however, a number of scholars have attempted to rectify that oversight with illuminating analyses of both Old Testament and New Testament sources. Derived from Haggai 2:6–7 and Hebrews 12:26–27, "Yet once more" has been ably placed in its scriptural contexts by scholars such as David S. Berkeley and most notably Joseph A. Wittreich, Jr.[3] Consolidating the findings of recent

1. References to Milton's poetry in my text are to *The Complete Poetry of John Milton*, ed. John T. Shawcross, 2d ed. (Garden City: Doubleday, 1971). I wish to thank the staffs of the Newberry Library, the Regenstein Library of the University of Chicago, and the Lutheran School of Theology Library for their assistance.

2. Gen. ed. Merritt Y. Hughes, 4 vols. to date (New York: Columbia University Press, 1970–   ). For *Lycidas*, see the commentary and notes of A. S. P. Woodhouse and Douglas Bush, vol. 2, pt. 2, p. 639. Updating Woodhouse with bracketed insertions, Bush alludes to David S. Berkeley's note in *Notes & Queries* 8 (1961): 178 on the scriptural context but does not elaborate on Berkeley's findings.

3. In addition to Berkeley's note cited above, see his *Inwrought with Figures Dim: A Reading of Milton's "Lycidas"* (The Hague: Mouton, 1974), pp. 33–34. For Wittreich, see "'A Poet Amongst Poets': Milton and the Tradition of Prophecy," in *Milton and the Line of Vision*, ed. Joseph A. Wittreich, Jr. (Madison: University of Wisconsin Press, 1975), pp. 117–23, and the chapter on *Lycidas* in his *Visionary Poetics: Milton's Tradition and His Legacy* (San Marino, Calif.: Henry E. Huntington Library, 1979), esp. pp. 138–41. Additional insights may be found in Edward Tayler, *Milton's Poetry: Its Development in Time* (Pittsburgh: Duquesne University Press, 1980), pp. 45–59.

criticism and offering insights of his own, James H. Sims has duly recorded in the first volume of the *Milton Encyclopedia* the primacy of the Haggai and Hebrews texts.[4] Given the reputation encyclopedias have enjoyed from the Renaissance onward, the format accorded those insights in the *Milton Encyclopedia* has bestowed upon them something of the status of a commonplace. If we can find this information in an encyclopedia, we reason, it must be common knowledge. With the many new discoveries that the *Milton Encyclopedia* embodies, such, of course, is hardly the case. Nor is it, we have seen, true of the issue under discussion. Not only are the scriptural underpinnings of phrases like "Yet once more" not commonly known, but our knowledge of them is still very much "in the making," as Milton would say.

In response to this situation, I hope to augment the atmosphere of discovery surrounding the language of *Lycidas* and, in the process, extend the insights of my earlier article on the subject.[5] As a point of departure, I shall review briefly the findings of this article. The initial formulaic phrase "Yet once more" recalls not only the classical and Renaissance pastoral elegiac tradition of Theocritus, Moschus, Alamanni, and Marot but also the scriptural tradition founded upon the texts from Haggai and Hebrews. At the same time, Milton associates the phrase with the redemptive mission of Christ, culminating in the Last Judgment and the experience of heavenly bliss by those who are redeemed. In the framework of *Lycidas*, the counterpart of "Yet once more" is to be seen, of course, initially in the pronouncement "smite no more" (131) and ultimately in the consolation "Weep no more" (165). Like "Yet once more," "Weep no more" is indebted not only to classical and Renaissance pastoral elegy but also to specific passages of Scripture, such as Isaiah 30:18–19 and 65:17–19, on the one hand, and Revelation 7:16–17 and 21:1–5, on the other. Through those passages, "Weep no more" becomes a formulary in its own right, one that signifies the remission of

4. *A Milton Encyclopedia*, gen. ed. William B. Hunter, Jr., 8 vols. (Lewisburg, Pa.: Bucknell University Press, 1978–1980), 1:149.
5. "'Yet Once More': The Formulaic Opening of *Lycidas*," *Milton Quarterly* 12 (1978): 23–28.

wrath and the promise of joy.[6] With its two counterbalancing formulas ("once more"—"no more"), *Lycidas* opens with one scriptural declaration and culminates with another, the first anticipating the second, the second recalling and reformulating the first. There is nothing new in this juxtaposition: *Lycidas* accords structurally with a multitude of classical and Renaissance pastoral elegies that employ the same architectonic device. What is interesting, however, is the extent to which that device functions in *Lycidas* to bring into play an entire complex of nuances embodied in the formulaic language of Scripture and particularly in the language that characterizes the prophetical books. It is this aspect of the formulaic diction of *Lycidas* that I shall now explore: the unique significance of "once more" and "no more" as scriptural formulas.

A word first about formulas. Although recent practitioners of "formula criticism" would have us believe otherwise, the concept of the scriptural formula is not new.[7] Indeed, it flourished in Milton's own time in the many scriptural thesauri that his age produced. Anticipating modern dictionaries like the Botterweck and Ringgren *Theologisches Wörterbuch zum Alten Testament* and the Kittel *Theologisches Wörterbuch zum Neuen Testament*,[8] Renaissance thesauri distinguish what might be called "key" words and phrases that occur with formulaic consistency throughout both the Old Testament and the New. As might be expected, two such

6. Ibid., pp. 25–26. The expression "smite no more" has no specific scriptural antecedent. It represents a collocation of several passages (1 Sam. 26:8; Matt. 26:31; Mark 14:27; and Rev. 19:15).

7. Basically concerned with the Old Testament, "formula" critics derive many of their insights from the work of Parry, Lord, Bowra, and Magoun, among others. For the most important formula critics, see Stanley Gevirtz, *Patterns in the Early Poetry of Israel* (Chicago: University of Chicago Press, 1963); William Whallon, *Formula, Character, and Context: Studies in Homeric, Old English, and Old Testament Poetry* (Washington, D.C.: The Center for Hellenistic Studies, 1969); Robert C. Culley, *Oral Formulaic Language in the Biblical Psalms* (Toronto: University of Toronto Press, 1967); and William Watters, *Formula Criticism and the Poetry of the Old Testament* (Berlin and New York: Walter de Gruyter, 1967).

8. These works may be had in translation. See the *Theological Dictionary of the Old Testament*, ed. G. Johannes Botterweck and Helmer Ringgren, trans. John T. Willis, 3 vols. to date (Grand Rapids, Mich.: William B. Eerdmans, 1974), and the *Theological Dictionary of the New Testament*, ed. Gerhard Kittel and trans. Geoffrey W. Bromiley, 10 vols. (Grand Rapids, Mich.: William B. Eerdmans, 1964).

key phrases for the Renaissance (as well as for the twentieth century) are "once more" and "no more." According to Thomas Wilson, for example, both phrases fall under the heading of what his *Christian Dictionary* calls "*the chiefe Words dispersed generally through Holy Scripture of the Old and New Testament, tending to increase Christian knowledge.*"[9] Other Renaissance compendia follow suit. Particularly those that deal with the phrases in their original Semitic and Greek contexts are careful to indicate precisely what theological ideas accrue to them as they are used repeatedly throughout Scriptures. So the seventeenth-century exegetes Salomon Glass and Jacque Gousset in their respective works (*Philologia sacra* and *Commentarii Linguae Ebraicae*) provide extensive commentaries on such key phrases as "אחט מעט היא עוד" ("Yet once it is a little while") and "Ἔτι ἅπαξ" ("Yet once") that underlie the "once more" formula, on the one hand, and "לא . . . עדד" ("not . . . any more") and "ὸν μὴ . . . ἔτι" ("not at all . . . [any] longer") that underlie the "no more" formula, on the other.[10] Although we shall discuss these formulas in more detail later, suffice it to say that, during Milton's time, they formed the basis of a theological perspective as sensitive to the formulaic significance of key terms as any that the twentieth century has produced.

For our purposes, twentieth-century formula criticism is use-

9. The statement is taken from Wilson's subtitle to *A Christian Dictionary*, 3d ed. (London, 1622). This is Thomas Wilson the exegete, not Thomas Wilson the rhetorician. For his discussion of "once more" and "no more," see sigs. Ooo5ᵛ, Fff4⁴, Kkkgʳ, and Lll6ᵛ.

10. For Salomon Glass (1593–1656), I am using the 1705 edition of *Philologia sacra, qua totius SS. Veteris et Novi Testamenti scripturae* (Leipzig, 1705); for Jacques Gousset or Jacobo Gussetio (1635–1704), I am using the 1702 edition of *Commentarii Linguae Ebraicae* (Amsterdam, 1702). In Glass's *Philologia sacra*, see, in particular, the discourse on "*non amplius*" and "*semel*" as repeated formulas, pp. 966–72. Glass ties in all the motifs associated with "once more" and "no more" that I am dealing with here. In Gousset's *Commentarii*, see the discourses on "יסף," "עוד," and "מעט," pp. 331–32, 475–77, and 588–89. For comparable thesauri, see the *Christiani Noldii Concordantiae Particvlarvm Ebraeo-Chaldaicarvm* (Jena, 1734), sigs. Yyy4ʳ, B4⁴–B6ᵛ, Ttt3ʳ, of Christian Nold (1626–1683); John Buxtorf, *Lexicon Hebraicum et Chaldaicum* (London, 1646), pp. 301–2, 501–3, 506; [Alexander Rowley], חבך לתלמידים, *Sodalis Discipulis* (London, 1648), pp. 48, 136; William Robertson, *Thesaurus Linguae Sanctae* (London, 1680), pp. 323–24; and John Udall, מפתה לשין הקדש, *That Is the Key of the Holy Tongue* (Leyden, 1593), pp. 66, 99.

ful as it elaborates upon the significance of formulaic repetition, particularly in the Old Testament. Rooted in what the formula critics see as the oral formulaic character of specific texts, this kind of repetition gives rise to what they call formulaic systems, defined "as a group of phrases having the same syntactical pattern, the same metrical structure, and at least one major lexical item in common."[11] I am not enough of a Hebraist to vouch for the authenticity of such "systems," and there is as much bickering about the fine points in Old Testament formula criticism as there is in the allied disciplines that allegedly got there first.[12] What I do find significant, however, is the way in which certain formulas common to one text (Isaiah, for example) are assimilated into the framework of another (Micah, for example), either through automatic recourse to a stockpile of such formulas or through conscious borrowing and adaptation. From the second point of view, the formula critics have found that "literate poets resort to the fixed word pair much as the oral poets do."[13] In other words, the use of set formulas can be a characteristic of the most sophisticated poetic practices. Such is true not only of the Hebrew Scriptures but also of the Greek. There, Old Testament formulas are reformulated and provided with a context specifically in keeping with the New Testament frame of mind.[14]

Appropriately, this phenomenon is most graphically demonstrated by the author of Hebrews himself. Invoking Haggai 2:6–7 ("Yet once, it *is* a little while"), the author of Hebrews maintains, "This *word*, Yet once more, signifieth the removing of those things that are shaken, as of things that are made, that those things which cannot be shaken may remain" (Heb. 12:27). The point is that the author of Hebrews has taken a phrase ("היא אחת מעט," in the original) and made a formula of it: "Τὸ δὲ Ἔτι ἅπαξ, δηλοῖ," literally, "But the Yet once, signifies." More precisely, the author of Hebrews has reformulated what was already

11. Culley, *Oral Formulaic Language*, p. 12.
12. See, in particular, Watters, *Formula Criticism*, which reviews and calls into question some of the basic assumptions of formula criticism. His discussion of the allied disciplines (Homeric, Old English, and so on) is also interesting.
13. Watters, *Formula Criticism*, p. 74.
14. Whallon, *Formula, Character, and Context*, pp. 204–10. Whallon examines this phenomenon with particular reference to the language of Jesus.

formulaic, since "עוד מעט" ("Yet a little while") itself had the status of a formula by the time the old Testament prophet adopted it for his own use.[15] It is this act of formulating or reformulating (giving meaning to meaning) that the author of Hebrews both engaged in and alluded to with the term "δηλοῖ."[16] In doing so, he provided his own hermeneutic of the formula.

Formulaic language, that hermeneutic implies, reformulates what was previously understood to be embodied in a particular signifier (a word or a phrase) and infuses it with new meaning. More than that, it removes those layers of meaning it considers impermanent and lays bare what it considers lasting.[17] It is a radical hermeneutic that the author of Hebrews embraced. As indicated in his use of the term "δηλοῖ," this kind of formulaic language is essentially revelatory and finally apocalyptic: "Yet once more I shake not the earth only, but also heaven. . . . For our God is a consuming fire" (Heb. 12:26, 29). For the author of Hebrews, the formula itself thereby "signifieth the removing of those things that are shaken, as of things that are made, that those things which cannot be shaken may remain." This is how formula gives meaning to meaning. Such an outlook is, of course, fully in accord with Milton's poetic practices in *Lycidas*.

As I suggested in my earlier article, Milton, at the outset of *Lycidas*, uses "Yet once more" to invoke the pastoral elegiac tradition as a way of dramatizing the inability of traditional form to

15. For examples of the "עוד מעט" formula, see, among other texts, Job 24:24; Ps. 37:10; Isa. 10:25, 26:20, 29:17; Jer. 51:33; and Hos. 1:4. The formula is particularly characteristic of prophetic utterance. Comparative scriptural citations for the AV, the Hebrew, and the Greek are drawn from the *Biblia Polyglotta*, 6 vols. (London, 1657).

16. According to *A Greek-English Lexicon of the New Testament and Other Early Christian Literature*, trans. and ed. W. F. Arndt and F. W. Gingrich, 4th ed. (Chicago: University of Chicago Press, 1957), s.v., "δηλοῖ," from "δηλόω," suggests not only the idea of "signifying," "notifying," and "setting forth," but the concept of "revealing" (as of a revealing of secrets).

17. In the case of Heb. 12:26–27 versus Hag. 2:6–7, what the author of Hebrews considers impermanent about Haggai's "yet once more" is its focus upon the restored Temple as that which is made. In contrast, the author of Hebrews's "Yet once more" focuses upon the "kingdom which cannot be moved" (Heb. 12:28), the antitype prefigured in the restored Temple of Haggai. Typology, of course, is a fundamental constituent of the outlook that the author of Hebrews embodies.

sustain the weight of his vision. As a result, convention is undermined by means of convention. Calling up the pastoral elegiac tradition with repeated insistence ("Yet once more . . . and once more"), Milton "shatters" it. From the Miltonic perspective, "those things that are shaken" are the pagan world embodied in pastoral form, whereas "those things which cannot be shaken" are the Christian world embodied in the new pastoral form of *Lycidas*. Accordingly, "Yet once more" embodies its own consolation: it results in its own reversal through the climactic declaration, "Weep no more, wofull shepherds weep no more." With this declaration, the tradition of pastoral elegy, undermined at the outset, gives way to a new pastoral form, founded upon "those things which cannot be shaken."[18] It is this movement from the "once more" formula to the "no more" formula that I now wish to examine. As I hope to show, that transition is fundamental not only to the action of *Lycidas* but also to the formulaic disposition of scriptural language. It is particularly within the prophetic contexts of that language that the transition becomes meaningful.

According to Robert Culley, a major aspect of scriptural formula resides in phonetic iteration: once pronounced, the formula reverberates through repeated patterns of sound, orchestrated to recall the formula as originally uttered. The technique is basic to the phonetic constitution of *Lycidas*, in which such rhetorical devices as epanalepsis figure prominently.[19] From the formulaic perspective, these devices are implicit in the *or* sound of "once m*ore*," which reverberates throughout the poem as in an echo chamber. We hear *or* repeatedly in the phonetic insis-

18. Lieb, "Yet Once More," pp. 25–26.
19. Culley, *Oral Formulaic Language*, p. 15. For the most recent treatment of this dimension, see Heather Asals's "Echo, Narcissus, and Ambiguity in *Lycidas*," delivered before the Modern Language Association meeting in San Francisco, 1979. Although Asals is concerned primarily with epanalepsis (the act of ending a line with its opening word or words), other reverberative devices (such as anadiplosis, anaphora, atanaclasis, ploce, epiphora) are also important. See Edward S. LeComte, *Yet Once More: Verbal and Psychological Pattern in Milton* (New York: Liberal Arts Press, 1953), p. 25. Convenient explanations of individual devices may be found in the *Encyclopedia of Poetry and Poetics*, ed. Alex Preminger et al. (Princeton: Princeton University Press, 1965).

tence of "L*au*rels" (1), "bef*ore*" (5), "m*orn*" (26, 187; var. "m*ourn*," 41), "h*orn*" (28), "*o'*reg*rown*" (40), "th*orn*" (48), "rem*orse*less" (50), "b*ore*" (58, 110), "r*oar*" (61), "g*oary*" (62), "sh*oar*" (63, 183), "sp*ort*" (68), "n*or*" (54, 55, 79, 80; var. "*ore*," 170), "prom*ont*o*ry*" (94), "st*ory*" (95), "d*ore*" (130), "fl*oar*" (167), "m*orn*ing" (171), "gl*ory*" (180), "D*or*ick" (189), as well as in the iteration of "more" itself, repeated seven times throughout the poem. In the process, "once more" becomes "no more," at first imperceptibly in the lament "the willows, and the hazel copses green / Shall now *no more* be seen" (42–43; my italics), then disturbingly in the prophetic denunciation, "But that two-handed engine at the *dore* / Stands ready to smite *once* and smite *no more*" (130–31; my italics). In that denunciation, the "Ἔτι ἅπαξ" that initiates the poem is transformed: "once more" becomes "no more." A new formula has emerged. Its initial appearance is disturbing, just as the "yet once more" is at first disturbing. Both betoken a shaking of the heavens and the earth: both betoken an apocalypse. But just as "once more" embodies its own consolation, the reward of "a kingdom, which cannot be moved," "no more" ultimately emerges in a consolatory form: "Weep no more, wofull shepherds weep no more" (165).

In this sense, *Lycidas* subscribes to what Claus Westermann has called the "basic forms of prophetic speech." Underlying scriptural prophecy, Westermann maintains, is the "announcement" of "judgment," on the one hand, and of "salvation," on the other. Prophetic utterance is structured according to the categories of "judgment proclamation" and "salvation proclamation," each with its own formulas.[20] Among those formulas are the ones of most immediate concern to us, "once more" and "no more." In its own way, each embodies the dialectic of "judgment" and "sal-

20. Westermann, *Basic Forms of Prophetic Speech*, trans. Hugh Clayton White (Philadelphia: The Westminster Press, 1967), pp. 93–95, 116, and *passim*. Westermann's discussion is also of importance for anyone interested in the significance of "woe" as a formula (pp. 190–94). In this context, I am thinking, of course, of "woe" and its phonetic variations in Milton's Sonnet 18. For a review of Westermann's approach, as well as of "form criticism" (of which formula criticism is a kind) applied to the scriptural prophets in general, see W. Eugene March, "Prophecy," in *Old Testament Form Criticism*, ed. John H. Hayes (San Antonio: Trinity University Press, 1974), pp. 159–77.

vation" essential to prophetic speech. That such is true of the scriptural contexts of the "once more" formula as "עוֹד אַחַת מְעַט" (Hag. 2:6–7) and "Ἔτι ἅπαξ" (Heb. 12:26–27) we have already seen. It is the "no more" formula in its scriptural setting that must engage us now.

Let us begin with the "no more" formula as an expression of the "judgment proclamation." The *locus classicus* for the use of "no more" in this form is Revelation 18:21–24: "And a mighty angel took up a stone like a great millstone, and cast *it* into the sea, saying, Thus with violence shall that great city Babylon be thrown down, and shall be found no more at all [οὐ μὴ εὑρεθῇ ἔτι]. And the voice of harpers, and musicians, and of pipers, and trumpeters, shall be heard no more at all in thee [οὐ μὴ ἀκουσθῇ ἐν σοὶ ἔτι]; and no craftsman, of whatsoever craft *he be*, shall be found any more in thee [οὐ μὴ εὑρεθῇ ἐν σοὶ ἔτι]; and the sound of a millstone shall be heard no more at all in thee [οὐ μὴ ἀκουσθῇ ἐν σοὶ ἔτι]; And the light of a candle shall shine no more at all in thee [οὐ μὴ φανῇ ἐν σοὶ ἔτι]; and the voice of the bridegroom and of the bride shall be heard no more at all in thee [οὐ μὴ ἀκουσθῇ ἐν σοὶ ἔτι]: for thy merchants were the great men of the earth; for by thy sorceries were all nations deceived."

Although Saint John the Divine does not proclaim directly that "no more" "signifieth" any meaning in particular, his "δηλοῖ" is implicit in the formulaic context his prophetic denunciation creates with the constant iteration of "οὐ μὴ . . . ἔτι." In that way, it recalls the "Ἔτι ἅπαξ" of the author of Hebrews. The recollection, in fact, is both verbal and thematic, verbal because of the repeated adverb "Ἔτι" and thematic because of the significance of the destruction of the kingdom (the "τῶν σαλευομένων τὴν μετάθσιν" or the "removing of those things that are shaken" [Heb. 12:27]) embodied in the "οὐ μὴ . . . ἔτι" formula. In keeping with this formulaic pattern, *Lycidas* itself, of course, reflects precisely that concern with which kingdoms will endure and which will not. Those that will not, because they are both corrupt and transitory, will be "removed" by "that two-handed engine at the dore" (130). So it must be before "the blest kingdoms meek of joy and love" (177) are attainable. One of the primary features of both "judgment proclamation" and "salvation proclamation," as might be expected, is the role of the kingdom in prophecy. Whether as "ἡ βασιλεία" or as "ממלכה," the kingdom itself becomes the object either of castigation or of fulfillment that underlies the basic forms of prophetic speech.[21] Such is no less true of Saint John the Divine than of the author of Hebrews. For our purposes, the primacy of the kingdom is figured forth most compellingly in the "once more"—"no more" dialectic that engages us here. Implicit in the "οὐ μή . . . ἔτι" of Saint John the Divine, it is equally as discernible in the Old Testament prophetic formulations upon which the "οὐ μή . . . ἔτι" formula is based.

According to James Hope Moulton, the formula, which occurs repeatedly in Revelation (sixteen times) and is almost a distinguishing characteristic of that book, has its roots in "Semitic originals," particularly among the prophets. There, it is rendered "לא . . . עוד" ("not . . . any more"), as in Ezekiel 26:13, with Tyre as the object of "judgment proclamation": "And I will make cease the noise of your songs; and the sound of your harps shall not be heard any more [לא ישמע עוד]."[22] Especially as it incorporates various renderings of "יסף" ("more," "again"), the formula becomes very emphatic, as in Ezekiel 36:12–15, with Idumea as the object of "judgment proclamation": "Yea, I will cause men to walk upon you, *even* my people Israel; and they shall possess thee, and thou shalt no more [ולא־תוסף עוד] bereave them *of men*. . . . Therefore thou shalt devour men no more [עוד לא־תאכלי], neither bereave thy nations any more [לא תכשלי־עוד], saith the Lord God. Neither will I cause *men* to hear in thee the shame of the heathen any more [ולא־אשמיע אליך עוד], neither shalt thou bear the reproach of the heathen any more [תשאי־עוד לא], neither shalt thou cause thy nations to fall any more [עוד לא־תכשלי], saith the Lord GOD."[23] This passage is of particular

21. Ibid., pp. 95, 169–98.

22. *A Grammar of New Testament Greek*, 2 vols. (Edinburgh: T. & T. Clark, 1906), 1:187–92. See further William Francis Gallaway, *On the Use of Μή with the Participle in Classical Greek*, 2d ed. (Cambridge: Cambridge University Press, 1959), p. 156; and William Watson Godwin, *Syntax of the Moods and Tenses of the Greek Verb* (Boston: Ginn and Co., 1900), pp. 388–96.

23. See also Isa. 10:20, 23:12. For accounts of the Hebrew negative, see A. B.

interest because in it the "no more" formula undergoes a transformation in the movement from "judgment proclamation" (against the heathens) to "salvation proclamation" (on behalf of the Israelites). In scriptural terms, it is particularly this latter aspect with which we are already quite familiar.

The seminal passages for that aspect may be found, of course, in Revelation. There is consummated what the author of Hebrews calls the "receiving" of a "kingdom which cannot be moved [βασιλείαν ἀσάλευτον παραλαμβάνοντες]" (Heb. 12:28). Accordingly, Saint John the Divine proclaims: "They shall hunger no more [οὐ πεινάσουσιν ἔτι], neither thirst any more [οὐδὲ δι-ψήσουσιν ἔτι]; neither shall the sun light on them, nor any heat. For the Lamb which is in the midst of the throne shall feed them, and shall lead them unto living fountains of waters: and God shall wipe away all tears from their eyes" (Rev. 7:16–17). "And there shall be no more death [καὶ ὁ θάνατος οὐκ ἔσται ἔτι], neither sorrow, nor crying [οὔτε πένθος, οὔτε κραυγή], neither shall there be any more pain [οὔτε πόνος οὐκ ἔσται ἔτι]: for the former things are passed away" (Rev. 21:4). These passages, we recall, harken back to Isaiah: "Thou shalt weep no more [עוד . . . לֹא־יִשְׁמַע]" in Jerusalem (Isa. 65:19). Even more compelling, however, is Jeremiah, who incorporates a rendering of "יסף" into the "עוד . . . לֹא" formula: "Therefore they shall come and sing in the height of Zion . . . ; and they shall not sorrow any more at all [וְלֹא־יוֹסִיפוּ לְדַאֲבָה עוֹד]" (Jer. 31:12). In these cases, as in others, the "no more" formula that underlies the "salvation proclamation" becomes the occasion for celebrating the redemption of those chosen to participate in the renewed Jerusalem. As vehicle both for salvation and for judgment, this formula gives shape and meaning to prophetic utterance. Through it, that utterance embodies a resonance that distinguishes it as the uniquely charged language of the prophet. In this, it performs the same function

---

Davidson, *Hebrew Syntax* (Edinburgh: T. & T. Clark, 1901), p. 118; and Dean A. Walker, *The Semitic Negative* (Chicago: The University of Chicago Press, 1896). For the uses of "יסף," see *A Hebrew and English Lexicon of the Old Testament*, trans. Edward Robinson and ed. Francis Brown (Oxford: Oxford University Press, 1907).

as its counterpart, "once more." Each gives rise to the proclamations of judgment, on the one hand, and salvation, on the other, that characterize the basic forms of prophetic speech.

That *Lycidas* subscribes to these forms in its adoption of a formulaic system, the foregoing discussion has attempted to demonstrate. Such is only natural, however, given the character of what might be called Milton's disposition to repeat words and phrases not only within a single poem but throughout all his writings. This Edward S. LeComte long ago established in his book appropriately entitled *Yet Once More*, which examines the nature of Miltonic iteration from a psychological point of view. Although that is hardly my purpose here, I do wish to emphasize what treasures can be mined through a study of selected phrases iterated in such a way as to establish a complex of significations, at once unique to the settings in which they appear and commonplace to the traditions to which they are indebted. So it is with the "once more"—"no more" dialectic that informs the texture of *Lycidas*. Defined by a hermeneutical tradition rooted in scriptural formula, this dialectic becomes meaningful only when we are in a position to understand the formulaic contexts that distinguish it.

Paradise Lost and Its Biblical Epic Models

Leland Ryken

his essay is an attempt to bring together two significant themes of recent Milton criticism. One is the growing consensus that Milton's poetic forms or genres are modeled on the literary forms of the Bible. Annotators of Milton's poetry have for more than two centuries shown that Milton used the Bible as a source of imagery, allusions, and doctrine. From that accurate but too simple view of the relationship between Milton's poetry and the Bible, criticism moved toward an awareness of how specific passages or stylistic effects in Milton's poetry are indebted to the Bible.[1]

But it remained for recent criticism to suggest the extent to which Milton (a) looked upon the Bible as a model for literary form and (b) based his own poetic genres on the Bible. The result is a critical climate in which it has become acceptable to say that Milton "looks back for his aesthetic not to Homer and Vergil

---

1. The definitive and most comprehensive work in this category continues to be James H. Sims's *The Bible in Milton's Epics* (Gainesville: University of Florida Press, 1962). Other notable examples of criticism in this vein include Harold Fisch, "Hebraic Style and Motifs in *Paradise Lost*," in *Language and Style in Milton*, ed. Ronald D. Emma and John T. Shawcross (New York: Frederick Ungar, 1967), pp. 30–64; Kitty Cohen, *The Throne and the Chariot: Studies in Milton's Hebraism* (The Hague: Mouton, 1975); Emory Elliott, "Milton's Biblical Style in *Paradise Regained*," *Milton Studies VI*, ed. James D. Simmonds (Pittsburgh: University of Pittsburgh Press, 1975), pp. 227–41; John N. Wall, Jr., "The Contrarious Hand of God: *Samson Agonistes* and the Biblical Lament," in *Milton Studies XII*, ed. James D. Simmonds (Pittsburgh: University of Pittsburgh Press, 1979), pp. 117–39.

For a general overview of the topic of Milton's indebtedness to the Bible, one should consult Sims's "Milton and the Bible" in *A Milton Encyclopedia*, ed. William B. Hunter (Lewisburg, Pa.: Bucknell University Press, 1978), 1:142–63.

but to the Bible,"[2] or that he drew upon the Bible "not only . . . for telling images and phrases" but for "structures and . . . repeated patterns" in "the overall shaping" of his poems,[3] or that he belongs to a Protestant tradition of "biblical poetics" in which the Bible affords the poet "a literary model which he can imitate in such literary matters as genre, language, and symbolism."[4] I do not wish to overstate the scope of this movement,[5] but it seems to me that criticism has never been in a better position than it is now to understand what it means to say that *Paradise Lost* "is the work of a man who has read the *Bible* with a poet's heart."[6]

A second significant discovery of recent criticism is that *Paradise Lost* transformed (some would say killed) the Western epic tradition by destroying its heroic ethos and the forms that expressed that ethos. I am speaking of the climate of criticism that has made it common to speak of *Paradise Lost* as "counter-epic," "anti-epic," a "critical reassessment" of epic, a "radical . . . redefinition" of epic, "nonepic," "more than an epic," a "devaluation of the epic tradition," and "the anti-heroic epic."[7] The critic

2. Joseph A. Wittreich, Jr., *Angel of Apocalypse: Blake's Idea of Milton* (Madison: University of Wisconsin Press, 1975), pp. 175–76.

3. Mary Ann Radzinowicz, *Toward "Samson Agonistes": The Growth of Milton's Mind* (Princeton: Princeton University Press, 1978), p. 208.

4. Barbara K. Lewalski, *Protestant Poetics and the Seventeenth-Century Religious Lyric* (Princeton: Princeton University Press, 1979), pp. ix, 6–7.

5. Despite the plenitude of sources cited here, it would be easy to exaggerate the extent to which recent criticism has explored Milton's use of the Bible as a model for literary form. The studies that relate Milton's poetry to postbiblical traditions (both Christian and Hebraic) and to Renaissance exegetical traditions far outnumber the studies that relate Milton's work to the Bible itself.

6. Elbert N. S. Thompson, *Essays on Milton* (New Haven: Yale University Press, 1914), p. 130.

7. These descriptions of *Paradise Lost* belong, seriatim, to John M. Steadman, *Milton and the Renaissance Hero* (Oxford: Oxford University Press, 1967), p. xx; T. J. B. Spencer, "*Paradise Lost*: The Anti-Epic," in *Approaches to "Paradise Lost*," ed. C. A. Patrides (Toronto: University of Toronto Press, 1968), pp. 81–98; Judith A. Kates, "The Revaluation of the Classical Heroic in Tasso and Milton," *Comparative Literature* 26 (1974): 299–317; George M. Ridenour, *The Style of Don Juan* (1960; rpt. Hamden, Conn.: Archon Books, 1969), p. 92; Fisch, "Hebraic Style and Motifs," p. 58; A. S. P. Woodhouse, *The Heavenly Muse: A Preface to Milton* (Toronto: University of Toronto Press, 1972), p. 182; Peter Hagin, *The Epic Hero and the Decline of Heroic Poetry: A Study of the Neoclassical English Epic with Special Reference to Milton's "Paradise Lost"* (1964; rpt. Folcroft, Pa.: Folcroft, 1970), p. 146; and

who has treated the subject in virtually definitive terms is John Steadman, though he has had predecessors and corroborators.[8] Most helpful of all is Steadman's revelation that Milton achieved his "Copernican revolution" by bringing together two divergent approaches to the epic hero—the philosophical/theological definition of the hero and the literary portrayal of the hero.

Exactly how did Milton effect the reconciliation between these two traditions? Analysis will show that his basic strategy was threefold: (1) he replaced the heroic (military) values of epic tradition with pastoral and domestic values; (2) he changed the traditional epic theme of human greatness to an emphasis on divine greatness and human smallness; (3) he spiritualized epic motifs (such as warfare, kingship, heroism) that in the earlier tradition had been physical and earthly.[9]

In each case, Milton's poem requires us to read an "intertext." The crucial action occurs *between* the epic tradition and Milton's transformation of it. *Paradise Lost* is not self-contained. It repeatedly depends for its full effect on being read against the background of its predecessors, which it often evokes only to challenge and refute them.[10]

Louis L. Martz, *Poet of Exile: A Study of Milton's Poetry* (New Haven: Yale University Press, 1980), p. 203. The accuracy of the designation *anti-epic* is defended by E. R. Gregory, "Three Muses and a Poet: A Perspective on Milton's Epic Thought," in *Milton Studies X*, ed. James D. Simmonds (Pittsburgh: University of Pittsburgh Press, 1977), pp. 35–61.

8. See especially Steadman's *Milton and the Renaissance Hero* and "The Arming of an Archetype: Heroic Virtue and the Conventions of Literary Epic," in *Concepts of the Hero in the Middle Ages and the Renaissance*, ed. Norman T. Burns and Christopher J. Reagan (Albany: State University of New York Press, 1975), pp. 147–96. Some corroborators and predecessors include C. M. Bowra, *From Virgil to Milton* (London: Macmillan, 1945), pp. 194–246; Burton O. Kurth, *Milton and Christian Heroism: Biblical Epic Themes and Forms in Seventeenth-Century England* (1959; rpt. Hamden, Conn.: Archon Books, 1966); and Michael Wilding, "The Last of the Epics: The Rejection of the Heroic in *Paradise Lost* and *Hudibras*," in *Restoration Literature: Critical Approaches*, ed. Harold Love (London: Methuen, 1972), pp. 91–120.

9. This threefold scheme omits a fourth part of Milton's anti-epic strategy, his denigration of military heroism, achieved by associating it with Satan and fallen reality. This feature of *Paradise Lost* has been so thoroughly covered that little remains to be said on the topic, nor can I find biblical models for the motif comparable to the three that I discuss in this essay.

10. Some may find the term *refute* too strong, but the discussion that follows

Where did Milton receive the impetus for such a revolutionary venture? The tendency of critics has been to assume that Milton's Christian beliefs adequately explain what he did with the epic tradition. Yet Christian doctrine by itself does not account for Milton's strategy. Christian writers of heroic story had struggled for centuries to reconcile the theological and literary traditions of the hero without hitting upon Milton's solution. There was certainly no paucity of attempted solutions: the "holy war" epics, in which the military exploits of the hero were regarded as being fought (like Israel's in the Old Testament) for the cause of God; the allegorical solution of poets like Spenser, who tried to make the military trappings symbolize moral or spiritual realities; and "divine poetry," in which the fact that the story was taken from the Bible was supposed to make the story Christian, even though the work might remain infused with the content and spirit of military epic. Springing from the same Christian doctrinal base that Milton accepted, these works are remote from the transvaluation of Western epic that we find in *Paradise Lost*.

The best explanation for Milton's drastic changes in epic tradition lies not only in Christian doctrine but also in his use of biblical narratives as literary models. That Milton looked upon the literary parts of the Bible as examples of literary genres is indisputable.[11] The key piece of evidence occurs in *The Reason of Church Government*, in which Milton classifies the book of Job as a "brief" epic, the Song of Solomon as "a divine pastoral Drama," the New Testament Apocalypse as "a high and stately Tragedy," and parts of "the law and prophets" as "songs."[12] These com-

---

lends support to Steadman's claim regarding *Paradise Lost* that "if it imitates the established models of heroic poetry, it also refutes them" (*Milton and the Renaissance Hero*, p. xx). J. B. Broadbent similarly says about the opening invocation that it "is different from its predecessors: for as it imitates, it condemns them" (*John Milton, Paradise Lost: Books I–II* [Cambridge: Cambridge University Press, 1972], p. 12).

11. For commentary on the subject, see James H. Sims, "Milton, Literature as a Bible, and the Bible as Literature," in *Milton and the Art of Sacred Song*, ed. J. Max Patrick and Roger H. Sundell (Madison: University of Wisconsin Press, 1979), pp. 3–21.

12. *CPW*, 1:813, 815–16.

ments are, however, rudimentary at best, nor do Milton's generic labels always inspire confidence by modern standards. We should note, though, that "Milton describes his plans for an epic not so much in terms of theory as of models,"[13] confirming the general approach that I have taken in this essay.

Joan Webber is doubtless correct in her claim that "Renaissance readers thought of the Bible as an epic,"[14] though it would not be easy to find Renaissance commentators or poets who used the precise word *epic* for the Bible. The absence of the designation *epic* means little, however, for, as Steadman notes, Milton does not call *Paradise Lost* an epic but a heroic poem.[15] The key element in epic for the Renaissance was the image of the hero, and we can recall that in casting about for an epic subject Milton expressed the need to find "the pattern of a Christian *Heroe*."[16] That Renaissance writers viewed the Bible as a repository of such heroic stories is abundantly clear from the frequency with which they used stories from the Bible as the subject matter for epic poems.[17]

In writing an epic poem, Milton would have been especially sensitive to those biblical narratives that have the most claim to being considered epics. As Amos Wilder has noted, parts of the Bible "represent a kind of epic," and Milton "could base his Puritan-humanist epics upon the biblical storytelling."[18] Without claiming that Milton's indebtedness is limited to the three biblical epics that I am about to discuss, I wish to explore how Milton found in the Bible a model for each of the transformations of classical epic that he undertook in *Paradise Lost*. In the epics of Genesis, Exodus, and Revelation, Milton found a pattern, respectively, for his substitution of domestic values for heroic ones,

13. Brian Wilkie, *Romantic Poets and Epic Tradition* (Madison: University of Wisconsin Press, 1965), p. 20.
14. *Milton and His Epic Tradition* (Seattle: University of Washington Press, 1979), p. 157.
15. "The Arming of an Archetype," pp. 163–65.
16. *The Reason of Church Government, CPW*, 1:813–14.
17. For surveys of such poems, see Lily B. Campbell, *Divine Poetry and Drama in Sixteenth-Century England* (Cambridge: Cambridge University Press, 1959), and Kurth, *Milton and Christian Heroism*.
18. *The New Voice: Religion, Literature, Hermeneutics* (New York: Herder and Herder, 1969), p. 42.

his substitution of divine strength and human weakness for the epic motif of human glory, and his substitution of spiritual for physical versions of some common epic motifs. In drawing these connections between *Paradise Lost* and biblical epic, I will be uniting two leading strands of recent Milton criticism that have largely existed side by side—Milton's use of the Bible as a model for literary forms and his writing of what can truly be called an anti-epic.[19]

In the Renaissance there flourished a tradition of "divine poetry" that championed the practice of putting biblical material into the forms of classical literature. The aim of such poetry was, in the words of Du Bartas, "*not so much . . . to follow the phrase or text of the Bible, as . . . to imitate* Homer *in his* Iliades *and* Virgil *in his* Aenidos."[20] There is, of course, a sense in which Milton did exactly this in *Paradise Lost*. But there is also a sense in which he did virtually the opposite: having decided to write an epic in the classical tradition, he turned to the example of biblical epic as a model for the specific form into which he cast the motifs and formulas of classical epic. Classical epic prescribed a certain type of content for Milton; biblical epic served as a literary model for how to treat that content.

I

Milton's choice of Adam and Eve's life in Paradise as the subject of a long epic resulted in a story that can validly be called a

19. The term *anti-epic* continues to be accurate, even in the face of Joan Webber's thesis that epic has always been a subversive form. Epic may be, as Webber calls it, "essentially subversive," but it was never *primarily* subversive until Milton made it so. No other literary genre prescribes such a strong sense of continuity with the earlier tradition as does epic. Despite the variety that exists from one epic to another, virtually every Western epic until *Paradise Lost* presents as a norm some version of the warrior as hero. The tradition as a whole accepts as an axiom that the epic feat is military in nature, that the decisive events in the story should occur on the battlefield, and that earthly victory or fame is an adequate motivation for the epic hero. Whatever subversive traits an individual epic might display, it displays them within a framework that is common to the epic tradition. Milton, by contrast, rejects the framework itself.

20. The most complete study of the tradition is Campbell, *Divine Poetry and Drama*. Du Bartas, preface to *Judit*, as quoted by Barbara K. Lewlaski, *Milton's*

domestic epic. With only two human characters on the scene throughout most of the story, the focus is perforce on the private rather than the public roles and virtues of the epic protagonists. The distinctiveness of "Milton's household epic," as one critic calls it,[21] becomes obvious if we compare it with its classical predecessors.

The hero of Western epic and romance had traditionally been a person of national or international importance. His role was primarily that of a leader of a nation, and his personal fate was at the same time the destiny of a nation. Even the homecoming of Odysseus is more than the story of a family man returning to his wife and son; Odysseus is also the king returning to establish order in a kingdom. In the military world of classical epic, the decisive events occur in the public arena of the battlefield, and the ultimate reward of heroic achievement is kingship. Corresponding to these public roles of the conventional epic hero are his public virtues, which Steadman lists as fortitude, sapience, leadership, *amor*, and magnanimity.

The divergence of *Paradise Lost* from this epic preoccupation with public glory is at once evident. The relationship of Adam and Eve is not that of warrior to comrade, or king to subject, or even king to queen or mistress, but rather that of husband to wife. This is true even though Adam and Eve, as progenitors and representatives of the whole human race, are elevated above ordinary married couples. The memorable speeches in the middle books of *Paradise Lost* are expressions of love and discussions about daily work between husband and wife at the supper table or in their bower. In this domestic climate, Eve gets more space and prominence than does the heroine in any classical epic, giving the lie to claims about Milton's supposed misogyny. The vignettes that we remember from the human scenes in *Paradise Lost* are domestic in nature: Adam and Eve eating supper and

---

Brief Epic: The Genre, Meaning, and Art of "Paradise Regained" (Providence: Brown University Press, 1966), p. 76.

21. Harold E. Toliver, "Milton's Houschold Epic," in *Milton Studies IX*, ed. James D. Simmonds (Pittsburgh: University of Pittsburgh Press, 1976), pp. 105–20.

conversing at the end of a day of work, discussing their work and relationship to each other, recalling their first meeting and their marriage, entertaining a visitor with ideal hospitality, praying together, retiring for the evening, enjoying wedded sexual love, waking and planning the day's work, discussing a troublesome dream of the preceding night. In Milton's story we are far removed from the public, military world of classical epic and medieval romance, even though the representative status of Adam and Eve makes their story less private than it would otherwise be. It is no wonder that Northrop Frye can say that Adam and Eve are suburbanites, and "like other suburbanites they are preoccupied with gardening, with their own sexual relations, and with the details of their rudimentary housekeeping." [22]

Even Milton's epic crisis is domestic. As E. M. W. Tillyard noted, in book 9 we find Milton "substituting a domestic for a heroic crisis." The entire story of the Fall in *Paradise Lost* illustrates this, from the morning conversation between husband and wife about working apart (Irene Samuel calls it "their first domestic spat"), to Adam's inability to say "no" to Eve's whim about working separately ("In persuading Adam to work alone, Eve is a typical woman having the last word in a household argument"),[23] to his wife's temptation to join him, to Adam's inability to forego married companionship for a life of solitude, to the scene of sexual lust (deliberately juxtaposed to earlier scenes of pure conjugal love), to a domestic quarrel between husband and wife over who is to blame for the latest crisis. Adam's fall is part of a decidedly domestic act, a choice of love and wife over obedience to God's command; as Dennis Burden puts it, "Marriage is the crucial issue in the fall of Adam." [24]

When set against the epic background of aristocratic gran-

22. *The Return of Eden: Five Essays on Milton's Epics* (Toronto: University of Toronto Press, 1965), p. 66.

23. Tillyard, *The English Epic and Its Background* (London: Chatto and Windus, 1966), p. 530; Samuel, "Paradise Lost as Mimesis," in *Approaches to "Paradise Lost,"* ed. Patrides, p. 25; John E. Seaman, *The Moral Paradox of "Paradise Lost"* (The Hague: Mouton, 1971), p. 100.

24. *The Logical Epic: A Study of the Argument of "Paradise Lost"* (Cambridge: Harvard University Press, 1967), p. 150.

deur, some of Milton's domestic scenes emerge as obvious parodies of their counterparts in previous epics. The lavish banquet that Dido orders to be prepared for Aeneas and his men is replaced in Milton's domestic epic by the hospitality that husband and wife show to the visiting Raphael (*PL,* 5.308–403).[25] The descriptions of the simple bower of Adam and Eve are a pastoral inversion of the courtly splendor of the palaces of Alcinoos or Odysseus or Priam. In scenes such as these, *Paradise Lost* becomes a "mocking epic."[26]

Even more striking than the prominence that Milton gives to scenes of domestic life in his epic is the fact that he elevates these scenes to the status of epic norm. They are the image of heroism that Milton, as an epic poet writing a poem doctrinal and exemplary to a nation, offers as his standard of moral virtue. In the process, Milton elevates the common and domestic to a status that they never have in classical epic; as Wilding comments, Milton locates virtue "not in military glory, noisy splendour . . . but in the everyday, the domestic."[27]

Within the framework of classical genres, domestic scenes are much more likely to be the subject of comedy than of serious epic. Domestic conversations, sexual relations between husband and wife, the quibbling wife—these are proper subjects for comedy but not for epic. And when they do appear in epic, among the gods and goddesses, we laugh at the incongruity of divine beings behaving like human couples. Milton himself draws upon these classical expectations at the end of book 2; as Joseph Summers noted, when Satan descends from his public role as the grand ruler of Hell to a domestic role when he encounters his wife and son at the gates of Hell, we sense at once that the domestic represents a deflation of the heroic ("Here is the family

25. Spencer, "*Paradise Lost,*" pp. 87–88, discusses the scene as a parody of epic parallels.

26. The phrase *mocking epic* is applied to two epics that parallel what Milton did to Christianize the epic tradition by Dennis M. Kratz, *Mocking Epic: Waltharius, Alexandreis and the Problem of Christian Heroism* (Madrid: Studia Humanitatis, 1980).

27. Wilding, "Last of the Epics," p. 117.

life of Hell"). Mainly, though, Milton was revolutionary in putting the hero's private, domestic role in the center of the epic stage and investing it with ultimate moral and spiritual seriousness. *Paradise Lost* is, as Ian Watt noted, "the greatest and indeed the only epic of married life."[28]

When Milton wrote an extended epic account of the domestic life of Adam and Eve, pastoral became a natural ally to him.[29] Pastoral reinforced the nonaristocratic bias of the story and the emphasis on a personal rather than a public role for the hero. The pastoral version of humble daily work is far closer to the domestic sphere than is heroic endeavor on the battlefield, and, because of its long associations with romantic love, pastoral lent itself to Milton's domestic theme in a way that heroic epic would not have done.

Although pastoral conventions reinforced the domestic emphasis of *Paradise Lost*, it would be wrong to conclude that pastoral and domestic are often thus combined in Western literature. The lovers in pastoral literature have only infrequently been husband and wife. Courtship, not marriage, is the normal subject. Milton, however, went out of his way to make his portrayal of Adam and Eve a full-fledged depiction of his hierarchical philosophy of the institution of marriage and of Puritan ideals of marriage and family.[30] We might say that corresponding to the shift from public heroism to domestic heroism in *Paradise*

28. Summers, *The Muse's Method: An Introduction to "Paradise Lost"* (1962; rpt. New York: W. W. Norton, 1968), pp. 46–48; Watt, *The Rise of the Novel: Studies in Defoe, Richardson, and Fielding* (1957; rpt. Berkeley: University of California Press, 1965), p. 137.

29. The best treatment of the pastoral element in *Paradise Lost* continues to be John R. Knott, Jr., *Milton's Pastoral Vision: An Approach to "Paradise Lost"* (Chicago: University of Chicago Press, 1971).

30. The extent to which *Paradise Lost* embodies a full range of Puritan attitudes toward married love has been shown in detail by William and Malleville Haller, "The Puritan Art of Love," *Huntington Library Quarterly* 5 (1942): 234–72; Roland M. Frye, "The Teachings of Classical Puritanism on Conjugal Love," *Studies in the Renaissance* 2 (1955): 148–59; John Halkett, *Milton and the Ideal of Matrimony: A Study of the Divorce Tracts and "Paradise Lost"* (New Haven: Yale University Press, 1970), pp. 98–121; and Levin L. Schucking, *The Puritan Family: A Social Study from the Literary Sources* (New York: Schocken Books, 1970), pp. 103–8.

Lost is Milton's shift of focus "from the *amour courtois* to the *amour bourgeois.*"[31] It is not enough to say, as Knott does, that Milton "replaced heroic values with others that can be characterized as pastoral."[32] The distinctiveness of Milton's pastoral vision is that he "makes the life in his Garden marital and domestic."[33]

On several counts, then, Milton's epic completely reversed the expectations of classical epic. It replaced the warrior/ruler hero with the domestic hero, it substituted domestic and pastoral values for heroic values, it made the family rather than the kingdom the central sphere of action, and it replaced the conquering warrior with the Christian saint as the norm of virtue. There can be no mistaking that Milton did something revolutionary with the epic genre, and it remains to ask where he would have found the literary model for such a venture.

The most likely source is the biblical book from which Milton took his basic plot. Milton was alert to the epic dimension of the book that Tolstoy called "the epic of Genesis" and that in current scholarship is known as "epic material," a text "equally epic" as Homer's *Odyssey*, "royal epic," "epic narrative," and "Israel's epic."[34] Milton could not have viewed the book of Genesis very

31. William Haller, "'Hail Wedded Love,'" in *Milton: Modern Judgements*, ed. Alan Rudrum (London: Macmillan, 1968), p. 298. John Broadbent and Jane Powell make a similar comment: Milton "has in mind a new epic, a better and more heroic epic, and he specifically rejects two sorts of love interlude: . . . not violent sexual passions and not elaborate courtly amours but the transfigured love in marriage will be his subject" (*John Milton, "Paradise Lost": Books VII–VIII* [Cambridge: Cambridge University Press, 1974], p. 63).

32. Knott, *Milton's Pastoral Vision*, p. xii.

33. Burden, *The Logical Epic*, p. 42. Cohen, *The Throne and the Chariot*, notes the surprisingly small amount of use that Milton made of the Song of Solomon and concludes that it was "not, after all, in the epic tradition in which he was writing" (p. 82). The real reason is that the Song of Solomon lacks the domestic atmosphere of *Paradise Lost*, even though it possesses the motif of idealized love in a garden setting.

34. Tolstoy, "What Is Art?" in *Criticism: The Major Statements*, ed. Charles Kaplan (New York: St. Martin's Press, 1975), p. 452. The descriptions of Genesis as an epic come, respectively, from Jacob Licht, *Storytelling in the Bible* (Jerusalem: Magnes Press, 1978), p. 36; Erich Auerbach, *Mimesis: The Representation of Reality in Western Literature*, trans. Willard R. Trask (1953; rpt. Princeton: Princeton University Press, 1968), p. 7 (the claim is repeated on p. 11); Cyrus H. Gordon, *Before*

differently, since he took his epic story from the opening chapters of Genesis and based much of his poem on it.[35]

Even though Genesis lacks a single unifying epic hero, it is replete with the type of heroism that the Renaissance, especially, associated with epic. Martin Luther suggested the prevailing Renaissance attitude toward the patriarchs of Genesis when he commented, "We must not think that these are ordinary . . . people; but, next to Christ and John the Baptist, they were the most outstanding heroes this world has ever produced. . . . Those patriarchs were most holy men endowed with superior gifts, being the heroes, as it were, of the entire world."[36] In addition to being a story with epic heroes, Genesis is a story of national destiny and scope, inasmuch as it recounts the patriarchal history of the line that became the nation of Israel. The feat around which the story revolves is an epic feat—the formation of a nation under divine providence. Genesis has the historical seriousness that epic traditionally has. The stories of its heroes—Abraham, Isaac, Jacob, Joseph—are quest stories filled with encounters with the supernatural, in a manner reminiscent of the stories of Odysseus and Aeneas. And certainly Genesis fills "the supreme role of epic . . . to focus a society's self-awareness" and to define "the genesis and values" of a culture.[37]

If Genesis belongs to the genus *epic*, it belongs to the species *domestic epic*. The domestic/pastoral emphasis of Genesis begins with chapters 2 and 3, where both the state of innocence and the Fall have a domestic identity. In the words of Fisch, "The tone of the narration of Genesis 3—there is only one word for it—is *do-*

---

the Bible: The Common Background of Greek and Hebrew Civilisations (London: Collins, 1962), p. 285; Jeremy Ingalls, "The Epic Tradition: A Commentary," East-West Review 1 (1964): 46; Frank Moore Cross, Canaanite Myth and Hebrew Epic: Essays in the History of the Religion of Israel (Cambridge: Harvard University Press, 1973), p. 182.

35. While not concerned directly with the epic identity of Genesis, Mother Mary Christopher Pecheux, "Abraham, Adam, and the Theme of Exile in Paradise Lost," PMLA 80 (1965): 365—71, shows how such motifs as exile and quest in Paradise Lost are modeled on the story of Abraham in Genesis.

36. Luther's Works, ed. Jaroslav Pelikan (St. Louis: Concordia Publishing House, 1958), 1:334, 354.

37. Hugh M. Richmond, The Christian Revolutionary: John Milton (Berkeley: University of California Press, 1974), p. 124.

mestic."[38] At the very moment of the Fall, in fact, Eve passes the fruit to Adam in a manner that calls to mind a wife serving her husband at a meal: she "gave also unto her husband with her; and he did eat" (Gen. 3:6). But the brief domestic story of Genesis 2–3 is insufficient to account for Milton's lengthy treatment of Adam and Eve in *Paradise Lost.* The real model is the entire epic of Genesis.

Throughout the book of Genesis we observe family life in a rural and pastoral milieu. Abraham, for example, is a domestic hero. His wife, Sarah, and concubine, Hagar, engage more of his attention by far than any other human characters in the story. His quest is a domestic quest—for land, a son, and descendants. The crises of his life center on family matters, such as disguising his identity as Sarah's husband to preserve his life and marriage, settling disputes between his wife and concubine, showing himself willing to sacrifice his son, and finding a suitable wife for his son. Although his status as the father of believers makes Abraham more than an ordinary husband and father, his typical roles and sphere of action are domestic rather than kingly and military.

The emphasis in the stories of Isaac and Jacob is equally domestic. What, after all, do we most remember from the story of Isaac? His "courtship" (by proxy) of Rebekah, his tension with his wife over which of the two sons should be favored, and his being deceived by his son Jacob. And all of this action occurs not in a palace, as in traditional epic, but in the field and tent, in a manner similar to *Paradise Lost.* The heroic story of Jacob repeats the pattern. His crises are family ones, his heroic acts occur in the context of his family, and his love is domestic and pastoral in flavor.

With the story of Joseph, it is true, we have the action occurring in the more typically epic setting of an emperor's court. But the story begins in the countryside and with the family, and throughout even the public phase of Joseph's life the story of the hero's destiny remains firmly tied to the story of his relations with his family, as well as to such pastoral motifs as harvest and grain. Even in Egypt, Joseph's story bears the marks of what

38. Fisch, "Hebraic Style and Motifs," p. 37.

Northrop Frye calls "the patriarchal pastoral period" of biblical history.[39]

Corresponding to this domestic action in a pastoral setting is the private scope of the heroes' actions. One of the most conspicuous features of the heroes of Genesis is their social obscurity. Whereas Western epic and romance have taken aristocratic figures as their heroes, the heroes of Genesis were not prominent national or international figures within the world of their stories. They were obscure individuals in their day, wanderers without a country. They were, moreover, family leaders in charge of their small domestic sphere, not leaders of nations. Hermann Gunkel wrote regarding them,

> The material of Genesis . . . contains no accounts of great political events, but treats rather the history of a family. We hear a quantity of details, which certainly have for the greater part no value for political history, whether they are attested or not: that Abraham was pious and magnanimous, and that he once put away his concubine to please his wife; that Jacob deceived his brother; that Rachel and Leah were jealous—"unimportant anecdotes of country life, stories of springs, or watering-troughs, and such as are told in the bedchamber," attractive enough to read, yet everything but historical occurrences. Such minor incidents aroused no public interest when they took place.[40]

In this emphasis on the private rather than the public role of the epic hero we can find, I believe, the likely source of Milton's similar strategy in *Paradise Lost*.

A related similarity that Genesis and *Paradise Lost* share is the absence of the military hero as the epic protagonist. Whereas Western epic and romance are variations on the theme of the warrior hero, the heroes of Genesis, like Adam in *Paradise Lost*, are family leaders and tillers of the soil who depend for their livelihood on the land. Only once (in Genesis 14) are their ex-

---

39. *The Great Code: The Bible and Literature* (New York: Harcourt Brace Jovanovich, 1982), p. 143.

40. *The Legends of Genesis: The Biblical Saga and History*, trans. W. H. Carruth (1901; rpt. New York: Schocken Books, 1964), p. 5.

ploits military in nature. The same pattern is true of Milton's Adam, but not of other epic heroes.[41]

Even the epic quest and epic feat in a story like the Abraham story fall into the private and domestic mode. The epic feat in other epics is public in nature and national in its importance; it consists of winning a war or founding an empire or defeating a monster. Even in the *Odyssey*, the ancient epic that is atypical because it celebrates domestic values, the hero is not only the family man returning as a private person to his home, but he also fills the public role of king of Ithaca. When we look closely at the great epic feat in the story of Abraham, it is laughable by contrast. It consists of having a baby and raising a boy. It is thoroughly private and domestic. As Auerbach comments (and it is equally true of *Paradise Lost*), "In the Old Testament stories . . . the sublime working of God . . . reaches so deeply into the everyday that the two realms of the sublime and the everyday are . . . basically inseparable."[42]

We should perhaps note in passing that because the epic feat in the Abraham story is producing a son, it is a feat in which the male protagonist is dependent on his female partner. Joan Webber is thus wrong to claim regarding Adam and Eve in Milton's epic that "theirs is the first epic story to accept absolutely the joint necessity and active heroism of male and female."[43] A predecessor exists in the form of the story of Abraham and Sarah.

By what logic can the birth of a baby become an epic feat? By the same logic that can make pruning a garden an epic action, and eating an apple the crucial event in an epic. We must remember that in biblical literature, as in *Paradise Lost*, the signifi-

---

41. Ulrich Simon, after describing the conventional hero of Western literature, concludes, as I do, that "the biblical stories in Genesis are remarkably free from this pattern of heroism" ("Samson and the Heroic," in *Ways of Reading the Bible*, ed. Michael Wadsworth [Sussex: Harvester Press, 1981], pp. 154–55). Northrop Frye has said that "the hero of most human traditions is not the worker but the leader against the human enemy" (*The Great Code*, p. 187). Because *Paradise Lost* deviates so notably from the main heroic tradition, we are justified in looking for a model, which turns out to be the biblical epic of Genesis.

42. Auerbach, *Mimesis*, pp. 22–23.

43. Webber, *Milton and His Epic Tradition*, p. 161.

cant action is spiritual in nature. External events provide the occasion for spiritual choice, which is the truly significant action. Thomas Greene has said regarding the Fall in *Paradise Lost* that "Milton welcomed the triviality in the act of eating the apple because that triviality demonstrates the primacy of interior action."[44] In a similar way, the story of Abraham focuses on an event that, given the standards of heroic epic, is trivial but that has the advantage of allowing the emphasis to fall on the spiritual rather than the physical action. Externally the process by which Abraham received his child was unheroic (he waited twenty-five years), but the spiritual struggles and victories that were occasioned by that event were epic in their stature.[45] In *Paradise Lost*, similarly, the external life of Adam and Eve in the garden is dull by comparison with traditional epic. Yet their life in the garden is Milton's moral norm, and it rises to epic stature because of the spiritual realities represented by that life.

Not only did Milton duplicate the domestic spirit of Genesis; he also modeled some specific domestic scenes on this biblical epic. The most famous example is Adam and Eve's hospitable reception of Raphael (5.297ff.), which is modeled on Abraham and Sarah's similar reception of three angelic visitors in Genesis 18.[46] Adam's pleading with God for a human mate (8.357–436) bears a resemblance to Abraham's interceding for the safety of his nephew Lot.[47] Critics have tended to view the tone of such

44. *The Descent from Heaven: A Study in Epic Continuity* (New Haven: Yale University Press, 1963), p. 405.

45. Norman Habel says regarding the heroes of Genesis, "There is something epic and mighty in the way these men of God grapple with their Lord. They are giants of prayer and intercession" (*Literary Criticism of the Old Testament* [Philadelphia: Fortress Press, 1971], p. 48).

46. For commentary on the parallels, see Sims, *The Bible in Milton's Epics*, pp. 202–3; Fisch, "Hebraic Style and Motifs," pp. 54–56; Cohen, *The Throne and the Chariot*, pp. 93–97; Jason P. Rosenblatt, "Celestial Entertainment in Eden: Book V of *Paradise Lost*," *Harvard Theological Review* 62 (1969): 411–27; Jack Goldman, "Perspectives of Raphael's Meal in *Paradise Lost*, Book V," *Milton Quarterly* 11 (1977):31–37; Thomas Kranidas, *The Fierce Equation: A Study of Milton's Decorum* (The Hague: Mouton, 1965), pp. 147–54. Fisch stresses the domestic tone of the episode and links it to Genesis: Milton has welded "the heroic matter of the epic on to the quotidian realism of a Biblical story."

47. For commentary, see Sims, *The Bible in Milton's Epics*, pp. 203–4, and Fisch, "Hebraic Style and Motifs," pp. 55–56.

episodes in *Paradise Lost* as comic. But I have already noted that Genesis invests domestic, commonplace events with ultimate significance by accepting the principle of the primacy of the spiritual. In the words of Auerbach, biblical narrative "engenders a new elevated style, which does not scorn everyday life"; it "created an entirely new kind of sublimity, in which the everyday and the low were included."[48] Failure to realize how thoroughly Milton assimilated the biblical example perhaps accounts for the consistency with which critics have misread the tone of Milton's domestic scenes. Assuming that commonplace domestic reality is perforce subject matter for comedy (a conclusion based on classical models), they automatically equate "the domestic and the comic," or treat Raphael's visit as a low-brow "breakfast scene," or interpret the episode as containing "a good deal of comedy." Actually, as Cohen observes, Milton treats the domestic scenes before the Fall with full "epic dignity."[49]

Nowhere in classical epic tradition do we find a work that resembles *Paradise Lost* in its focus on the private, domestic life of a human couple living in pastoral surroundings. When domestic and pastoral interludes occur in other epics (for example, Odysseus' visit in Phaiacia or reunion with Penelope in book 23 of the *Odyssey*, Hector bidding farewell to Andromache, Aeneas seeking out his family during the sack of Troy), they are always moments that the hero leaves behind in order to accomplish the epic feat on a public, military plane. The model for Milton's domestic epic, I suggest, comes from Genesis, with its blend of domestic activity and pastoral simplicity, both invested with a quality of ultimate spiritual significance.

II

A second part of Milton's anti-epic strategy was to discard the theme of human greatness in favor of the twin themes of divine greatness and human weakness. The shift of focus from human

48. Auerbach, *Mimesis*, pp. 72, 154.
49. Tillyard, *The English Epic*, p. 439; Kranidas, *The Fierce Equation*, p. 153; Rosenblatt, "Celestial Entertainment," p. 427; Cohen, *The Throne and the Chariot*, p. 96.

to divine glory is perhaps most evident in Milton's treatment of God (especially the Son) as epic hero, that is, as exemplar of supreme virtue. Whereas "classical epic centered . . . on man," Milton "reverses this tradition and has put God back in the center of the epic world."[50] The epic tradition that Milton inherited praised a human hero or patron. Milton, by contrast, reserves his praise for God:

> thy Name
> Shall be the copious matter of my Song
> Henceforth, and never shall my Harp thy praise
> Forget, nor from thy Fathers praise disjoine (3.412–15).

Earlier epics had praised a self-reliant human hero; Milton praises the only self-reliant hero, God. As Adam says to God, "Thou in thy self art perfet, and in thee / Is no deficience found; not so is Man" (8.415–16).

Milton's substitution of a divine for a human level extends to other motifs as well. Traditional epic had been based on the motifs of glory and merit, conceived humanly. *Paradise Lost* presents the same motifs, but they center on the Son, not a human hero.[51] The usual subject of warfare appears in Milton's war in Heaven, where it becomes a story of creaturely (angelic) inactivity as the Son wins the battle in a supernatural manner.[52] The action of classical epic centers around the founding of an empire

50. Francis C. Blessington, *"Paradise Lost" and the Classical Epic Tradition* (Boston: Routledge and Kegan Paul, 1979), p. 49.

51. Blessington, ibid., pp. 83–85, notes that *glory* "is a key word in the epic tradition" and shows that in *Paradise Lost* true glory belongs to God. As John T. Shawcross has stated, epic is always "a kind of praise," but *Paradise Lost* is unconventional in being "a praise of God rather than of hero and nation" ("The Style and Genre of *Paradise Lost*," in *New Essays on "Paradise Lost,"* ed. Thomas Kranidas [Berkeley: University of California Press, 1969], p. 26).

52. Critics who discuss the war in Heaven as an important part of Milton's revaluation of the heroic ideals of classical epic include Kates, "Revaluation of the Classical Heroic"; Summers, *The Muse's Method*, pp. 122–37; Stanley Fish, *Surprised by Sin: The Reader in "Paradise Lost"* (New York: St. Martin's Press, 1967), pp. 158–207; Stella Revard, "Milton's Critique of Heroic Warfare in *Paradise Lost* V and VI," *Studies in English Literature* 7 (1967): 119–39; James A. Winn, "Milton on Heroic Warfare," *Yale Review* 66 (1976):70–86; George deForest Lord, *Heroic Mockery: Variations on Epic Themes from Homer to Joyce* (Newark: University of Delaware Press, 1977), pp. 67–77.

by human heroism on the battlefield. *Paradise Lost* gives us a divine equivalent in God's creation of the world by his supernatural power.

Milton balances this exaltation of God with a denigration of man. His very theme, "Of Mans First Disobedience," announces a revolution. As Steadman has said so eloquently about this statement of theme,

> The uniqueness of *Paradise Lost* is implicit in the first enunciation of its theme. . . . Unlike the usual heroic poem, it does not propose a victory, but a defeat. Its action is not some illustrious "act of benefit", but a crime. Its hero is not a paragon of heroic virtue, but the archetypal sinner. The results of this conflict are not glory but shame, not dominion or deliverance, but servitude and death. Instead of celebrating his merit, the poem chastises his vice. Its argument is in reality an "argument of human weakness rather than of strength."[53]

Paradise Lost is "the Anatomy of Failure," built on Milton's own "experience of heroic failure."[54]

This rejection of the humanistic premises of classical epic entails specific epic motifs as well as the general theme. The usual epic theme of human merit appears in *Paradise Lost*, but Milton gives it a novel twist by showing that what his human characters merit is condemnation and death. The epic feat is not winning a victory but losing the world. Most conspicuous of all, perhaps, is Milton's parody of the prophetic vision of future history. Whereas Virgil and Spenser had used this epic convention to celebrate their nation, Milton transforms it into a nightmare of human vice and depravity, relieved only by occasional instances of solitary figures who exhibit moral heroism.

Milton, in other words, stands apart from the tendency of Western epic to put the human and divine on a single continuum and to narrow the gap between the two. The gods of classical mythology are basically superior humans, and the human heroes become godlike. "How could I forget godlike Odysseus?"

---

53. *Milton and the Renaissance Hero*, p. v.
54. Richmond, *The Christian Revolutionary*, p. 129; Webber, *Milton and His Epic Traditions*, p. 105.

Zeus asks regarding Odysseus in the opening lines of Homer's *Odyssey*, while the closing pages of Virgil's *Aeneid* assert that "Aeneas is a divine hero."[55] Someone has rightly said that "in the societies that we might call 'mythological' . . . man's culture and the world of the gods exist in a kind of cosmic continuum with little or no gap between them."[56] Someone has quipped that God made man in his image and man returned the compliment. Milton, by contrast, follows the biblical pattern and goes out of his way to accentuate the infinite disproportion between divine and human merits. He stresses the "antagonism between, instead of identification of, hero and God."[57] The result is an epic in which the chief heroic example is a divine being, the truly heroic exploits divine works, and the heroic virtues divine virtues.

Where, we might well ask, did Milton find a literary model for such a consistently executed subversion of the humanistic emphasis of Western epic? In the Old Testament epic of the Exodus (by which I mean the book of Exodus and the narrative portions of the subsequent books in the Pentateuch) Milton would have found in kernel form virtually everything that he himself did in exalting the divine and disparaging the human. Of all the narrative parts in the Bible, the story of the Exodus probably would have struck Milton as the most thoroughly epic in its content.[58] It

55. *The Odyssey of Homer*, trans. Ennis Rees (Indianapolis: Bobbs-Merrill, 1977), p. 5; *The Aeneid of Vergil*, trans. Kevin Guinagh (New York: Holt, Rinehart and Winston, 1970), p. 330.

56. Herbert Schneidau, *Sacred Discontent: The Bible and Western Tradition* (Baton Rouge: Louisiana State University Press, 1976), p. 4.

57. Hagin, *The Epic Hero*, p. 82.

58. Criticism to date has skirted the issue of Milton's use of Exodus as a literary model for epic. Fisch, "Hebrew Style and Motifs," pp. 42–51, shows how allusions to Exodus are woven into the texture of Milton's poem; he also cites the liabilities of the biblical story as an epic subject (God overshadows the human characters, the central hero lacks military prowess and is noted for meekness), overlooking the ways in which Milton used Exodus as a guide for achieving these very qualities in *Paradise Lost*, even though he chose early Genesis as his subject. John T. Shawcross discusses the myth or archetype of exodus as it informs Milton's poem in *With Mortal Voice: The Creation of "Paradise Lost"* (Lexington: University Press of Kentucky, 1982), pp. 119–38. Jason P. Rosenblatt, "Structural Unity and Temporal Concordance: The War in Heaven in *Paradise Lost*," *PMLA* 87 (1972): 31–41, draws a number of specific parallels between the Exodus of the Bible and of Jewish tradition and Milton's portrayal of the war in Heaven.

is a story that has been appropriately called "a prose epic," "the most 'epical' of all biblical stories," a "national epic," "Epic material," "the Epic of Moses," "an epic narration," and a work belonging to "the epic ideology of the ancient Near East."[59]

Milton would have been particularly struck by the parallels between the epic of the Exodus and the classical epic that *Paradise Lost* is generally considered to most closely resemble, Virgil's *Aeneid*. Like the *Aeneid*, the biblical epic of the Exodus is a national epic that tells about the formation of an empire and the decisive events in the early history of a nation. Both epics are quest stories in which a group of people travels from one geographic area to another in order to establish a new nation in a promised land. Both epics are strongly religious epics in which the nation and religion are interrelated. Both epics are built around the twin motifs of the transfer of an empire and of an epic leader who embodies the normative values of a culture and whose personality permeates the larger epic action of the nation.

But, along with the similarities, Milton would have sensed a crucial difference in spirit and in specific narrative motifs between classical and biblical epic. Classical epic is humanistic and exists to glorify a human hero and his nation. In the words of Joseph Summers, traditional epics "dealt with the great actions of the heroes of a tribe or nation or civilisation. In hearing or reading them, later men could feel that their heritage was both defined and glorified by the ancestral deeds."[60] The epic of the Exodus, by contrast, reserves its praise for God. I have elsewhere demonstrated how the terms by which John Steadman describes *Paradise Lost* are exactly the ones that best identify the

59. Ferdinand S. Schenck, *The Oratory and Poetry of the Bible* (New York: George H. Doran, 1915), p. 212, Fisch, "Hebrew Style and Motifs," p. 38; Cyrus H. Gordon, *Homer and the Bible* (Ventnor, N.J.: Ventnor Publishers, 1967), p. 21; Cross, *Canaanite Myth and Hebrew Epic*, p. 134; Roland M. Frye, *The Bible: Selections from the King James Version for Study as Literature* (Boston: Houghton Mifflin, 1965), p. 63; Luis Alonso Schokel, *The Inspired Word: Scripture in the Light of Language and Literature* (New York: Herder and Herder, 1965), p. 203; and Meredith G. Kline, *The Structure of Biblical Authority* (Grand Rapids, Mich.: William B. Eerdmans, 1972), p. 79.
60. "The Embarrassments of *Paradise Lost*," in *Approaches to "Paradise Lost*," ed. Patrides, p. 67.

Old Testament's anti-epic.[61] As in *Paradise Lost*, the anti-epic bias of Exodus has a double thrust: the greatness of God and the depravity of people.

From the beginning of the epic of the Exodus, God is the chief actor, as a few typical specimens of action will show. When the Israelites finally leave Egypt, the writer tells us, "And they spoiled the Egyptians" (Exod. 12:36). This is the standard epic formula, and its military imagery, if we encountered it out of this context, would prompt us to conclude that the Israelites had defeated their enemy on the battlefield. The truth, of course, is that there has not been a battle at all. Nor has the victory been achieved by human effort. During the ten plagues, the Israelites have been passive spectators of the mighty acts of God, while the epic leader's activity has been largely limited to initiating God's miracles with his rod.

In classical epic, the exploits of the conquering hero are the subject of epic boasts, either by the hero himself or by a court bard. Against such a background, Moses' speech to his followers after God's deliverance by means of the plagues is a parody of the usual epic pattern. Moses boasts of God's epic feats and ascribes to God what in ordinary epic is ascribed to a human warrior: "by strength of hand the Lord brought you out from this place" (Exod. 13:3); "the Lord shall bring thee into the land of the Canaanites" (13:3, 11); "And thou shalt shew thy son in that day, saying, This is done because of that which the Lord did unto me when I came forth out of Egypt" (13:8); "by strength of hand the Lord brought us out from Egypt" (13:14); "the Lord slew all the firstborn in the land of Egypt" (13:15). In such a story of divine deliverance there is simply no room for the conventional epic emphasis on human glory.[62]

The deliverance at the Red Sea follows the same pattern. The

---

61. *The Literature of the Bible* (Grand Rapids, Mich.: Zondervan, 1974), pp. 82–85.

62. D. F. Rauber, "Observations on Biblical Epic," *Genre* 3 (1970): 331, 333–34, notes that "in view of the universality" of the heroic value of honor in the epic tradition "its near absence in biblical accounts is notable. . . . A Hebraic hero rests upon the rock of the Lord, not the foundation of personal glory."

episode itself allows for a demonstration of what is dear to the heart of every epic writer, the theme of glory. But in this story it is God, not a human hero, who is able to say, "I will get glory over Pharaoh and all his host" (Exod. 14:4, RSV). In the encounter that follows, the people are again the passive spectators of God's mighty acts. "Fear ye not," Moses tells the Israelites; "stand still, and see the salvation of the Lord. . . . The Lord shall fight for you, and ye shall hold your peace" (14:13–14). The actual epic encounter turns out to be a divine conquest: "the Lord overthrew the Egyptians" (14:27); "thus the Lord saved Israel that day out of the hand of the Egyptians; and Israel saw the Egyptians dead upon the sea shore" (14:30); "And Israel saw that great work which the Lord did upon the Egyptians" (14:31). It is no wonder that Moses' Song of Victory (Exod. 15) substitutes God for the customary human victor of classical epic: "I will sing unto the Lord, for he hath triumphed gloriously. . . . The Lord is my strength and song. . . . The Lord is a man of war: the Lord is his name" (15:1–3). In the epic of the Exodus, it is clear, the acts that merit the storyteller's praise are the acts of God, not of people. In classical epics the gods sometimes participate in battles, but they do not, as God does in Exodus, replace the human warriors entirely.

How do we know that Milton followed the anti-epic pattern of Exodus in *Paradise Lost*? It is obvious that Milton drew heavily on the model of Exodus for one of his great anti-epic episodes, the war in Heaven, especially its culmination with the Son's intervention. As the Son addresses the faithful angels on the last day of the battle, he declares,

> Stand still in bright array ye Saints, here stand
> Ye Angels arm'd, this day from Battel rest. . . .
> . . . stand onely and behold
> Gods indignation on these Godless pourd
> By mee. (6.801–2, 810–12)

This is a virtual paraphrase of Moses' command to the Israelites at the Red Sea: "Fear ye not, stand still, and see the salvation of the Lord. . . . The Lord shall fight for you, and ye shall hold

65

your peace" (Exod. 14:13–14).[63] What the narrator in *Paradise Lost* says in summary of the faithful angels is equally true of the Israelites in such episodes as the plagues and the Red Sea deliverance: "who silent stood / Eye witnesses of his Almightie Acts" (6.882–83).

And this is only part of the use that Milton makes of the story of the Exodus in his account of the war in Heaven. He keeps alive in our minds the way in which he is modeling his picture of Satan and his rebellious angels on Pharaoh and his army. The fallen angels are as numerous as the locusts of the eighth plague (1.338–43). As the confounded enemies of God who perished in a lake, the fallen angels are linked in an epic simile to the army of Pharaoh as it was overwhelmed in the Red Sea (1.306–13). Like Pharaoh, the fallen angels refuse to be quelled by God's signs and wonders, instead hardening themselves in rebellion (6.789–93).

It is not primarily the details, however, that show Milton's indebtedness to the biblical epic of the Exodus. Even more important than the specific allusions is the prevailing spirit of both works. As we read Milton's accounts of both the war in Heaven and the creation of the world, we sense the same atmosphere that we experience as we read the epic of the Exodus—an emphasis on the transcendent greatness of God, the chief hero whose acts alone are truly glorious.

Corresponding to the greatness of God in the story of the Exodus is the consistent smallness of people. It is not simply that they are passive spectators while God performs the feats of the plagues and numerous miracles and rescues. The people are actively depraved in their behavior. The Israelites are portrayed as chronic complainers whose ignoble behavior serves as a continuous foil to the mercy and goodness of God. The stock epithet *children of Israel* begins to resonate with connotations of immaturity and childish behavior as the epic unfolds. And all of this, we must remember, in an epic that is nationalistic and patriotic in nature.

63. For further commentary on the correspondence, see Sims, *The Bible in Milton's Epics*, pp. 151–52.

Virtually every episode connected with the journey from Egypt to Canaan reenacts a common pattern consisting of crisis or test—complaint by the people—deliverance by God, often accompanied by a revelation from God. In the incident at Marah, for example (Exod. 15:22–26), the bitter waters become a test of the Israelites' faith in God; they fail the test by murmuring; Moses cries to God; and God works a miracle, revealing at the same time that he will be the Israelites' healer if they will obey him.

The most notable feature of this series of tests is that the people fail every major test. In fact, near the end of the story God castigates the Israelites with the charge that they "have put me to the proof these ten times and have not hearkened to my voice" (Num. 14:22, RSV). It so happens that if we catalog the events of the story we will find ten occasions when the Israelites as a whole failed the test by murmuring against God, against God's chosen leaders, or against the circumstances into which God brought them. The events, which are a rollcall of the main episodes in the story, are the oppression by the taskmasters in response to Moses' early activity (Exod. 5:20–21); the Red Sea crisis (Exod. 14:10–12); the bitter waters of Marah (Exod. 15:24); the lack of food near Elim (Exod. 16:2–3); the disobedience regarding the gathering of manna (Exod. 16:20, 27); the lack of water at Rephidim (Exod. 17:2–3); the golden calf incident (Exod. 32); the complaining at Taberah (Num. 11:1); the craving for meat (Num. 11:4–5); the unbelief of the ten spies (Num. 13–14).

Milton thoroughly assimilated the Exodus motif of human waywardness, most notably when he came to write his epic vision of future history in the last two books of *Paradise Lost.* Again it is the spirit of the vision that is important rather than the specific details taken from the Pentateuch. "Good with bad / Expect to hear," Michael tells Adam as he previews the vision, "supernal Grace contending / With sinfulness of Men" (11.358–60). Whereas in other epics the vision of the future is an occasion to praise the greatness of the poet's nation, Milton transforms it into what has been variously called "a detailed survey of . . . depravity," a "chronicle of human backslidings," an exposure of "the spiritual bankruptcy of natural man," and "a darkly pessimistic view of human history." [64]

The anti-epic strategy of *Paradise Lost* is based partly on the disproportion between divine greatness and human weakness. This is precisely the dual theme of the biblical epic of the Exodus. It is the interpretive framework that is suggested by the Song of Moses at the end of the Pentateuch (Deut. 32). Part of the song catalogs God's great acts of mercy: "ascribe ye greatness unto our God. He is the Rock, his work is perfect; for all his ways are judgment: A God of truth and without iniquity, just and right is he" (Deut. 32:2–3). This is balanced by repeated emphasis on the theme that "they are a perverse and crooked generation" (Deut. 32:5). The same doubleness pervades the catalogs in the most famous of the historical psalms, Psalm 78.

We need not wonder where Milton received the impetus for the transformation of epic tradition that he effected when he made his epic hero divine rather than human and made the human actors on his epic stage deeply flawed instead of paragons of strength and virtue. There are only two epics that are mainly satiric in their portrayal of the human characters in the story. What Joseph Summers says of *Paradise Lost* is equally true of the biblical epic of the Exodus: "No heroic poem was ever less a glorification of a nation or a civilisation." [65] Milton found this pattern, not primarily in classical epic, nor even simply in Christian doctrine, but in biblical epic, especially the epic of the Exodus.

III

Despite the large influence of Old Testament epic on the spirit and ethos of *Paradise Lost*, there is also a distinctive New Testament flavor to Milton's poem. This tone comprises a Christo-

---

64. Steadman, *Milton and the Renaissance Hero*, p. 197; Fish, *Surprised by Sin*, p. 287; H. R. MacCallum, "Milton and Sacred History: Books XI and XII of *Paradise Lost*," in *Essays in English Literature from the Renaissance to the Victorian Age Presented to A. S. P. Woodhouse*, ed. Millar MacLure and F. W. Watt (Toronto: University of Toronto Press, 1964), p. 161; and Louis L. Martz, *The Paradise Within: Studies in Vaughan, Traherne, and Milton* (New Haven: Yale University Press, 1964), p. 141.

65. Summers, "The Embarrassments of *Paradise Lost*," p. 68.

centric focus, an emphasis on the spiritual as distinct from the physical, and an elevation of the heavenly over the earthly. This New Testament atmosphere is closely tied to yet another element of Milton's anti-epic procedure: *Paradise Lost* repeatedly presents a spiritualized or heavenly or divine version of the standard motifs of classical epic.

Warfare and conquest, for example, are the established subject for classical epic. But the form in which these motifs appear in *Paradise Lost* is drastically altered from classical sources. Warfare in *Paradise Lost* is spiritual (good versus evil, obedience versus disobedience to God), not secular and political. Conquest is not national and military but is pictured by Adam and Eve's repentance from sin and faith in Christ; it is a conquest of sin and spiritual death, not of a rival warrior. The decisive conflict in *Paradise Lost* does not occur on the battlefield, as ancient epic would have it. It is instead "a wholly moral conflict" that consists of "doing battle within the soul, with defeat or victory defined only in spiritual terms."[66] Near the end of the poem, as the story moves toward Adam's ultimate moment of epiphany, the old heroic formulas make an appearance ("overcoming," "accomplishing great things," "fortitude," "highest victorie"), but they are radically redefined in spiritual and moral terms:

> Henceforth I learne, that to obey is best,
> And love with fear the onely God, . . .
>   . . . with good
> Still overcoming evil, and by small
> Accomplishing great things, by things deemd weak
> Subverting worldly strong, and worldly wise
> By simply meek; that suffering for Truths sake
> Is fortitude to highest victorie. (12.561–62, 565–70)

Not only are these motifs given a spiritual rather than a physical importance in *Paradise Lost*; they are also frequently shifted from an earthly to a heavenly plane. For example, the greatest example of the theme of epic battle in *Paradise Lost* is a war in

66. Kates, "Revaluation of the Classical Hero," p. 317. Hagin, *The Epic Hero*, p. 154, similarly notes, "Milton conceives of his theme as a conflict of the soul which can only insufficiently be treated in direct action."

Heaven fought by angels instead of by human warriors. In Milton's celestial battle the final conquest is not military in the ordinary sense. Instead, on the climactic third day the physical modes of warfare are replaced by the supernatural power of the Son as he rides forth in his celestial chariot.

Another epic feature that becomes spiritualized in *Paradise Lost* is the motif of dominion or empire. In conventional epic the standard goal of the quest and the final reward of heroic achievement is a kingdom. *Paradise Lost* gives us several versions of this motif. On a human level, dominion is not the political rulership of a king but Adam and Eve's life of pastoral perfection and their obedience to God before the Fall, as Adam makes clear in his first speech in the poem (4.426–32). Dominion, in other words, consists of ruling a garden and one's individual soul. After the Fall, dominion is still spiritual in nature and consists of repentance and coming to believe in the Son as savior (this being the climax to which the vision of the future moves).

On the divine level, empire in *Paradise Lost* is God's spiritual, heavenly kingdom, yet another substitution for the earthly kingdom of conventional epic. The dialogue in Heaven in book 3 (especially lines 274–343) contains the motif in kernel form. It pictures the Son as the one who, through his incarnation, will win as a kingdom the church, which he will bring to Heaven and reign over as "universal King" (3.318).

Another epic convention that becomes spiritualized in *Paradise Lost* is heroism. In conventional epic the hero is imaged as a military hero whose great feat is victory on the battlefield. Horace accurately summarized the subject matter of heroic epic as "the deeds of kings and captains and the sorrows of war."[67] Milton, however, replaced the warrior as hero with the Christian saint as hero. Such heroism is displayed before the Fall by Adam and Eve's virtuous life in Paradise and after the Fall by their repentance, mutual forgiveness, faith in God to forgive them, and willingness to take up life in a fallen world sustained, not by the promise of earthly success, but by the providence of God and the

---

67. *Art of Poetry*, in *Criticism: The Major Texts*, ed. Walter Jackson Bate (New York: Harcourt, Brace and World, 1952), p. 52.

hope of redemption. It can be rightly said of Milton's concept of the hero that "his main characteristic is not physical strength but moral strength."[68] Near the end of the poem, after the preview of fallen history and just before Adam is expelled from Paradise, Adam expresses a heroic ideal that is solidly Christian and spiritual in nature:

> Henceforth I learne, that to obey is best,
> And love with fear the onely God, to walk
> As in his presence, ever to observe
> His providence, and on him sole depend. (12.561–64)

And Michael reinforces this revolutionary epic norm with a summary of virtues that is equally spiritual:

> onely add
> Deeds to thy knowledge answerable, add Faith,
> Add vertue, Patience, Temperance, add Love. (12.581–83)

A final New Testament emphasis in *Paradise Lost* is its Christocentricity.[69] A number of epic formulas come to focus on the Son before the story is complete. The dialogue in Heaven in book 3 exalts the worthiness of the Son and invests his redemptive life with the quality of being the ultimate feat in the history of the universe. In the war in Heaven, moreover, it is the Son alone who wins the victory,

> that the Glorie may be thine
> Of ending this great Warr, since none but Thou
> Can end it. (6.701–3)

In the creation of the world, the Son, though not the only person of the Godhead who is active,[70] is conspicuously present.

---

68. William R. Herman, "Heroism and *Paradise Lost*," *College English* 21 (1959): 13.
69. Woodhouse, *The Heavenly Muse*, p. 188, calls the Son "the real hero of *Paradise Lost* in the sense that, like Achilles and Aeneas, he sets the standard of heroism." Important discussions of the Son as the hero of *Paradise Lost* include Seaman, *Moral Paradox*, pp. 9–58; Boyd M. Berry, *Process of Speech: Puritan Religious Writing and "Paradise Lost"* (Baltimore: John Hopkins University Press, 1976), pp. 223–32; and Robert J. Wickenheiser, "Milton's 'Pattern of a Christian Hero': The Son in *Paradise Lost*," *Milton Quarterly* 12 (1978): 1–3.
70. For the data on which this comment is based, see Leland Ryken, *The Apoca-*

And the entire vision of the future comes to focus on the incarnation of the Son.

To summarize, an important part of Milton's anti-epic strategy in *Paradise Lost* consists of transforming motifs that had been earthly and physical in the previous epic tradition into something spiritual or heavenly or related to the Son. If we are looking for the model for this treatment of the inherited epic traits, we can look to a New Testament book that is filled with epic features, the book of Revelation.

It is obvious that *Paradise Lost* is deeply indebted to the book of Revelation, but the critics' account of the relationship between the two works has never struck me as satisfactory. We know from Milton's own comments that he regarded Revelation as a literary model, but exactly how he used Revelation remains an open question.[71] Generally the critics' claims have exceeded in scope what they actually demonstrate.[72]

Michael Fixler, for example, shows conclusively that it is possible to draw many parallels between *Paradise Lost* and Revela-

---

lyptic Vision in "Paradise Lost" (Ithaca: Cornell University Press, 1970), pp. 168–73, and "Milton's Dramatization of the Godhead in *Paradise Lost*," *Milton Quarterly* 9 (1975): 1–6.

71. Milton's remarks occur in the autobiographical digression of *The Reason of Church Government* and the preface to *Samson Agonistes*. Several important studies of Milton are concerned not with the book of Revelation but Protestant commentary on it as a literary influence on Milton. See, for example, Barbara K. Lewalski, "*Samson Agonistes* and the 'Tragedy' of the Apocalypse," *PMLA* 85 (1970): 1050–62, and Stella P. Revard, "The Warring Saints and the Dragon: A Commentary Upon Revelation 12:7–9 and Milton's War in Heaven," *Philological Quarterly* 52 (1974): 181–94, rpt. in *The War in Heaven: "Paradise Lost" and the Tradition of Satan's Rebellion* (Ithaca: Cornell University Press, 1980), pp. 108–28.

72. For strictures similar to mine on the claims by Fixler, Dobbins, and Wittreich, see C. A. Patrides, "'Something Like Prophetic Strain': Apocalyptic Configurations in Milton," *English Language Notes* 19 (1982): 198–99. Patrides, in turn, understates the influence of Revelation on Milton's epic techniques because he is looking upon Revelation as a source of Milton's imagery, structure, and themes, instead of as a literary model for some specific epic techniques and transformations that we find in *Paradise Lost*. Patrides's caution that a critic will find Revelation yielding what he or she is looking for is true enough, but his own essay illustrates that very point: given the grid of interests through which he puts the data, there is relatively little correspondence between the book of Revelation and *Paradise Lost*.

tion.[73] His bigger claim that the structure of *Paradise Lost* is modeled on the sevenfold structure of Revelation, however, is based on such a complex and intricate system of alleged parallels and inversions and "transversions" that the whole structure collapses under its own weight, in the process refuting Fixler's claim that the blind Milton used the scheme as a simple mnemonic device. Even Fixler's division of *Paradise Lost* into seven "visions" (to apply the term in this way to *Paradise Lost* already begs the question), while plausible and helpful, is far from conclusive. In an encyclopedic work like *Paradise Lost*, many divisions are possible: Northrop Frye finds twelve units, Arthur Barker six units of two books each and three units of four books, Ernest Sirluck five units, Francis Blessington six units (but not the same as Barker's arrangement), Robert M. Adams a "ring" construction of six units, and so forth.[74]

Austin C. Dobbins's *Milton and the Book of Revelation: The Heavenly Cycle* is a heterogeneous and confusing collection of specific details from the book of Revelation and Renaissance exegesis of it, all of them alleged sources for specific effects in *Paradise Lost*.[75] Here, too, the sheer quantity of details threatens to obscure the main outlines of the thesis; yet if one stands at a sufficient distance, the final impression (especially that created by the chapter on the war in Heaven) is undoubtedly correct: Milton did, in fact, use the book of Revelation as a model for his epic, and many facets of *Paradise Lost* that are usually attributed to the classical tradition can just as plausibly (and sometimes more plausibly) be ascribed to the influence of the Bible.

Joseph A. Wittreich's epoch-making *Visionary Poetics: Milton's Tradition and His Legacy* similarly establishes as indisputable that the book of Revelation influenced *Paradise Lost*. Wittreich's argu-

73. "The Apocalypse within *Paradise Lost*," in *New Essays on "Paradise Lost,"* ed. Kranidas, pp. 131–78.
74. Frye, *Return of Eden*, pp. 18–21; Barker, "Structural Pattern in *Paradise Lost*," *Philological Quarterly* 28 (1949): 17–30; Sirluck, *"Paradise Lost": A Deliberate Epic* (Cambridge: W. Heffer's and Sons, 1967), pp. 11–13; Blessington, *Classical Epic Tradition*, pp. 74–78; Adams, *The Norton Anthology of English Literature*, 3d ed. (New York: W. W. Norton, 1974), 1:1360.
75. (University: University of Alabama Press, 1975).

ment is strong when he is content to treat Revelation as exemplary of a visionary spirit, tone, and rhetoric, but weak when he asserts that Revelation provided Milton with the basic genre (identified as prophecy) for *Paradise Lost*. The truth is that prophecy is not a well-defined genre, as becomes clear when one begins to apply some of Wittreich's tidy definitions to Old Testament prophetic books.[76] Prophecy is a spirit or tone or quality or atmosphere that can occur in a wide range of genres. To use Northrop Frye's terminology, it is a "pregeneric form," which explains why Wittreich can apply it to such diverse works (in terms of literary genre) as *Lycidas* and *Paradise Lost*. We are also on firmer ground when we use the adjectival form *prophetic* rather than the noun form *prophecy* (with its implication of a well-defined genre). Once we begin to speak of the *prophetic* element in literature, it turns out that we are really talking about a quality of discourse, a stance of the writer as a person and narrator, and a set of poetic and rhetorical techniques, not about a genre of literature.

One of the greatest contributions that Wittreich makes is his demonstration of the epic qualities of Revelation. In fact, he repeatedly acknowledges that the traits he attributes to prophecy (encyclopedic scope, mixture of genres, use of visions, the legislative role of the writer, the use of dramatized scenes) are equally characteristic of epic. Having shown how thoroughly the book of Revelation resembles epic, Wittreich offers a non sequitur—that Milton subdued "epic within prophecy" (p. 76), writing a prophecy, in the final analysis, rather than an epic. Yet no amount of special pleading will convince us that *Paradise Lost* is, in terms of genre, anything other than an epic. The parallels that Wittreich draws between Revelation and epic pave the way for a conclusion opposite to the one he draws and that I think is correct: Milton looked upon Revelation as an epic and used it, not as a model

76. (San Marino, Calif.: Henry E. Huntington Library, 1979). Wittreich also slights the ways in which the book of Revelation belongs to the intertestamental and New Testament genre known as apocalypse, as distinct from prophecy. The salient features of the genre include dualistic structure (conflict between good and evil), eschatological outlook, messianic focus, spiritism, use of animal symbolism and numerology, and a judgmental tone.

for writing something other than epic, but as a literary model for writing the particular type of epic that he produced. As Wittreich notes elsewhere, "There are many points of correspondence between Revelation prophecy and Milton's conception of epic."[77] Revelation did not give Milton a new genre with which to replace epic; it showed him how to write a spiritual epic.

The fact that Milton twice refers to the book of Revelation as a "tragedy" does not cast doubt on my conclusion, for several reasons. Milton's citation of Pareus to support the idea of Revelation as a drama in the preface to *Samson Agonistes* is strictly apologetic. To my knowledge, no one has suggested that the book of Revelation is a model for the dramatic *genre* of Milton's play. The reference to the Apocalypse as a tragedy in *The Reason of Church Government* is also apologetic, lending credence to William Riley Parker's view that Milton simply wished to invoke biblical authority to silence Puritan objections against drama.[78] Furthermore, Milton's designation of Revelation as a "high and stately Tragedy" has little to do with literary form and instead belongs to the Protestant tradition of exegesis that interpreted "the Church as tragic protagonist enduring painful agony and suffering."[79] The book of Revelation, moreover, is a mixed form that encompasses both epic and drama, as well as lyric. Milton did not necessarily regard it as only a drama. Finally, a text can influence a poet's handling of a genre without adhering in every respect to that genre; Milton called the book of Job a brief epic, but its influence on Milton's drama *Samson Agonistes* is well established.

The affinities of Revelation to epic are obvious. The work consists of a great and heightened battle or conflict conducted partly by spiritual beings using supernatural means of warfare (see especially Rev. 12). There is a cosmic setting for the action, including Heaven as well as earth and Hell. References to the earth often extend to the whole earth, not just a localized part of

77. Wittreich, *Angel of Apocalypse*, p. 169.
78. "On Milton's Early Literary Program," *Modern Philology* 33 (1935–1936): 49–53.
79. For details, see Lewalski, "*Samson Agonistes* and the 'Tragedy' of the Apocalypse."

it, reinforcing the expansiveness of the action. As we read the book, we follow the exploits of a hero (Christ) who conquers his enemies and establishes his eternal empire. The story is the record of the mighty feats of the central hero. We also observe many scenes set in Heaven, where decisions are made that are then enacted on earth. These scenes resemble, both in construction and function, the epic councils of the gods. The work is built on the pattern of the quest—the believer's quest for Heaven and the movement of history toward its consummation and goal. There are also visions of future history. What does it all add up to? That the work is composed of a whole host of familiar epic motifs. In the book of Revelation there is, indeed, an "approximation to the epic."[80]

When we look at the style in which the work is written, we also find much that is epic in nature. The writer uses similes in an effort to do justice to his vision and theme: "a great voice, as of a trumpet" (1:10); "eyes . . . as a flame of fire" (1:14); "feet like unto brass, as if they burned in a furnace" (1:15); "a sea of glass like unto crystal" (4:6); "as it were a great mountain burning with fire" (8:8); "a loud voice, as when a lion roareth" (10:3); "as it were a sea of glass mingled with fire" (15:2). We find also that the writer uses epithets in referring to the characters in the story: "him which is, and which was, and which is to come" (1:4); "Jesus Christ, who is the faithful witness, and the first begotten of the dead, and the prince of the kings of the earth" (1:5); "him that loved us, and washed us from our sins in his own blood" (1:5); "Lord God Almighty, which was, and is, and is to come" (4:8); "the Lion of the tribe of Juda, the Root of David" (5:5); "King of Kings, and Lord of Lords" (16:16).

Revelation is also replete with other features of epic style. There are catalogs—of churches, of the beings around God's throne in Heaven, of the tribes of Israel, of the jewels in the heavenly city. There are allusions to the Old Testament (350 of them) and to the redemptive life of Christ. At the level of style, we find sheer fullness and exuberance. All of the words that

---

80. Richard G. Moulton, *The Modern Reader's Bible* (1895; rpt. New York: Macmillan, 1966), p. 1510.

C. S. Lewis uses to describe the style of secondary epic are typical of the style of Revelation: "solemnity," "ritualistic," "incanta-
tory," "grandeur," "elevation."[81]

A brief look at how the book of Revelation begins will confirm
its epic identity. The work opens with a formal statement of
theme: "The Revelation of Jesus Christ." The work as a whole
does, in fact, unveil the central figure, much as Homer's *Odyssey*
centers on the man who is never at a loss and Virgil's *Aeneid* centers on arms and the man, in each case as announced in the
opening statement of theme. Having announced his theme, the
narrator claims a divine source for his vision, much as epic poets
have always done: "which God gave unto him . . .; and he sent
and signified it by his angel unto his servant John" (1:1). The
narrator emerges as a mediator between his audience and the
supernatural vision, just as Milton does in the invocations of
Paradise Lost. And as the prologue continues to announce what
will follow, the epic nature of the material comes into fuller view.
The keynotes are such epic motifs as kingship, conquest, glory,
dominion, and power: "and from Jesus Christ, . . . the prince of
the kings of the earth. . . . To him be glory and dominion for
ever and ever. Amen. Behold, he cometh with clouds; and every
eye shall see him" (1:5–7).

In reading through the book of Revelation, we are constantly
reminded of standard epic motifs. Nineteenth-century critics
were right in considering the book of Revelation "one grand
epic poem."[82] If we wish to put the book of Revelation into the
literary family that it most resembles outside of the Hebraic-
Christian tradition of apocalyptic literature, that literary family
would be epic. The chief difference between Revelation and
conventional epic is that in Revelation we get a series of brief
pictures instead of smooth narrative flow from one extended
event to another. A less striking difference is that although both
epic and the book of Revelation deal with history, epic is retro-
spective and Revelation is prophetic or prospective.

If we now proceed to ask what type of epic Revelation is, it is

---

81. *A Preface to "Paradise Lost"* (Oxford: Oxford University Press, 1942), p. 40.
82. Their attitude is thus summarized by Wittreich, *Angel of Apocalypse*, p. 176.

at once evident that virtually everything I have said about Milton's anti-epic strategy of replacing physical and earthly versions of epic motifs with spiritual and heavenly versions is true also of Revelation. This, in turn, is the basis for my claim that Revelation is a literary model for one dimension of Milton's transformation of the epic tradition in *Paradise Lost*.

Everywhere we turn in Revelation we find the familiar epic motifs in an altered, spiritual setting. The quest for a kingdom, for example, is a quest for the spiritual, heavenly, and eternal kingdom of Christ, not an earthly political kingdom. The goal of the quest is pictured in kernel form with the seventh trumpet midway through the book: "The kingdoms of this world are become the kingdoms of our Lord, and of his Christ; and he shall reign for ever and ever" (12:15). Conquest in the book of Revelation is not primarily national and military but consists rather of the defeat of Satan and the forces of spiritual evil—during the war in Heaven (chapter 12), during the millennial binding of Satan (20:1–4), and when Satan's forces are defeated and cast into the lake of fire (20:7–10). Glory is not the fame that human warriors win for themselves through prowess on the battlefield but the spiritual glory that God confers on those who enter Heaven through the merits of Christ. In the great battle of chapter 12, for example, we read that the saints conquer Satan and his angels "by the blood of the Lamb, and by the word of their testimony" (12:11).

In addition to spiritualizing some of the conventional epic motifs, the book of Revelation achieves its aim by shifting the focus of some epic formulas from the human to the divine. It dispenses with the classical paraphernalia of a semidivine human hero and pictures instead a divine hero, Christ. The motif of empire takes the form of the spiritual kingdom of God, not the kingdom that a human hero establishes or regains. Victory is not a human hero's victory but Christ's defeat of Satan and redemption of his church. It is Christ who appears as a warrior on a white horse (19:11–16), who destroys the dragon (20:7–11), marries the bride (19:1–10), and lives happily ever after in a palace glittering with jewels (chapters 21–22). Warfare is not primarily human and earthly but is usually conducted by supernatural beings. Human action often consists of the passive activity of patient endurance until Christ appears. The epic motif of glory focuses not on a human hero but on God ("Blessing and glory, . . . and honour, and power, and might, be unto our God for ever and ever," 7:12) and Christ ("Worthy is the Lamb that was slain to receive power, . . . and honour, and glory, and blessing," 5:12). Revelation has the usual epic emphasis on history, but its focus is not on political or national history. Instead, it brings to a climax what biblical scholars have taught us to call salvation history. Heroes in classical epic exerted themselves to win or establish a city; the same motif appears at the end of Revelation, but here it is a supernatural and heavenly city—a "holy city . . . having the glory of God" (21:10–11).

It is not difficult, in my view, to explain why it is so easy and natural to discuss some features of *Paradise Lost* and the book of Revelation in identical terms. Milton, I suggest, had thoroughly assimilated the epic features of Revelation, and he used that book as the model for many of the specific forms that the traditional epic formulas take in *Paradise Lost*. This is especially true of the shift from earthly to heavenly and from physical to spiritual. Nor need we doubt where Milton got the idea for a Christocentric epic. The pattern came from the New Testament book that from start to finish attributes to Christ what in humanistic epic had been linked with human heroes.

IV

Several conclusions about the influence of the Bible on *Paradise Lost* emerge from the foregoing discussion. My analysis confirms the paradoxical comment of Philip Neve that Milton is most biblical and Christian "where he is thought most to follow a classic original."[83] Superficially it would appear that the epic genre is a thoroughly classical form. But there are also epics within the Bible, and when we scrutinize exactly what type of epic *Paradise Lost* is we will find Milton's predecessors in the domestic epic of Genesis, the anti-epic of Exodus, and the spiritual epic of Revelation. Thus, while it is too much to claim that the

83. Quoted by Wittreich, *Visionary Poetics*, p. xviii.

Bible gave Milton his basic form for *Paradise Lost*, it is accurate to say that the Bible taught him to write the specific type of epic that he wrote.

No single book of the Bible by itself explains what Milton did in *Paradise Lost*. Milton's epic is too complex in its effects to support such a simplification. We should remember, too, that the Bible is itself a tradition in which the individual parts are written by many authors over many centuries. The biblical tradition (by which I mean the canon itself) afforded Milton a library of diverse literary models in a single volume. It is small wonder that the anti-epic strain in *Paradise Lost* should have taken us to three separate and very different epics in the Bible, nor do those three exhaust Milton's biblical models for his anti-epic strategy.

I have tried to suggest that Milton was influenced to write as he did by literary models, not simply by theory. We know that Milton was influenced by both. In a key passage in *The Reason of Church Government*, Milton talks theoretically about such topics as "diffuse" and "brief" epics and "the rules of Aristotle." But in the same passage he describes his epic plans in terms of epic models, both biblical and classical. Recent studies by such scholars as Steadman, Lewalski, and Wittreich have uncovered an amazing amount of data about Renaissance epic theory and Renaissance traditions of biblical exegesis. Milton scholarship to date lacks a critical examination of the poet's use of biblical literary models as extensive and competent as the tradition that places his poetry in a context of epic and theological theory. Until such a critical balance emerges, we are in danger of giving the impression that Milton was far more deeply influenced by sermons and treatises of literary theory than by biblical literary models. This I take to be a misleading picture, running counter to the actual practice of writers.

My analysis confirms the importance that recent critical theory has attached to the idea of "intertexts." *Paradise Lost*, in fact, interacts with two such "texts." One is the classical epic tradition, partly paralleled by medieval heroic romances. Again and again, Milton evokes our awareness of an epic motif only to call our attention to how thoroughly he has changed and transcended his predecessors. *Paradise Lost* also asks to be read with an awareness of biblical epic models. In the process, *Paradise Lost* becomes a spokesman for the biblical/Christian tradition as something that "corrected, rather than fulfilled, the classics." [84] If we read *Paradise Lost* with a simultaneous awareness of classical and biblical epic, we get a clearer picture of what Milton says in his opening invocation about his intention to soar "Above th' *Aonian* Mount, while it pursues / Things unattempted yet in Prose or Rhime" (1.15–16). There had been numerous attempts to put the biblical content into the form of classical epic, but none that adapted classical epic to the form of biblical epic.

It might be questioned whether linking *Paradise Lost* to three biblical works adheres to what is promised in the title of this volume. How does relating *Paradise Lost* to the Bible itself constitute a relationship between Milton and scriptural *tradition*? The answer is twofold. As I have said, the Bible itself is not a single work but a tradition that produced a series of works. And secondly, as recent scholarship has shown, the Renaissance habit of viewing the Bible as a model of literary form to be emulated belongs especially to the Protestant religious tradition of the sixteenth and seventeenth centuries.

Finally, I have combined two major thrusts of recent Milton criticism. Two of the greatest glories of that criticism are the discovery of Milton's indebtedness to the Bible for his literary forms and his transformation of the Western epic tradition into something that redefines and displaces as well as perpetuates the inherited tradition. I trust that I have given a reason for believing that in the case of *Paradise Lost* these two tendencies in Milton are in fact a single phenomenon.

84. The formulation comes from Georgia B. Christopher, *Milton and the Science of the Saints* (Princeton: Princeton University Press, 1982), p. 67.

The Council Scenes in
Paradise Lost

Sister M. Christopher Pecheux

he existence of classical precedents for the coun-
cil scenes in *Paradise Lost* has long been taken for
granted.[1] Since Milton so often combined classical elements with scriptural, an inquiry into specific scriptural influences seems appropriate.
The present study will examine the tradition of
the divine council in the Old Testament and in-
dicate some ways in which this tradition enriched *Paradise Lost*.

At first glance it might seem that the idea of a divine council
would be entirely foreign to Hebrew monotheistic thought; yet
the concept is stated or implied in a number of Old Testament
passages. Probably the best-known example is found in the prologue to the book of Job: "Now there was a day when the sons of
God came to present themselves before the Lord, and Satan
came also among them" (1:6).[2] Most exegetes see the same idea
behind certain plurals in Genesis, such as "Let us make man in
our image" (1:26) and "Go to, let us go down, and there con-
found their language" (11:7).

---

1. Olin H. Moore, "The Infernal Council," *Modern Philology* 16 (1918): 169–93;
Mason Hammond, "*Concilia Deorum* from Homer through Milton," *Studies in
Philology* 30 (1933): 1–16; and Francis Blessington, "*Paradise Lost*" *and the Classical
Epic* (Boston: Routledge and Kegan Paul, 1979), esp. pp. 1–2, 14, 75, have dealt
specifically with this topic.

2. In addition to the examples from the Bible that will be cited in the essay,
other relevant passages are Gen. 3:22, Ps. 89:5, 2 Chron. 18:18–21, and Ezek.
13:9. The concept of the Council of Yahweh has attracted a fair amount of attention from exegetes during the past forty years. A lucid survey of the subject can
be found in G. Ernest Wright, *The Old Testament Against Its Environment* (London:
SCM Press, 1950), pp. 30–41. See also H. Wheeler Robinson, *Inspiration and Revelation in the Old Testament* (Oxford: Clarendon Press, 1946), pp. 166–70, and his
article "The Council of Yahweh," *Journal of Theological Studies* 45 (1944): 151–57;
Frank M. Cross, Jr., "The Council of Yahweh in Second Isaiah," *Journal of Near*

More explicit and more detailed is the account of an incident in the career of the prophet Micaiah. Micaiah speaks to the king:

> And he said, Hear thou therefore the word of the Lord: I saw the Lord sitting on his throne, and all the host of heaven standing by him on his right hand and on his left. And the Lord said, Who shall persuade Ahab, that he may go up and fall at Ramoth-gilead? And one said on this manner, and another said on that manner. And there came forth a spirit, and stood before the Lord, and said, I will persuade him. And the Lord said unto him, Wherewith? And he said, I will go forth, and I will be a lying spirit in the mouth of all his prophets. And he said, Thou shalt persuade him, and prevail also: go forth, and do so. (1 Kings 22: 19–22)[3]

Whatever the ambiguities in this account, certainly the scene presents a full-fledged council, with the Lord asking for and accepting suggestions from the members of his court.

Such a council undoubtedly had its origin, as far as the biblical writers are concerned, in the beliefs of their Canaanite neighbors, who in turn may have derived the concept from their own political structures. In ancient Near Eastern thought, the general assembly of the gods was presided over by the chief god, who might listen to proposals made by the lesser gods; after these had been discussed, a final decision would be made.[4]

In its earliest stages in the Bible, the lesser gods—the gods of the nations—are actually present in an assembly presided over by Yahweh. The original pagan concept was, however, in Albright's phrase, rapidly demythologized;[5] the members of the council were soon envisaged as angels, and eventually as men. A brief account of these developments will help to make clear how Milton took over the tradition.

Eastern Studies 12 (1953): 274–77; Raymond E. Brown, "The Pre-Christian Semitic Concept of 'Mystery,'" *Catholic Biblical Quarterly* 20 (1958): 417–21; William F. Albright, *Yahweh and the Gods of Canaan* (Garden City: Doubleday, 1968); and in other works that will be cited later.

3. Milton included in the Trinity MS a plan for a tragedy based on this episode; see *Works*, 18:238.

4. Thorkild Jacobsen, "The Cosmos As State," in *The Intellectual Adventure of Ancient Man*, ed. H. Frankfort et al. (Chicago: University of Chicago Press, 1946), p. 136.

5. Albright, *Yahweh*, p. 193.

The eighty-second Psalm, which on a literal level embodies the primitive concept,[6] offers a good example of the variety of possible interpretations.

> God standeth in the congregation of the mighty; he judgeth among the gods. How long will ye judge unjustly, and accept the persons of the wicked? . . . They know not, neither will they understand; they walk on in darkness: all the foundations of the earth are out of course. I have said, Ye are gods; and all of you are children of the Most High. But ye shall die like men, and fall like one of the princes. Arise, O God, judge the earth: for thou shalt inherit all nations. (82: 1–2, 5–8)

The first verse refers clearly to the gods of the foreign nations. In the seventh verse these gods are either condemned to death or, more probably, stripped of their immortality.[7]

Even though the psalm as it stands attests the superiority of Yahweh, the pagan overtones were not really acceptable; hence the members of the assembly came to be seen as angels. In an ancient Syriac version the word *angels* is used instead of *gods* in the first verse.[8] This development was part of a general trend in the Old Testament; in a similar transformation, the phrase *heavenly host*, originally referring to the sun, moon, and stars (often as objects of worship), was applied to the angels who were the attendants at God's throne and the bearers of his messages. When Micaiah describes "all the host of heaven" standing around the throne, he probably envisages angels. Angels seem to be the attendants also in the blessing of Moses in Deuteronomy 33, which Cross translates as follows:

> Yahweh from Sinai came . . . .
> with Him were myriads of holy ones . . . .
> Yea, the guardians of the peoples.

6. It is probably an early psalm; Mitchell Dahood in the Anchor Bible, *Psalms II* (Garden City: Doubleday, 1968) dates it as premonarchical (p. 269).

7. After demonstrating that "gods" in verse 6 can mean only divine beings, Julian Morgenstern asserted that verse 7 means that a sentence of mortality is being passed on beings originally immortal ("The Mythological Background of Psalm 82," *Hebrew Union College Annual* 14 [1939]: 33).

8. Harris Fletcher, *Milton's Semitic Studies* (New York: Gordian Press, 1966), p. 101.

All the holy ones are at Thy hand
They prostrate themselves at Thy feet
They carry out Thy decisions.[9]

The next logical step was to dilute the literal meaning still further by applying the notion of the assembly to human beings. In the exegesis of Psalm 82 this interpretation was usually concerned with the second part of the psalm (verses 6 and 7). According to a popular rabbinic interpretation, the occasion of the psalm was thought to be the revelation of the Law on Sinai: the coming of this word to the Israelites made them gods, sons of the Most High.[10]

This approach is implied in the New Testament passage in which verse 6 is quoted: "Jesus answered them, Is it not written in your law, I said, Ye are gods? If he called them gods, unto whom the word of God came" (John 10:34–35). Saint Augustine espoused this meaning, while Saint Justin contended that all men are deemed worthy of becoming gods, since they are all sons of the Most High.[11]

A further narrowing can be seen in some Reformation commentators. Luther understood the gods of verse 1 as rulers, and the Geneva headnote explains: "The Prophet declar[es] God to be present among the Judges and Magistrates."[12] Later exegetes have favored one or other of these possibilities, which, as Morgenstern points out, resolve themselves basically into a dichot-

9. Frank M. Cross, Jr., and David Noel Freedman, "The Blessing of Moses," *Journal of Biblical Literature* 67 (1948): 193, 201–2. In his "The Council of Yahweh in Second Isaiah," Cross discusses the dual use of the term *heavenly host* for heavenly bodies and angels (p. 274). The many Old Testament passages in which heaven and earth sing or rejoice may be related to this concept, as suggested by Herbert B. Huffmon, "The Covenant Lawsuit in the Prophets," *Journal of Biblical Literature* 78 (1959): 291.

10. Raymond E. Brown, in the Anchor Bible, *The Gospel According to John (i–xii)* (Garden City: Doubleday, 1966), p. 410.

11. Saint Augustine, "Expositions on the Book of Psalms," *The Nicene and Post-Nicene Fathers,* 1st ser., vol. 8, ed. Philip Schaff (Grand Rapids, Mich.: Eerdmans, 1956), p. 395; Saint Justin, "Dialogue with Trypho," *The Ante-Nicene Fathers,* vol. 1, eds. Alexander Roberts and James Donaldson (Grand Rapids, Mich.: Eerdmans, 1956), p. 124.

12. Luther, *Works,* ed. Jaroslav Pelikan, vol. 13, *Selected Psalms II* (St. Louis: Concordia Publishing House, 1956), p. 44; *The Geneva Bible: A Facsimile of the 1560 Edition* (Madison: University of Wisconsin Press, 1969).

omy between divine beings (gods or angels) and human (foreign rulers, native kings, or native judges).[13]

Most of the English translations of the sixteenth and seventeenth centuries struck some sort of compromise, especially in the first two verses. The Coverdale Bible of 1535 has a congregation of gods in the first part of the verse, and one of judges in the second; the Great Bible of 1539 reverses this arrangement, as does the Authorized Version. The metrical versions are by their nature less close to the original, so Sternhold and Hopkins felt free to omit entirely the supernatural elements; the assembly is of "men of might . . . Judges of the land."[14]

Some notice must be taken of Milton's own translation of this psalm, made in 1648, although the circumstances surrounding its composition and the fact that as a paraphrase it permits certain changes for the sake of rhyme and rhythm reduce its significance in the present context. Although he modified and expanded the text, Milton was meticulous in indicating by italics which words he had added and in noting in the margin some of the original Hebrew words. His translation begins:

> God in the great assembly stands
>   *of Kings and lordly States*,
> Among the gods on both his hands
>   He judges and debates.
> How long will ye pervert the right
>   With judgment false and wrong
> Favouring the wicked *by your might*,
>   *Who thence grow bold and strong*.[15]

13. Morgenstern, "Mythological Background," pp. 30–31.
14. Fletcher, *Milton's Semitic Studies*, p. 102.
15. Milton's version appears in *Works*, 1:140–41; I have retained his italics but omitted the rest of his scholarly apparatus (asterisks, daggers, and marginal notes). Almost all the scholars who have studied his versions of the 1648 psalms posit some topical relevance. Most helpful in comparing his translations with other versions are Fletcher, *Milton's Semitic Studies*, pp. 100–107, and William B. Hunter, Jr., "Milton Translates the Psalms," *Philological Quarterly* 40 (1961): 485–94; see also Edward C. Baldwin, "Milton and the Psalms," *Modern Philology* 17 (1919–1920): 457–63; Marian H. Studley, "Milton and His Paraphrases of the Psalms," *Philological Quarterly* 4 (1925): 364–72; Margaret Boddy, "Milton's Translation of Psalms 80–88," *Modern Philology* 64 (1966): 1–9; and Carolyn

All the italics in this quotation are Milton's own; and, whatever the exact reason for his undertaking the translation of nine psalms in 1648, it is difficult not to see a political orientation in what he has chosen to expand. And any republican would have been happy, in 1648, to remind his readers of the mortality of princes, as does the translation of verse 7: "But ye shall die like men, and fall / As other Princes *die*" (the second "die" is the only word Milton italicizes here).

There can be no question that Milton was familiar with the psalm. When he began writing *Paradise Lost*, it may have been one of the many scriptural sources he planned to utilize. At any rate, he seems to have incorporated more than one of its possible interpretations into his epic.

To begin, as Milton does, with the infernal councils: the reader who may have been misled by the rhetoric and false grandeur of the assembly in book 2 is able to view that assembly from an altered (and truer) perspective after he has read book 3, when he can see the council in Hell as a parody of the one in Heaven. The force of this shift in perspective has often been commented on. A similar manipulation of perspective can be seen if we observe that certain features of the council in Hell correspond to the more primitive biblical tradition, which was corrected by the viewpoint of later interpreters. Specifically, it is notable that the fallen angels are frequently addressed and described as "gods," whereas with one exception (to be discussed later) this term is never applied to the good angels in Heaven. The point is worth stressing precisely because the scriptural tradition countenanced the application of the word either to angels or to men; Milton himself in the *Christian Doctrine* cites John 10:35 to indicate that the term can be used somewhat loosely.[16] His consistent use of it only for the devils therefore implies a conscious purpose.

In his first address to the fallen spirits, Satan speaks of their strength as the united force of gods (1.629). In the council itself,

---

Collette, "Milton's Psalm Translations," *English Literary Renaissance* 2 (1972): 243–59.

16. *CPW*, 6:233–34.

Beelzebub, speculating on the creation of man (and turning his speculation into fact) asserts that this decision was pronounced among the gods (2.352). The assembly is a "synod of gods" (2.319).

This passage is especially interesting. After the final vote has been taken, Beelzebub congratulates the council members:

> Well have ye judg'd, well ended long debate,
> Synod of Gods, and like to what ye are,
> Great things resolv'd; which from the lowest deep
> Will once more lift us up, in spight of Fate,
> Neerer our ancient Seat. (2.390–94)

The idea of judgment and debate recalls the first verse of Psalm 82, which Milton had translated "Among the gods on both his hands / He judges and debates," using, as Fletcher remarks, two verbs, *judge* and *debate*, instead of the single one a more literal translation would require.[17] Beelzebub, of course, is ignoring the fact that in reality it is God who does the judging, in the sense of condemning, but perhaps he glances at that fact when he refers to "Fate," which is responsible for their present situation in the "lowest deep." He cannot ignore the fact that they have fallen, though he can express the hope that the great things they have resolved will once more lift them up.

In book 6 Satan berates Abdiel for his opposition to the rebels' party, which he describes as "a third part of the Gods, in Synod met / Thir Deities to assert" (156–57), and in the same book Nisroc speaks of their rights as gods. Even when he is alone Satan retains this manner of speaking: he suggests that earth may be even worthier of gods than Heaven was (9. 99–100) and thinks that Eve is a fit love for gods (9. 489).

The climax of the irony inherent in this practice occurs at the end of Satan's speech in book 10—the last sentence he utters in the poem, just before the metamorphosis into serpents: "Ye have th' account / Of my performance: What remains, ye Gods, / But up and enter now into full bliss" (501–3). The "Gods" who are

---

17. Fletcher, *Milton's Semitic Studies*, p. 100; on p. 103 he explains the justification for this expansion and the evidence it affords of Milton's command of Hebrew.

invited upward are those wicked and unjust beings who in Psalm 82 are condemned to die and "fall like one of the princes." "They know not, neither will they understand," an earlier verse of the psalm had said. Satan's perverse misunderstanding and scorn of the sentence that has been passed on him ("A World who would not purchase with a bruise?") and his proud expectation of rising are fittingly followed by the actual event: "*down* he *fell* / A monstrous Serpent on his Belly *prone*" (513–14). His followers, "that revolted Rout / Heav'n *fall'n*" (534–35) share in the degradation: "*down* thir arms, / *Down fell* both Spear and Shield, *down* they as fast" (541–42; my italics).

Satan does not yet know that in human history he and his followers will be given new names—the names of false gods—corrupting mankind "by falsities and lyes" and inducing them to adore Devils for Deities (1. 364–75). But since the reader knows it, there is a vast irony in Satan's consistent mode of address: he uses the epithet to connote nobility and grandeur, whereas the word reminds us each time that the fallen spirits are destined to be false gods, empty idols.

The four infernal councils in *Paradise Lost* have several other relevant characteristics. They show a gradual discarding by Satan of the pretense of democracy. As the archetypal tyrant, he does not intend to use the advice of his followers, but he flatters them by pretending to do so. In this, and in his plan of seducing man by fraud, he has some resemblance to the lying spirit that in Micaiah's vision is used to deceive Ahab. In the first council, which occupies the first half of book 2, he begins with his own unproved premise that Heaven has not been lost irretrievably. Debate is permitted only on the subject of what means to use to regain it. Within these limits there is, however, freedom of speech: "Whether of open Warr or covert guile, / We now debate; who can advise, may speak" (41–42). The debate ends, however, when the scheme secretly devised by Satan is divulged by Beelzebub. Any possibility of further discussion after Satan has accepted his mission is cut off: "Thus saying rose / The Monarch, and prevented all reply" (466–67).

One of the most ironic features of this council is the uncertainty expressed by the demons as to whether or not they are immortal. Even that ultimate question can be decided only by the God against whom they have rebelled, who has the power to say, "Ye shall die like men." "They know not, neither will they understand; they walk on in darkness."

It is Beelzebub again who carries out Satan's injunction to gather his subordinates for the council that is described in book 5. Here the ostensible reason for the assembly is a false one: they are to plan the entertainment for the supposed royal progress of the Messiah. Once the angels approached by Beelzebub have assembled, Satan embroiders on the notion of the triumphal passage of the Messiah, the "knee-tribute" (782) he will demand, and the dignity of the angels which is being encroached on. Here there is no pretense of debate (the lone voice of Abdiel is quickly drowned out), but Satan's tone is one of persuasion rather than of command; he asks a series of rhetorical questions that imply a desire to secure agreement. He answers the questions himself, however: "Will ye submit your necks, and chuse to bend / The supple knee? ye will not, if I trust / To know ye right" (787–89).

This second council in the poem (the first in chronology) takes place on "the Mountain of the Congregation," "For thither he assembl'd all his Train" (5. 766–67). *Congregation* was the word used most commonly in English versions of Psalm 82: "God standeth in the congregation of the mighty," while *assembly* was a word alternately used, as in the 1560 edition of the Geneva Bible. Milton includes both in these two lines, one as a noun and the other as a verb.

The third council, a brief one, is held at the end of the first day of the battle, when Satan "His Potentates to Councel call'd by night" (6. 416). He has set this assembly up in order to enhance the announcement of his new weapon, gunpowder. He speaks of "due search and consultation" (445) and allows Nisroc to ask the right question before he reveals his own invention.

For the final council, in book 10, there is no need to gather the fallen angels together, since they are already in Pandemonium, awaiting the return of their mighty chief. Satan has consistently used the device of permitting his subordinates to demonstrate the inferiority of their debates and efforts so that his own plan, in each case already decided on, may appear more brilliant. This expedient he now translates into symbolic action by making his way through the ranks of the assembly in disguise so that the "sudden blaze" of his "false glitter" (452–53) may draw their acclaim. Now he has no need for the pretense of debate or for setting up a leading question; his speech is merely an announcement of his success.

None of the elements I have examined *demands* a biblical context for its explanation; but the various ironic allusions to the biblical tradition have a cumulative effect that makes the infernal councils more sinister than they would be if they were seen simply as classical conventions.

There is nothing sinister about the councils in Heaven, which are suffused in light—both the light of glory that emanates from God and the light of truth that is part of his essence. God deals with plain facts in plain language; there is no "lying spirit" involved. The members of the assembly know who they are and who God is, and so they are content to approve whatever God does.

In Heaven there are three major councils as well as four similar assemblies on a smaller scale. If the "gods" were the prototypes of the council members in Hell, it is the angels who serve that function here. In the Bible itself the divine assembly of the earliest period soon became less an actual council than a forum where God's orders were declared and given to his messengers, who would then go out from the assembly to transmit and execute the divine decrees.[18] This conception is reflected in the Geneva Bible; on 1 Kings 22:19, "the host of heaven standing by him on his right hand and on his left," the gloss explains, "Meaning, his Angels."

When the first council opens in book 3, the angels are already assembled around the Almighty Father, who is "High Thron'd above all highth" (3. 58). The double meaning of heavenly hosts (the heavenly bodies and the angels) is glanced at in the next phrase: "About him all the Sanctities of Heaven / Stood thick as Starrs" (60–61). The position of the Father, high above all other

18. Albright, *Yahweh*, p. 192.

beings, supernatural or natural, at once makes clear that the angels are in a subordinate position. Nevertheless, they are not nonentities. It may be significant that the word *stood* is used, for in Hebrew it carries the technical sense "to participate as a member."[19]

At first God does not address the angels directly; it is "to his onely Son" (79) that he first speaks. But the question at the end of his second speech is directed to the angels as well as to the Son. The proposal for an incarnation comes from the Father himself:

> Dye hee or Justice must; unless for him
> Som other able, and as willing, pay
> The rigid satisfaction, death for death.
> Say heav'nly powers, where shall we find such love,
> Which of ye will be mortal to redeem
> Mans mortal crime, and just th' unjust to save,
> Dwels in all Heaven charitie so deare? (210–16)

What happens here is an exact reversal of the situation envisaged in Psalm 82, where the "gods," against their will, are condemned to become mortal. Instead, there is here an invitation to a willing stripping of immortality, and the Son responds by offering to "Freely put off" (240) the glory he enjoys. The angels continue in a passive role; their function is to express their approval of the divine decisions. This role is, of course, no more democratic than is that of the councils in Hell; the difference is that in Heaven there is no pretense of any other expectation.

As with its infernal counterpart, the second council to be described is the first in chronology. It occurs in book 5:

> . . . on such a day
> As Heav'ns great Year brings forth, th' Empyreal Host
> Of Angels by Imperial summons call'd,
> Innumerable before th' Almighties Throne
> Forthwith from all the ends of Heav'n appeerd. (582–86)

19. Cross, "The Council of Yahweh in Second Isaiah," pp. 274–75. Milton uses the same verb in *CD*, 1.9: the angels "stand around the throne of God as ministers"; he cites Deut. 33:2, 1 Kings 22:19, Job 1:6 and 2:1, Dan. 7:10, Matt. 18:10, and Luke 1:19 (*CPW*, 6:345).

The angels are being informed, not consulted; the Father has assembled them to hear the decree "which unrevok't shall stand" (602) by which he exalts the Son.

A final formal assembly takes place in book 11. Man is now repentant; the way to his ultimate salvation is open; all that remains is to expel the fallen couple from the Garden. The Father will now communicate the final plans to the angels before he chooses one of their number to execute the decree of expulsion. He speaks to the Son, associating him with the summoning of the council: "But let us call to Synod all the Blest / Through Heav'ns wide bounds; from them I will not hide / My judgments, how with Mankind I proceed" (67–69). At the sound of the great trumpet blast, for which the Son gives the signal, the angels gather once more; from their blissful bowers,

> . . . where ere they sate
> In fellowships of joy: the Sons of Light
> Hasted, resorting to the Summons high,
> And took thir Seats; till from his Throne supream
> Th' Almighty thus pronounced his sovran Will. (79–83)

In this last council of the epic, as in the first, the Almighty is supreme upon his throne, freely and graciously condescending to share his plans with his faithful ministers.

In addition to the formal councils, which are called by the Father and attended by the angels in fixed ranks, whether standing thick as stars as in book 3, orb within orb as in book 5, or taking their seats as in book 11, there are a number of other assemblies of the angels that are somewhat spontaneous; the participants are not summoned but appear before the Throne for some particular purpose. One gets the impression that the Almighty is easier of access than is Satan. Another difference between Heaven and Hell apparent in these scenes is that the members of the heavenly assemblies show nothing of the anxiety or jostling for prestige that are concomitants of those in Hell.

At the beginning of book 6 the angels meet the returning Abdiel. There is no sign of jealousy or rivalry; they are proud of their comrade and eager to be present as he receives his decorations. "On to the sacred hill / They led him high applauded, and present / Before the seat supream" (25–27). In a similar scene at the beginning of book 10 the angelic guards, foiled by Satan, return to Heaven to report the failure of their mission. "About the new-arriv'd, in multitudes / Th' ethereal People ran, to hear and know / How all befell" (26–28). If they are subject to what we might describe as a very human curiosity, it is a sentiment unmixed with any malice; they accompany the guards to the Throne and with them are reassured by the Father's words: "Assembl'd Angels, and ye Powers return'd / From unsuccessful charge, be not dismaid" (34–35). Whether in triumph or in defeat, the angels love and support one another.

In the gathering in book 10 the Father reverses the process of book 3: he speaks directly to the angels as he begins his speech in line 34, turning to the Son in line 55 with a question that this time is only rhetorical: "But whom send I to judge them? whom but thee / Vicegerent Son." The Son responds appropriately, and the angels accompany him, apparently in silence, to the gate of Heaven.

Aside from these spontaneous gatherings, it seems that there is always a multitude of angels assembled around the Throne, an audience ready to receive any new pronouncement. They are present to hear the plan for creation; "th' Omnipotent / Eternal Father from his Throne beheld / Thir multitude, and to his Son thus spake" (7.136–38). Perhaps at this point they have not yet disbanded after they have escorted the Son in his triumphant return from the battle. They are present also when the Father once more explains how he intends to bring good out of evil, after Sin and Death have made their way into the world, "which th' Almightie seeing, / From his transcendent Seat the Saints among, / To those bright Orders utterd thus his voice" (10.613–15). He foretells the final judgment, and the angels, predictably, rejoice.

√ The sense of harmony and joy in all the heavenly assemblies contrasts with the uncertainty and fear of those in Hell. One key to this change of tone is found in the epithets applied to the angels. Most of the time, whether in council or dispersed through Heaven, they are simply angels. At other times they are the sanctities of Heaven (3.60), a holy choir (3.217), empyreal ministers

(5.460), progeny of light (5.600), armed saints (6.47), bright orders (10.615). Only in one instance are they spoken of as gods. The use of this term to signify the angels need not in itself create an insuperable difficulty (as has been noted, Milton himself remarked in the *Christian Doctrine* that the word could be applied to angels or men); but a difficulty does arise from the fact that whereas the term is used regularly by the inhabitants of Hell, and by the narrator in describing them, it is never used for the inhabitants of Heaven except in this one instance.

The exception occurs at a crucial point: the conclusion of the Father's final speech in the major council in book 3: "But all ye Gods, / Adore him, who to compass all this dies, / Adore the Son, and honour him as mee" (341–43). The problem is complicated by the fact that the lines just quoted allude directly to Hebrews 1:6, which is itself quoting Psalm 97:7, and that the commonly accepted text in each of these biblical citations is different.

The citation from Hebrews, in the Authorized Version, is: "And again, when he bringeth in the first-begotten into the world, he saith, And let all the *angels* of God worship him" (my italics). The original Greek of the Epistle to the Hebrews reproduces accurately the Greek text of Psalm 97 (the Septuagint was the text ordinarily used by early Christians), but the Hebrew word in the psalm, as reproduced in the Authorized Version, is "worship him, all ye *gods*" (my italics). Milton certainly knew both versions, and he could have counted on his audience to be familiar with both. The context in Hebrews—the exaltation of the Son and his evident superiority to the angels—fits much better the context of the Father's speech in *Paradise Lost*. Yet Milton chose to say not "all ye angels" but "all ye Gods."

I think it is possible to suggest an answer to the problem by disentangling one scriptural thread from the many that are fused in the Father's speech. After speaking of the Son's incarnation, death, and glorification, God foretells the final judgment, in terms very similar to those in Psalm 82, where an assembly, a judgment, and a falling are the dominant themes. In *Paradise Lost* the Son is to appear in Heaven while the archangels proclaim "Thy dread Tribunal" (327):

> Then all thy Saints *assembl'd*, thou shalt *judge*
> Bad men and Angels, they arraignd shall *sink*
> Beneath thy Sentence; Hell, her numbers full,
> Thenceforth shall be for ever shut. (330–33; my italics)

The connotations of this allusion to an assembly of "gods" may be designed to point up the fact that the councils of the devils, who appropriate to themselves a title that the good angels never claim, has its antitype in a final assembly that is to witness the downfall of these so-called gods, and the exaltation of the Son in both his Godhood and his manhood, to be adored by the inhabitants of Heaven, earth, and Hell.

While preserving and even accentuating the subordinate character of the angels that the Old Testament had emphasized, Milton has added a feature that seems to have been suggested by some passages in the New Testament. In the former, individual messengers may deal kindly with man, but the members of the council as such display no particular concern for the human race. Milton's angels, on the other hand, take a great interest in man's welfare and display all the appropriate emotions. When he discusses the government of the angels in the *Christian Doctrine* (1.9) Milton remarks that "the angels take great pleasure in examining the mystery of man's salvation," and he cites, among other supporting texts, the song of the angels at the Nativity and Luke 15:10: "Likewise, I say unto you, there is joy in the presence of the angels of God over one sinner that repenteth."[20] This conception gives a note of warmth to all the heavenly councils in *Paradise Lost*.

In book 3, once the Father has explained the divine economy whereby man's redemption will be accomplished, the angels cannot contain their joy:

> No sooner had th' Almighty ceas't, but all
> The multitude of Angels with a shout
> Loud as from numbers without number, sweet
> As from blest voices, uttering joy, Heav'n rung
> With Jubilee, and loud Hosanna's filld
> Th' eternal Regions. (344–49)

20. *CPW*, 6:344.

And so on, for some seventy lines. Each time the Father announces to them a new development, they show a similar reaction. They rejoice at the news of the new creation about to take place:

> Great triumph and rejoycing was in Heav'n
> When such was heard declar'd the Almightie's will;
> Glorie they sung to the most High, good will
> To future men, and in thir dwellings peace. (7.180–83)

When the Son returns from his great work they escort him and praise him with new jubilation; and their joy stems in part from the fact that they themselves will have some contact with this new creature, man:

> Open, ye everlasting Gates, they sung, . . .
> Open, and henceforth oft; for God will deigne
> To visit oft the dwellings of just Men
> Delighted, and with frequent intercourse
> Thither will send his winged Messengers
> On errands of supernal Grace. (7.565, 569–73)

As they gather in book 10, the angels, aware that the Fall has occurred, react with pity and sympathy for poor mankind: they are "mute and sad" (18); "dim sadness did not spare / That time Celestial visages, yet mixt / With pitie, violated not thir bliss" (23–25). When the judgment has been delivered, however, and the Father explains how even sin and death will finally be conquered, "the heav'nly Audience loud / Sung Halleluia" (641–42).

It seems possible to assert, on the basis of the analysis just given, that an awareness of the scriptural tradition enriches our interpretation of both the infernal and the celestial councils in *Paradise Lost*, making them much more significant and integral to the epic than are their counterparts in classical epics. In addition, Milton drew from the scriptural tradition something that the classics could not supply.

In the process of demythologization that took place within the Old Testament itself, the pagan concept of a council of pagan gods that gave way to a council composed of angels was eventually superseded by a viewpoint that saw the prophets being admitted to the council. It is precisely because he has been admitted that the prophet can identify his utterance with that of the Lord. The concept appears as early as Amos: "Surely the Lord God will do nothing, but he revealeth his secret unto his servants the prophets" (3:7). Jeremiah makes participation in the council of the Lord the criterion by which false prophets can be distinguished from true:

> Thus saith the Lord of hosts, Hearken not unto the words of the prophets that prophesy unto you; they make you vain: they speak a vision of their own heart, and not out of the mouth of the Lord.
> For who hath stood in the counsel of the Lord, and hath perceived and heard his word? . . .
> I have not sent these prophets, yet they ran: I have not spoken to them, yet they prophesied.
> But if they had stood in my counsel, and had caused my people to hear my words, then they should have turned them from their evil way, and from the evil of their doings. (Jer. 23:16–22)

There is a great difference between such references as these to a divine council and the more figurative and fantastic scenes that sometimes appear in apocalyptic literature. The word most commonly used in prophetic literature to describe these assemblies is *sôd* (it is used in both the quotations just given); Jeremiah uses the same word elsewhere for a gathering of young men (6:11) and for human fellowship (15:17); hence the heavenly assembly is to be viewed as in a certain sense realistic.[21]

Thus admission to the council becomes the criterion for the true prophet. The implications of the passages from Amos and Jeremiah are drawn out by two modern commentators. Of Amos, James Mays observes:

> The true prophet has stood in the divine council where Yahweh's policy is formulated and decreed before it is carried out in history. Because the heavenly counsel (sōd) has been revealed to the prophet, his messages are true and to be believed. The role of the

---

21. Robinson, *Inspiration and Revelation*, pp. 167–68, and Brown, "The Pre-Christian Semitic Concept of 'Mystery,'" pp. 417–21, emphasize this point.

prophet as messenger has become an institution of the divine government.[22]

And James Ross says of Jeremiah:

> Clearly Jeremiah claims that his ultimate authority as God's messenger is to be found at the highest level, in the divine council itself. He has heard words and has seen visions; he is under constraint to make the people hearken, to carry out the decisions of the *sôd*.[23]

A divine council forms the setting for the call of Isaiah. The Lord sits upon a throne, high and lifted up; he is surrounded by seraphim who cry one to another; and the prophet laments his unworthiness to have seen the King, the Lord of hosts. An angel purifies his lips with a live coal; this cleansing equips him for his task, but, as Robinson points out, its first result is to enable him to join in the deliberations of the council.[24] He takes part in the dialogue:

> Also I heard the voice of the Lord, saying, Whom shall I send, and who will go for us? Then said I, Here am I; send me. And he said, Go, and tell this people, Hear ye indeed, but understand not: and see ye indeed, but perceive not. . . . Then said I, Lord, how long? (6:8–11)

Another council takes place in Isaiah 40. The scene opens with God's directive to his messengers: "Comfort ye, comfort ye my people, saith your God." The repetition of an imperative form is characteristic of an address to a heavenly council,[25] and it should be noted that the verb here is indeed imperative, with "people" as its object.[26] This point is important, since it makes

22. James L. Mays, *Amos: A Commentary* (Philadelphia: Westminster Press, 1969), p. 62.
23. James F. Ross, "The Prophet as Yahweh's Messenger," in *Israel's Prophetic Heritage*, ed. Bernhard W. Anderson and Walter Harrelson (New York: Harper, 1962), p. 105.
24. "The Council of Yahweh," p. 154.
25. Cross, "The Council of Yahweh in Second Isaiah," p. 276.
26. James Muilenburg, in *The Interpreter's Bible* (New York and Nashville: Abingdon Press, 1956), 5:424.

clear that some members of the council are being instructed to carry a message of comfort to the people. In verse 3 a voice from the assembly ("to wit, of the prophets," explains the Geneva gloss) answers. "A voice cries: 'In the wilderness prepare the way of the Lord, make straight in the desert a highway for our God.'"[27]

Either the same voice or another continues the dialogue in verse 6: "The voice said, Cry. And he said, What shall I cry?" The Masoretic text, followed by the Authorized Version, reads "And he said," as here, whereas the Septuagint, the Vulgate, and now the Dead Sea Isaiah scroll give the first person, "And I said."[28] In the latter case, the prophet himself is evidently participating directly in the council. In any case, he is present to receive and deliver the message.

The relevance of this part of the tradition to *Paradise Lost* should be apparent. The plan of Milton's epic did not permit prophets, who in the time-scheme did not yet exist, to take part in the heavenly councils in the way that the angels do. Instead, it is the narrator himself who assumes this role. In recent years there have been several enlightening discussions on the role of the narrator of *Paradise Lost* as a blind bard who has received special illumination.[29] This prophetic personality shows the in-

27. A long but erroneous tradition has perhaps obscured the full dramatic force of the dialogue. The Septuagint, the Vulgate, and the Authorized versions all place the phrase "in the wilderness" with the main verb: "The voice of him that crieth in the wilderness, Prepare ye the way of the Lord." But the laws of parallelism, literary form, and Hebrew accentuation all require that the phrase be placed as it is now in RSV, making it clear that the voice cries out not from the wilderness but from the assembly (Muilenburg, *Interpreter's Bible*, p. 426).

28. Ibid., p. 429.

29. Anne Davidson Ferry, in *Milton's Epic Voice* (Cambridge: Harvard University.Press, 1963), was, I believe, the first to point out in an extended way the prophetic role of the narrator. Others who have developed the idea include Michael Fixler, "The Apocalypse within *Paradise Lost*," in *New Essays on "Paradise Lost*," ed. Thomas Kranidas (Berkeley: University of California Press, 1969); William Riggs, *The Christian Poet in "Paradise Lost*," (Berkeley: University of California Press, 1972); Leland Ryken, *The Apocalyptic Vision in "Paradise Lost*" (Ithaca: Cornell University Press, 1970); Austin Dobbins, *Milton and the Book of Revelation* (University: University of Alabama Press, 1975); William Kerrigan, *The Prophetic Milton* (Charlottesville: University Press of Virginia, 1974); John Spencer Hill, *John Milton: Poet, Priest and Prophet* (Totowa, N.J.: Rowman and Littlefield, 1979); Joseph Wittreich, *Milton and the Line of Vision* (Madison: University of Wisconsin

fluence of the biblical concept of the prophet who has been admitted to the council.

The initial justification for relating the councils of prophets in the Old Testament with *Paradise Lost* is that Isaiah's inaugural vision clearly lies behind the council in book 3, where the biblical "Who will go for us?" and "Here am I; send me" are echoed in the Father's "where shall we find such love" and the Son's "Behold mee then, mee for him, life for life / I offer, on mee let thine anger fall."[30] If the dialogue in Milton's council is modeled on that in Isaiah 6, it is reasonable to look for other elements from that scene, and in particular its main point: the role of the prophet as the sharer in God's secrets. In this context it is significant that Milton makes most explicit his own role as prophet in the prologue to book 3, which precedes the opening of the heavenly council. Here he (or, to speak more accurately, the narrator) likens himself to such pagan seers as Homer and Tiresias, but the functions he describes bear more resemblance to those of the biblical prophet. The celestial light he receives is given not for his own benefit alone; as God's messenger he must bear it to others: "that I may see and tell / Of things invisible to mortal sight" (3.54–55). Furthermore, the narrator assumes the prophet's proper place in the heavenly council when, in the angels' song of book 3, lines 372–415, he shifts from the third-person plural ("they sung," lines 372, 483) to the first-person singular:

> Hail Son of God, Savior of Men, thy Name
> Shall be the copious matter of my Song
> Henceforth, and never shall my Harp thy praise
> Forget, nor from thy Father's praise disjoin. (412–15)

In the invocation to book 1 the narrator claims a relationship with Moses and, through the reference to "*Siloa's* Brook that flow'd / Fast by the Oracle of God" (11–12), with Isaiah. In book 7 he reasserts his prophetic role; after addressing the muse who

---

Press, 1975), and *Visionary Poetics: Milton's Tradition and His Legacy* (San Marino, Calif.: Henry E. Huntington Library, 1979).

30. This has been pointed out by James H. Sims, *The Bible in Milton's Epics* (Gainesville: University of Florida Press, 1962), p. 163.

with Eternal wisdom "didst play / In presence of th' Almightie Father" (10–11), he implies that he himself has been admitted into that presence:

> Up led by thee
> Into the Heav'n of Heav'ns I have presum'd
> An Earthlie Guest, and drawn Empyreal Aire,
> Thy tempring. (12–15)

Like Isaiah, he combines fear because of his unworthiness with confidence drawn from the knowledge that he has become a messenger only at God's invitation. In common with many of his biblical predecessors, he lives amidst dangers and finds few to listen to him; but he is not alone while he receives the heavenly visions. Having been admitted at least to the outskirts of the heavenly assembly, having heard the secret counsels of God, he is able with authority to assert eternal Providence and justify the ways of God to men.

While it would be difficult to add substantially to the insights of the critics mentioned in note 29 regarding prophecy in general in *Paradise Lost*, the notion of participation in the divine council does suggest another dimension. It explains not only the what and the how but also the why. If Milton hoped to write an epic that would surpass the efforts of Homer and Virgil, he needed more than an exalted subject to elevate it; he needed to envelop the whole in an aura of the supernatural, to present his poem as a revelation from on high. The role of the prophet for his epic voice accomplished these ends.

What H. Wheeler Robinson says about the exegetical gains resulting from a consideration of the council concept seems to me to apply very well also to *Paradise Lost*, thinking of the narrator as an example of the prophetic consciousness:

> First of all there is the contribution made to our understanding of the prophetic consciousness. No question is more interesting or on the psychological side more important than this—how did the Hebrew prophets become convinced that theirs was indeed the voice of God to men? An essential part of the answer lies in the peculiar psychology of the Hebrews, which cannot here be discussed. But the conception of a council of Yahweh, to which the

prophet was in some real sense admitted, according to Jeremiah's explicit statement, usefully reinforces the strictly psychological explanation of inspiration. It offers an intelligible and graphic way of imagining that intercourse between God and man from which the prophetic consciousness springs. It provides a permanent basis of fellowship, so marked in the dialogues of Jeremiah, whilst also giving occasion for the "high lights" of special moments, as in the call of Isaiah. It introduces the idea of collaboration and of a personal relation more intimate than any external command suggests. In all generations men depend on the adequacy of such thought-forms to express and revive their deepest convictions. In the course of time these thought-forms may be transcended, but not necessarily the reality which for a measure of time they served to express.[31]

Milton found in the divine council an adequate objective correlative. It enabled him to imagine an intercourse between God and man; it provided a basis of fellowship; it introduced the idea of collaboration and of an intimate personal relation. It made the blind bard a true spokesman for God.

A commentator on Isaiah 6 has remarked that the use of the image of a divine assembly "is a good example of how the Hebrews could borrow from their neighbors and yet drastically transform the image in accordance with the demands of Israelite monotheism."[32] Similarly, the divine councils in *Paradise Lost* are a good example of how Milton could borrow from both the classics and the Bible and transform his borrowings in accordance with the demands of his poetic purpose.

31. Robinson, "The Council of Yahweh," p. 156.
32. Frederick L. Moriarty, in *The Jerome Biblical Commentary*, ed. Raymond E. Brown et al. (Englewood Cliffs: Prentice-Hall, 1968), p. 270.

Creation in Reverse:
The Book of Job and *Paradise Lost*

Harold Fisch

he echoes from Job found in the early books of *Paradise Lost* have a significance far greater than their frequency would lead us to suppose. They have a controlling function comparable to that of the cluster of images and references relating the Fall of the Angels and the Fall of Man to the Exodus of the Israelites from Egypt, which I pointed out some years ago.[1]

It will be best to start not with Milton but with the Book of Job, viewing it from the angle that would have suggested itself, I believe, to the author of *Paradise Lost*. Milton had a strong feeling for Job as a literary model for drama or brief epic—this is evidenced in *Paradise Regained* and *Samson Agonistes*. He also undoubtedly responded to it as theodicy. But in writing *Paradise Lost*, Milton was surely more aware of Job as a great Creation-poem. This is an aspect of the book not always fully appreciated by readers today.[2] Nevertheless, such a reading is part of an ancient and continuing exegetical tradition as well as being natural to any reader sensitive to the great lyrical passages describing the primeval order of Nature, such as 26 : 7–13, 28 : 1–11, 36 : 26–33, 37 : 3–16, and 38 : 4 to 39 : 30. In the latter passage, God's overwhelming question out of the whirlwind—"Where wast thou when I laid the foundations of the earth?"—is followed by a

1. "Hebraic Style and Motifs in *Paradise Lost*," in *Language and Style in Milton*, ed. R. D. Emma and John T. Shawcross (New York: Ungar, 1967), pp. 46–51; further developed by John T. Shawcross in "*Paradise Lost* and the Theme of Exodus," *Milton Studies* 2 (1970): 3–26.

2. Recently, however, John J. Miles has argued for the importance of the theme of world-creation in Job ("Gagging on Job, or the Comedy of Religious Exhaustion," in *Studies in Job, Semeia* 7 [University of Montana, 1977]: 79).

series of images of primordial magnificence for which Job is especially famous:

> When the morning stars sang together, and all the sons of God shouted for joy? Or who shut up the sea with doors, when it brake forth, as if it had issued out of the womb? When I made the cloud the garment thereof, and thick darkness a swaddling band for it? (Job 38:7–9)

The only comparable poetry is to be found in the great Creation-psalms, such as Psalms 24, 90, 93, and 104.

According to a Talmudic view well known in Milton's time, Moses, the author of the book of Genesis, was also the author of Job.[3] The link with Genesis is suggested by references in the text to Adam (15:7; 28:28), to the Flood (12:15), and (according to the Chaldaic paraphrase) to Eve and the serpent (28:7–8).[4] Such parallels are also common in medieval Christian sources. In the Middle English *Pety Iob* (circa 1400), Job compares himself to Adam.[5] Augustine and Chrysostom had made the point that Job, tempted like Adam by his wife, had (unlike Adam) successfully resisted temptation. All in all, there are suggestive parallels and these are not all the fruit of medieval fantasy. In a full-length philological study of the text of the Book of Job, the Israeli scholar N. H. Tur-Sinai has suggested that many sections of the poem "stem from an elaborate poetical account of the Creation and the first steps of Man"—an early *Liber Adami* that the author of Job had before him but that is now lost to us. Nahum N. Glatzer has taken up the subject of the parallel between Genesis 3 and Job with special reference to the theme of the knowledge of good and evil.[6]

3. Babylonian Talmud, tractate *Baba Batra*, folio 14b.
4. In Brian Walton's *Polyglot Bible* (1656) the relevant Chaldaic version is rendered as: "Semitam arboris vitae quam non novit Sammael, volans instaravis; nec intuitus est eam oculus Evae. Non ambulaverunt in ea filii hominis, nec declinavit ad eam serpens." Sammael is a name given to Satan in many rabbinic sources.
5. See Lawrence L. Besserman, *The Legend of Job in the Middle Ages* (Cambridge: Harvard University Press, 1979), p. 80.
6. Tur-Sinai, *The Book of Job: A New Commentary* (Jerusalem: Kiryath Sepher, 1957), p. 409; Glatzer, "Knowest Thou?" in *Studies in Rationalism, Judaism and Universalism in Memory of Leon Roth*, ed. Raphael Loewe (London: Routledge and Kegan Paul, 1966), pp. 73–86.

But the depth and breadth of the Creation-theme in Job are evident to the nonscholarly reader who brings to the poem an awakened poetic sensibility. Job creates an image of a world fresh from the hand of its Creator, as yet unsubdued by man, who stands in awe before its grandeur and mystery. Above all, the aspect of Creation stressed both in the speeches of Elihu and in the mighty epiphany of chapters 38 through 41 is that of power. God thunders marvelously with his voice: he does great things that we cannot comprehend (37:5). In that sense the work is complementary to Genesis. Genesis 1 and 2 are subdued; there are no mighty thunderings; there is rather an orderly procession of marvelous events, an unfolding design. The language is measured, the details are few—features that Erich Auerbach has noted as typical of Old Testament narrative.[7] In Genesis 2 the description of the act of Creation is positively domestic: God shapes man out of clay, breathing into his nostrils the breath of life and then planting a garden around him that will, presumably, shelter him from all that is savage and uncontrolled in the world. From this point of view, Job represents an alternative to Genesis: it is more elaborate, more lyrical; above all, it introduces the dimensions of power and mystery. It provides numenousness, the aspect of the "Sublime."[8]

In the Christian tradition, power and mystery were associated in particular with the two terrifying monsters that appear as the climax to God's speech from the whirlwind, namely, Behemoth and Leviathan. Augustine quotes the version of Job 40:19 found in the Septuagint: "He is the beginning of God's works, made to be derided by the angels."[9] The great sea-monster is identified with the Devil who rebels against God and the angels of light and is cast out of Heaven. He is the *beginning* of things (*reshit* in the Hebrew of this verse also echoes the first word in Genesis)—the

7. Erich Auerbach, *Mimesis: The Representation of Reality in Western Literature* (New York: Doubleday, 1957), pp. 6–9.

8. In Burke's definitions a major role in creating the sublime is given to the qualities of Power, Terror, and Obscurity. He draws his chief examples from Job. See Edmund Burke, "On the Sublime and the Beautiful," in *Works* (London: The World's Classics, Oxford University Press, 1906), 1:108–9, 114, 116–18. These qualities are well caught in some of Blake's illustrations to Job.

9. *The City of God*, book 11, chap. 15 (London: Everyman, 1945), 1:325.

key figure in a creation-myth parallel to, but different from, that intimated in the first chapters of Genesis. Instead of an unfolding world of light and blessing summed up at each stage with the words "And God saw that it was good," we have a more fearful symmetry culminating in the forms of Behemoth and Leviathan. The latter is "king over all the children of pride" (41:34). He is a figure at once portentous and terrible whom God alone is capable of subduing. The relevance of this entire vision, and of the figure of Satan/Leviathan in particular, to books 1 and 2 of *Paradise Lost* is clear.

Milton's need in the first two books of *Paradise Lost* was to find a system of imagery to balance the light-drenched world of books 3 and 4. This was necessary to the essential architecture of the poem. Michael Lieb has pointed to the importance in the poem of the "dialectics of creation." "Divine birth from Chaos finds its antithesis in the 'destruction' of the angels, who are plunged into a 'wide womb' of uncreativity. . . . Ironically, like God, Satan resorts to the Abyss in order to create."[10] The diabolical and divine worlds represent parallel and opposed systems of metaphor. The two first books of the poem, in fact, provide us with a kind of photographic negative of what follows. Birth and Creation are predicated by Hell also but they are strangely inverted. Here, instead of the vigorous life of Eden, we have a "universe of death" (2.622). We may now add that Job, through its typical imagery, provided Milton with just such a universe.

Let us take first the motif of darkness. Darkness is a key term and a key concept in the first two books of Milton's poem. As Satan takes his first view of Hell, he notes

> The dismal Situation waste and wild,
> A Dungeon horrible, on all sides round
> As one great Furnace flam'd, yet from those flames
> No light, but rather darkness visible
> Serv'd onely to discover sights of woe. (*PL*, 1.60–64)

A. W. Verity and James H. Sims have here properly pointed to

---

10. Michael Lieb, *The Dialectics of Creation: Patterns of Birth and Regeneration in "Paradise Lost"* (Amherst: University of Massachusetts Press, 1970), pp. 24, 28.

Job's great lament in chapter 10.[11] He is speaking of *She'ol*, the world of shades, "A land of darkness, as darkness itself; and of the shadow of death, without any order, and where the light is as darkness" (10:22; more properly from the Hebrew, "and it gleams like darkness"). It would be tedious to list all the references to cloud and thick darkness in Job (those that suggest themselves at first glance are 9:7, 22:13–14, 26:8, and 38:9), just as it would be in Milton's poem. In both texts they are pervasive, but in Job they are felt to be part of a dark creation, a visionary antithesis to the world of light annunciated in Genesis. This I think accounts for the special significance of the vision of the Book of Job for Milton. The key to these images of darkness is in chapter 3. There Job curses his day and does so in words that take us back to Genesis 1. Instead of "And God said, let there be light" we have the opposite:

> Let that day be darkness; let not God regard it from above, neither let the light shine upon it. Let darkness and the shadow of death stain it; let a cloud dwell upon it; let the blackness of the day terrify it. (Job 3:4–5)

The Hebrew text forces the contrast upon us: instead of *yehi 'or*—"let there be light"—in verse 4 we have *yehi hoshekh*—"let there be darkness."[12] Curiously, in verse 8 of this dark creation we already have our first mention of Leviathan. The phrase is obscure and has never been satisfactorily explained, but it must have been felt as peculiarly appropriate by the author of *Paradise Lost*: "Let them curse it that curse the day, who are ready to arouse Leviathan."[13]

11. See James H. Sims, *The Bible in Milton's Epics* (Gainesville: University of Florida Press, 1962), Index of Biblical References.

12. J. William Whedbee remarks perceptively that in this chapter "Job calls the old creation myth to mind in order to reverse its effects; he desires to throw all creation back into primordial chaos" ("The Comedy of Job," in *Studies in Job*, *Semeia* 7 [University of Montana, 1977]: 8–9). Michael Fishbane points out that Job 3:1–13 are "nothing less than a counter-cosmic incantation. . . . their sequence and rhythm are exactly paralleled by the archetypal cosmic pattern of Genesis" ("Jeremiah IV 23–26 and Job III 3–13: A Recovered Use of the Creation Pattern," *Vetus Testamentum* 21 [1971]: 153–54).

13. The AV reads, "who are ready to raise up their mourning." "Leviathan" as

Tur-Sinai finds a reference here to Lotan, a figure in some pre-Israelite cosmogony who reigns over "the kings of the earth" (mentioned later in verse 14) as they lie sleeping in *She'ol*. Leviathan "wakens them from their sleep in order that they might assist him in his war against the God of heaven and light."[14] Milton knew nothing of Lotan in the Ugaritic mythology, but the strange universe of death intimated in this chapter and the mention of the stirring up of Leviathan amid "the kings and counsellors of the earth" in a place where "the prisoners rest together and hear not the voice of the oppressor" (verse 18)—all this evidently fused in Milton's imagination with his vision of Hell and Pandemonium, the angels slumbering, "intrans't" upon the Flood, and Satan/Leviathan rousing himself to lead them. What is more, all this takes place in a context that suggests a kind of parody of the Creation-story—Genesis seen through a glass darkly. And this is precisely what Milton was seeking.

Darkness in these early books of *Paradise Lost* occurs in dialectical association with fire. This is illustrated by the passage just quoted (1.60–64). The allusion to "darkness visible" is framed by images of fire:

> As one great Furnace flam'd, yet from those flames
> No light, but rather darkness visible.

And in the lines following we have a reference to

> a fiery Deluge, fed
> With ever-burning Sulphur unconsum'd: . . .
> With Floods and Whirlwinds of tempestuous fire.
> (*PL*, 1.68–69, 77)

We are aware of "utter darkness" (72) but also of flames. The Lake of Hell is a "burning Marle" (296); the fallen angels are seen "Twixt upper, nether and surrounding Fires" (346).

This feature, which belongs to the essential core of Milton's vision of Hell, finds its authority in the peculiar imagery of Job.

---

in the Hebrew (which of course Milton knew) is adopted by the RSV as well as by most modern translations.

14. Tur-Sinai, *The Book of Job*, p. 57.

In the speech of Zophar in chapter 20 the wicked man is pictured in darkness but consumed also by fire: "All darkness shall be hid in his secret places: a fire not blown shall consume him" (20:26). Maimonides, in his *Guide for the Perplexed* (a text evidently known to Milton in the Latin translation of Johannes Buxtorf, the younger) glossing this verse,[15] proposes that it may be used to interpret the word *hoshekh* in Genesis 1:4 to mean not only darkness but also fire. He is thus able to construct a creation-model in which all four elements are included, the element of fire being adduced from this text in Job. He goes on to point out, "If it [this element] were luminous we should see at night the whole atmosphere in flames."[16] In Job 18 we are told that the light shall be darkened in the tabernacle of the wicked man; he dwells in terror and "brimstone shall be scattered on his habitation" (18:6, 11, 15). Milton had taken a deep imprint from this chapter, as illustrated by the "ever-burning Sulphur" of 1.69 and the "Sulphurous Hail" of 1.171. The "fiery Surge" of Hell in 1.173 may well have been suggested by a later chapter of Job where the luminous path created on the ocean by Leviathan is compared to a pot boiling on the fire: "He maketh the deep to boil like a pot, he maketh the sea like a pot of ointment" (Job 41:31).

But the combination of fire with darkness is not the only dialectical combination in Milton's poem. Closely associated with it we also find the combination of ice and snow. This compounds the dialectic, for we have a suggestion of ice and flames together and of black or blackened snow. This image pattern belongs to the essence of Milton's vision of Hell. In *Paradise Lost* (1.350), the fallen angels alight on the "firm brimstone," but they immedi-

15. As I argued in "Hebraic Style and Motifs in *Paradise Lost*," Milton did not know the early medieval Jewish sources firsthand, nor did he know the Cabala. But he knew Maimonides's *Guide* in the Latin translation of Buxtorf, and he was able to consult the materials in the great Hebrew Bible (edited by Buxtorf or Bomberg) as well as in Brian Walton's *Polyglot Bible*. The latter two items were standard equipment for any serious student of the Bible. On the dissemination of Maimonides in England at this time, see J. L. Teicher, "Maimonides and England," *Transactions of the Jewish Historical Society of England* 16 (1945–1951): 97–100.

16. *The Guide for the Perplexed*, trans. M. Friedlander (London: Routledge, 1947), pt. 2, chap. 30.

ately remind the poet of the multitudes (evidently Vandals) pouring over the Rhine and Danube from the "frozen loyns" of the North. The burning Lake is a lake of darkness and ice. The fallen angels in *Paradise Lost* (2.490–91) are like dusky clouds that "o'respread / Heav'ns chearful face," and "the lowring Element / Scowls oer the dark'nd lantskip Snow." The paradox is further articulated in the description of the "frozen Continent" lying beyond the river Lethe, which the fallen angels proceed to explore once the Stygian Council is ended:

> Beyond this flood a frozen Continent
> Lies dark and wilde, beat with perpetual storms
> Of Whirlwind and dire Hail, which on firm land
> Thaws not, but gathers heap, and ruin seems
> Of ancient pile; all else deep snow and ice,
> A gulf profound as that *Serbonian* Bog
> Betwixt *Damiata* and Mount *Casius* old,
> Where Armies whole have sunk: the parching Air
> Burns frore, and cold performs th'effect of Fire. (2.587–95)

Appropriately, this is the spot chosen for the torment of the damned who are made to endure "the bitter change" of fire and ice (598–603).

Behind all these references the special image system of Job may be discerned. The black snow of 2.491 has its parallel in Job's speech to Eliphaz in chapter 6 where the deceitfulness of the friends suggests by association dark streams of ice: "which are blackish by reason of the ice and wherein the snow is hid" (Job 6:16). In chapter 24, speaking of the wicked, especially of the adulterer who waits in the dark, Job is again reminded of the dark streams of snow—this time thawing in the fierce heat (a phenomenon not uncommon when the snows of the Hermon thaw in the early summer to feed the headwaters of the Jordan): "Drought and heat consume the snow waters: so doth the grave those which have sinned" (Job 24:19).[17]

What we have in fact is an image cluster of darkness: fire: snow: flood specific to books 1 and 2 of *Paradise Lost* and part

---

17. Sims, *Bible in Milton's Epics*. Also John Carey and Alastair Fowler, eds., *The Poems of John Milton* (Harlow: Longmans, 1968).

also of the special climate of the Book of Job. Milton finds these images useful not only for their descriptive value—for the local color they provide—but also because they have a structural role. They represent, taken together and within the context from which they are drawn, a dark antithesis to that sunnier creation which is to be the subject of the later books of *Paradise Lost*.

I now approach two specific echoes of Job in Milton's poem that have not been pointed out by the commentators. They seem to me to have more than local significance. The building of Pandemonium is preceded by a description of a hill "whose grisly top / Belch'd fire and rowling smoak" (1.670–71). The emphasis is on the precious minerals and metals hidden in its bowels. It

> Shon with a glossie scurff, undoubted sign
> That in his womb was hid metallic Ore,
> The work of Sulphur. Thither wing'd with speed
> A numerous Brigad hasten'd. . . .
>   *Mammon* led them on,
>   . . . by him first
> Men also, and by his suggestion taught,
> Ransack'd the Center, and with impious hands
> Rifl'd the bowels of thir mother Earth
> For Treasures better hid. Soon had his crew
> Op'nd into the Hill a spacious wound
> And dig'd out ribs of Gold. Let none admire
> That riches grow in Hell; that soyle may best
> Deserve the precious bane. . . .
> Nigh on the Plain in many cells prepar'd,
> That underneath had veins of liquid fire
> Sluc'd from the Lake, a second multitude
> With wond'rous Art found out the massie Ore.
>   (*PL* 1.672–75, 678, 684–92, 700–703)

If we set this passage beside the first six verses of Job 28, the similarity in conception and details (the latter indicated by italics) at once becomes apparent. Job is speaking of the mysteriousness of the hidden things of the creation:

> Surely there is a vein for the silver, and a place for *gold* where *they fine it*. Iron is *taken out of the earth*, and brass is *molten* out of the stone. He setteth an end to darkness, and searcheth out all perfec-

tion: the stones of darkness, and the shadow of death. The *flood* breaketh out from the inhabitant; even the waters forgotten of the foot: they are dried up, they are gone away from men. As for the earth, out of it cometh bread: and *under it is turned up as it were fire*. The stones of it are the place of sapphires, and it hath *dust of gold*.

There is nothing actually pejorative about this account of subterranean wealth. The "fining" of the gold is not being condemned as the work of Mammon; the fiery depths of the earth arouse in us rather a sense of wonder, terror, mystery.

But in the continuation of this chapter of Job the point clearly emerges that the search for the riches hidden in the womb of the earth is not the true path of wisdom:

But where shall wisdom be found? and where is the place of understanding? Man knoweth not the price thereof; neither is it found in the land of the living. The depth saith, It is not in me: and the sea saith, It is not with me. It cannot be gotten for gold, neither shall silver be weighed for the price thereof. (Job 28:12–15)

True wisdom is found by a path both higher and simpler: "Behold, the fear of the Lord, that is wisdom; and to depart from evil is understanding" (Job 28:28). We are better off confining our efforts to the more overt and well-lit aspects of creation. The fallen angels seek to express a more violent creativity. In "wounding" the earth to seek out its hidden treasures, they indicate their desire to penetrate and preempt that dark and fiery zone of creation which, according to Job 28, God had excluded from human reach. Milton is again using hints from Job to support the dialectical structure of his poem.

The second specific echo I wish to point out has a more central function in the strategy of the poem as a whole. The images of Sin and Death as wife and first-born son of Satan, respectively, have been seen as supplying a devilish parallel to the divine Trinity and also as paralleling the mode of existence in Eden where Eve (like Sin) is born out of the body of Adam who becomes in a sense her progenitor and who afterward begets on her the human race. Here in Hell we have a ghastly parody of this generation with the added feature that Death, after issuing from the womb of Sin, then rapes her and engenders with her a race of yelling monsters who feed on their mother's bowels. Sin describes her fate:

> into the womb
> That bred them they return, and howle and gnaw
> My Bowels, thir repast; then bursting forth
> Afresh with conscious terrours vex me round,
> That rest or intermission none I find.
> Before mine eyes in opposition sits
> Grim *Death* my Son and foe, who sets them on,
> And me his Parent would full soon devour
> For want of other prey . . . (2.798–806)

There is an obvious source for the idea in James 1:15:

> Then when lust hath conceived, it bringeth forth sin: and sin, when it is finished, bringeth forth death.

But there is nothing here of the drama in which the figures are involved after Sin and Death are conceived, nothing of their mutual love and hate, nothing about death as a devourer, and nothing about the monsters that he sires. A parallel has been found in Spenser's account of the monster Error and her vile breed (*Faerie Queene*, 1.1.15)[18] for the detail of the yelling monsters that feed on their mother, but no really satisfactory analogues have been found for Milton's account of the pattern of violent relationships involving Satan, Sin, and Death.[19]

I believe, however, that here again Milton's invention was pro-

---

18. John Milton, *Complete Poems and Major Prose*, ed. Merritt Y. Hughes (New York: Odyssey Press, 1957).

19. John M. Steadman cites a passage from Basil's *Sixth Homily on the Hexaemeron* (Migne, *Patrologia Graeca*, vol. 29, col. 118) where sin (harmartia), offspring of Satan, gives birth to death ("Milton and St. Basil: The Genesis of Sin and Death," *Modern Language Notes* 73 [1958]: 83–84). Steadman found a similar pattern in a thirteenth-century sermon by Robert Grosseteste ("Grosseteste on the Genealogy of Sin and Death," *Notes & Queries* 204 [1959]: 367–68). These examples and others, however, are essentially bald, allegorical statements based on the text of James 1:15. There is no vivid personification of any of the three figures as in Milton's poem. I am suggesting that the hint for a more dramatic relationship between them was provided by the verses in Job 18 as Milton read them with the help of the apparatus in the great Hebrew Bible.

foundly influenced by his reading of the Book of Job. In Bildad's speech in chapter 18, the wicked man is described as condemned to darkness and terror—"cast into a net by his own feet." The description rises to a climax with the verse, "His strength shall be hungerbitten, and destruction shall be ready at his side" (Job 18:12). The Authorized Version here is too vague to be of service to the visual imagination. A clearer dramatic picture emerges, however, if the verse is read with the help of the Jewish scholiasts and of the Chaldaic paraphrase (*Targum*) as set out in Buxtorf's rabbinic Bible (which Milton evidently made use of). They explain the verse as meaning that "His 'strength' [son, as in Genesis 35:18] shall hunger, and destruction shall beset his 'rib' [wife, as in Genesis 2:22]." This is the version given by the chief Hebrew commentators (Rashi and Nahmanides). The Chaldaic paraphrase (which underlies this reading) is translated in the *Polyglot Bible* as "Sit famelicus primogenitus ejus, et afflictio parata uxori ejuus." This reading is also credibly adopted by some modern glossarists. The expressions are figurative, but not more so than other parts of the text of Job. Again we have Genesis in reverse. Here the "rib" (Eve) and the firstborn who should have augured strength and blessing become parodies of their benign roles. The violent hunger of the son and the ruin visited upon the wife of the wicked man will surely remind the reader of *Paradise Lost* of the condition of Sin and her offspring; Death, says Sin, "me his parent would devour / For want of other prey."

But the verse that follows in the Authorized Version would seem to settle the matter: "It shall devour the strength of his skin: even the firstborn of death [Hebrew: the firstborn, death] shall devour his strength [Hebrew: limbs]" (Job 18:13). ("It" could as easily mean "He" in the Hebrew, and, grammatically, the sentence could refer to the firstborn devouring his own limbs or those of another, say his father.) Here we surely have the germ of Milton's idea according to which the Evil One has a firstborn named Death who devours, or threatens to devour, the body of his parent or parents. The Hebrew is consistent with such a reading, and Milton, reading Job in the great Hebrew Bible with an outline already forming in his mind of a dark creation antithetical to the good world of Paradise and Heaven, sensed here the hint of an iconography that would suit his purpose, a diabolical trio matching the heavenly one.

Milton's use of Job is more than an example of literary indebtedness in the ordinary sense. In the obscure and strangely phantasmagoric world of Job, Milton found, if not a complete mythology, a striking pattern of images suggesting the direction for his imagination and conferring a biblical authority upon his invention. A mind as ready as Milton's to transmute Scripture into poetic fable would also detect in the same chapter a hint of the ultimate fate of Satan as a prelude to the far-off divine event to which the whole Creation was moving. Had not the sacred poet of the Book of Job added to the image of the insatiable firstborn, Death, his forecast of the end of the wicked parent himself?

> His roots shall be dried up beneath, and above shall his branch be cut off. His remembrance shall perish from the earth, and he shall have no name in the street. He shall be driven from light into darkness, and chased out of the world. (Job 18:16–18)

The Evil One would be swallowed up in darkness. But that is not the last word either, for in the final chapters of Job the good creation is restored and with it the victory of life over death. Job/Adam would survive to see light sown for the righteous in the land of the living.

theodicy - a vindication of the justice of

All-Interpreting Love: God's Name
in Scripture and in *Paradise Lost*

Michael Fixler

t was William Empson who first found extraordinary Milton's use of the word *all*—612 times—in *Paradise Lost*, or about once every seventeen lines. Since the frequency is almost exactly that of Pope's use of *wit*, clearly the most significant word in *Essay On Criticism*, it seemed to him that the use of *all* in Milton's poem should suggest something equally significant. But this proved not to be the case. Or so Empson thought. *Wit*, as Pope used it, was a good example of what Empson called "the structure of complex words," whereas Milton's use of *all*, though it had "a good many connections with the whole theme" of *Paradise Lost*, remained in its meaning "very simple." It did "not actually collect meanings," as Empson's complex words were supposed to do; hence, he concluded it was not a particularly useful term with which to approach a reading of the poem. On the other hand, Empson thought *all* told us a great deal about Milton himself as an obsessive "absolutist, an all-or-none man," whose complex ulterior sympathies for Satan and fallen man were at odds in his poem with his "appalling theology."[1]

Empson, I believe, was quite wrong about the simplicity of *all* in *Paradise Lost*. *All* does collect meanings phenomenally and in a way connected with its extraordinary frequency of usage. The word works often within an apparently calculated range, signify-

---

1. The quotations are from "All in *Paradise Lost*," in Empson's *The Structure of Complex Words* (London: Chatto & Windus, 1951), pp. 101–4, a section preceded immediately by the discussion, "Wit in the *Essay on Criticism*." Empson's more considered objections to Milton's "appalling theology" are in his later work, *Milton's God* (London: Chatto & Windus, 1961).

ing at one end any sort of completeness, and at the other end a very specific designation, a name of God. The use of *all* to designate God was not observed by Empson, or perhaps not consciously, though Milton's conception of God's absoluteness is probably what cued Empson to the "absolutist" tonality he found throughout the poem. In any case, the use of *all* as a word to signify God may not be strange to readers who share Milton's awareness of how it is associated with God's name in the New Testament.

I

In the Old Testament, God has several names, El, Elohim, Shaddai, and most importantly the tetragrammaton YHWH, or Yahweh, commonly anglicized as Jehovah. The name means, Milton wrote, "approximately 'he who is,' or *who is, was, and shall be*," and theologically signifies "the existence not only of [God's] nature but also the fulfilment of his promises." *Jehovah*, Milton also noted, "both in the New Testament and in the Greek version of the Old . . . is always translated as Κύριος." But later Milton qualified this point, observing that in the New Testament *Kyrios* strictly means only "Lord"; *Jehovah* itself, as a name, is utterly abandoned in the New Testament, where God's promises "are most markedly fulfilled." What Milton seems to have meant is that in the New Testament the Father's name is known only through his Son, who is preeminently Love. In himself, Milton wrote, "The Father is greater than all."[2] Or, as the Son exclaims to God in *Paradise Lost* before he goes to cast out Satan at the end of the War in Heaven, he but assumes God's "Sceptre and Power" in his own "Glory and Exaltation," but

> gladlier shall resign, when in the end
> Thou shalt be All in All, and I in thee
> For ever, and in me all whom thou lov'st. (6.730–34)

The source for this telescoped term for God is of course 1 Corin-

<hr/>

2. The discussions of the meaning of *Jehovah*, of the name as *Kyrios* in the Septuagint, and of *Kyrios* as excluding Jehovah in the New Testament, are to be found, seriatim, in *CD*, 1.2 and 1.5, in *CPW*, 6:138, 139, 256, 275. All citations of Milton's poetry are from John Milton, *Complete Poems and Major Prose*, ed. Merritt Y. Hughes (New York: Odyssey Press, 1957).

thians 15:28: "And when all things shall be subdued unto him, then shall the Son also himself be subject unto him that put all things under him, that God may be all in all."[3] In Paul as in Milton the word *all* moves from an adjectival designation of completeness to a nominative absolute and seems intended to be the only accessible name of God beyond the name of his Son. But the word remains ambiguous in Milton's usage and indeed resonates suggestively throughout *Paradise Lost*.

In that regard there are two distinct but closely related points I want to make. The first is that, when *all* tends to become *All* or *All in All*, it never appears as a designation of the Father's transcendence without being somehow associated with the Son's identifiable name and function as Love. The second is that whenever *all* serves to signify any aspect of God's transcendence, and thus takes on the property of a name, it partakes of a certain enigmatic quality associated with God's names in Scripture and tradition. In *Paradise Lost* the use of *Love* as a name for the Son also partakes of that enigmatic quality, and it is these two uses I intend to explore. As to the mysteriousness of God's names, Milton himself concludes his discussion of them in the *Christian Doctrine* by acknowledging that since God's attributes, which are his names, extend transcendently into glory, finally "we must all call God WONDERFUL and INCOMPREHENSIBLE."[4] But even on the hither side of knowledge accessible to men, the terms for his name seemed to be for Milton designations, the meanings of which are graduated from clarity to obscurity, much as he also conceived the ways they might be understood, for the regeneracy and understanding of men also varied from smaller to greater measure.

It would follow that Satan, the first and most irrevocably to fall, would least recognize such attributes of God in the created

3. This is known as the "Unitarian text," and Milton's use of *All in All* for God's absoluteness into which the Son himself is finally absorbed is Socinian or Unitarian in its thrust. See also 1 Cor. 12:6, Col. 1:15–17 and 3:11, Eph. 1:23, and John 17:21–22. The association of the names of God with the word *all* seems to go back to the theophany at Sinai (Exod. 33:18–19) when Moses first says to God, "I beseech thee, show me thy glory. And [God] said, I will make all [Hebrew *kōl*] my goodness pass before thee, and I will proclaim the name of the Lord before thee."

4. *CD*, 1.2, in *CPW*, 6:152.

✓ world as might be shadowed forth in the ambiguities of the divine names. To a lesser degree this would be true as well of the
✓ fallen reader—where, that is, it served the purposes of the poem to make that point. Conversely, the divine names might seem almost perfectly clear behind a diaphanous transparency, where it served the purposes of the poem to stress the reader's identification with Milton's own penetration of heavenly glories and insights. Such participation I attribute to Milton's larger conception of the whole nature and function of his poem, and I shall turn to that in due course. But first we may, with respect to *All*, test our own capacities against Satan's inability to perceive the divine attributes veiled by a name in *Paradise Lost*.

It is, for example, not generally noted that the reader's first view of the heart of Eden is glimpsed over Satan's shoulder as he wings inward to reconnoiter the terrain he must destroy to avenge himself. At the outset we are fully aware of Satan's guidance, but the closer we approach to the center the more enraptured we are by a beauty that seems in no way tainted by Satanic perceptions. Indeed it is the poet himself who conducts us into Eden's very heart, while Satan, seemingly forgotten, stands by, for there at the new world's center we behold in a metaphorical figure something imparted only to us, not to Satan, in the allegorical language of myth. As a scene it is a poetic translation of Botticelli's *Primavera*, celebrating quintessential springtime, the perfection of all creation being signaled by natural music and symbolic dance:

> The Birds thir choir apply; airs, vernal airs,
> Breathing the smell of field and grove, attune
> The trembling leaves, while Universal *Pan*
> Knit with the *Graces* and the *Hours* in dance
> Led on th'Eternal Spring. (4.264–68)

There is nothing here that need not be taken at face value as a consummate image for Paradisal perfection drawn from the great cognate tradition of classical mythology by which Renaissance Christian poetry was enriched. But the personified Graces evoke also a sense of the divine blessings poured down from God. And if their dance signifies the grace of God descending, it must also entrain the aspiring upward return of earthly and human virtues, a cycle that sanctifies space itself as the medium for the communion of Heaven and earth. Similarly, the Hours signify sanctified time both in its diurnal and seasonal (the *Horae*) cycles, that is to say, an unfallen time whose perfection we can only recover in the unfolding mystery of the relationship of Alpha and Omega, of perfection's beginning and the ultimate Apocalyptic world renewal. Here the dancing figures, who substantially embody Creation's dimensions of space and time, are led onward by "Universal *Pan*." And *he* is, of course, a figure for the God of all-created nature. Pan is the All through whose love perfection is first endowed upon Creation and through whom it will be restored; mediating all through himself, he will return all to the All in All of ultimate transcendence.[5] It is significant that

5. *Pan* appears as a name for the as yet unborn Christ in the *Nativity Ode*, line 89, though Milton also uses Pan in his more limited mythological aspect—with specific reference to Adam and Eve's nuptial bed—in *PL*, 4.705–8. Perhaps more relevant, *Pan* was revived as the name for an allegorical mystery in Renaissance Neoplatonism. This association may derive from Macrobius's *Commentary on the Dream of Scipio*, in which "the whole 'body' of the universe . . . is represented [by] the *to pan* of the Greeks" (trans. and ed. by William Harris Stahl [New York: Columbia University Press, 1952], p. 156). Raphael tells Adam of the whole ontological cycle in something like alchemical terms, which represented less a practical art than a symbolic and allegorical language of speculative discourse: "one Almighty is, from whom / All things proceed, and up to him return . . . one first matter all" (*PL*, 5.469–70, 472). The latter is the *materia prima* of the alchemists. Thomas Vaughan, the alchemist brother of the poet Henry Vaughan, related *materia prima*, as the source and the end of the universal transformational cycle, to the mystery of Pan in Proteus, "for out of the Universal Nature or First Matter all these are made and Pan hath their properties in himself" (*Caelum Terrae*, in *The Works of Thomas Vaughan*, ed. Arthur Edward Waite [London: Theosophical, 1919], pp. 223–24).

Edgar Wind, discussing the Renaissance "doctrine that Pan is hidden in Proteus," explains it as the belief "that mutability is the secret gate through which the universal invades the particular." He goes on to cite Cusanus that God, being "hidden from the eyes of all sages," must be manifest in a pluralism accessible by all-inclusive metaphorical variation. Then Cusanus is quoted as to the many names of God: "All these names are but the unfolding of the one ineffable name, and insofar as the name truly belonging to God is infinite, it embraces innumerable such names derived from particular perfections. Hence the unfolding of the divine name is multiple, and always capable of increase, and each single name is related to the true and ineffable name as the finite is related to the infinite" (from *De ludo globi* 2 and *De docta ignorantia* 1.25. See Wind further in chap. 14, "The Concealed God," in *Pagan Mysteries in the Renaissance* [New York: W. W. Norton, 1968]).

immediately following this scene Satan sees Adam and Eve for the first time, and what he sees is so recognizably erotic but pure human love, the gift of divine love, that such bliss incontinently restores Satan's mind to his own hell.

The counterpart of the dance scene with the apparently perfect but flawed image of earthly beauty at the center of Paradise, seen but unseen by Satan,[6] is to be found in the heavenly dance of worship in book 5 celebrating the divine "begetting of the Son." As Raphael describes it to Adam, "All seem'd well pleas'd, all seem'd, but were not all." Whereupon there follows a song and

> Mystical dance, which yonder starry Sphere
> Of Planets and of fixt in all her Wheels
> Resembles nearest, mazes intricate,
> Eccentric, intervolv'd, yet regular
> Then most, when most irregular they seem:
> And in thir motions harmony Divine
> So smooths her charming tones, that God's own ear
> Listens delighted. (5.617, 620–27)

Here an apparently flawed performance (Satan, having intellectually conceived Sin, has already begun the "irregular" course the fallen angels are to follow), "about the sacred Hill" or Heaven's center, is really an image of the *concordia discors*, the harmonic perfection God makes out of the Fall. And all this is entrained by the begetting of the Son, whose function is by his existence to mediate between the two absolutes of God as All at either end of the divine scheme.

6. There is at least one other notable instance in *Paradise Lost* in which Milton has Satan stand in the presence of some special aspect of Creation within which he does not know that God is present. This is Satan's arrival on the surface of the Sun where among specifically symbolic jewels and precious stones is the philosopher's stone (3.598–612). The whole passage begs for an extensive commentary, but let it suffice that we remember the Vulgate's Psalm 18 (19 in the AV): "*In sole (Deus) posuit tabernaculum suum*" ("The Lord has set his tabernacle in the sun," hence, there God is present). The particular presence of the philosopher's stone expresses, I suggest, the divine transformational power, which in context means the power to transmute evil (Satan's malevolent intent as he gazes earthward from the sun) into good. Indeed, throughout Satan's whole approach, which climaxes at the dance of Pan, we are reminded that God's spiritual presence can only be spiritually perceived through appropriate allusions and symbols, things, in short, inapprehensible to the fallen Satan.

The "Mystical dance" of heavenly worship about which Raphael tells Adam is a piece of knowledge somehow anticipated by Adam in his own and Eve's earlier morning worship service, as they invoked the universal praise Creation sings to its maker, each part in its own sphere, so that the stars "that move / In mystic Dance not without Song, resound / His praise" (5.177–79). As worship the great hymn of hierarchical degrees descends through Creation to evoke finally the earth's rejoicing, with winds and birds and all things in Paradise "made vocal" by human "Song, and taught his praise" (5.204). The prayer ends with an evocation of Universal Pan that is a nearly explicit allusion the reader may sense: "Hail universal Lord, be bounteous still" (5.205).

The significance of these three scenes is their typological relationship in a kind of essential identity, each being a creaturely expression of worship involving a dance figure as a partial or entire metaphor for the universal concord of praise, and each expressing some element of mystery or enigmatic figuration. In Adam's prayer that element is signified first in the confessional acknowledgment of the wonderful incomprehensibility of God,

> who sit'st above these Heavens
> To us invisible or dimly seen
> In these thy lowest works, yet these declare
> Thy goodness beyond thought. (5.156–59)

But more particularly it finds expression in Adam's instinctual grasp of the essence of the tetragrammaton, the name of all-inclusive Jehovah who is addressed, in a paraphrase of the traditional sense of the name, as "Him first, him last, him midst, and without end" (5.165).[7] I suggest that the scriptural source for

7. See Michael Lieb, "'Holy Name': A Reading of *Paradise Lost*," *Harvard Theological Review* 67 (1974): 329. Commenting on this line, Lieb goes on to remark of Adam and Eve's hymn: "The entire thrust of the celebration becomes a formulaic rendering of God's name." Lieb focuses sharply on two aspects of Milton's concern with God's "Holy Name," taking as his point of departure Milton's explanation in *CD* of the divine names as signifying first God's nature or attributes, and then God's promises to his elect, or the fulfillment of those promises. He then goes on to show how both conceptions relate to the Holy Name, the tetragrammaton, in *Paradise Lost*. Lieb particularly places Milton within the context of the exegetical traditions elaborating in the name the dual aspects of God's nature

Adam and Eve's hymn is Psalm 148, which is a descending sequence of praise involving all creation from heaven downward until at its climax it celebrates "the name of the Lord / For his name alone is excellent" (148:13). In a pattern characteristic of the theme in the Old Testament, God's name is in this psalm cojoined with "His glory [Hebrew *kabod*] above the earth and heaven" and the exaltation of his elect. Psalm 149 was Milton's inspirational mandate for his own poetic worship and for the essential characteristic of the three worship scenes we have looked at. It begins with "Praise ye the Lord. / Sing unto the Lord a new song," and it goes on to enjoin, "Let them praise his name in the dance" (149:1, 3). With the next and final hymn, the doxology of the Psalter, so to speak, the three Psalms, 148, 149, and 150, constitute a universal song of praise.

The key, then, to Milton's allusive juxtaposition of God's praise and the evocation of his names is the way the worship of God involves the knowledge of God's nature manifest through his names. This is a proposition that has an immediate significance for our theme and a more extended range of implications with respect to what Milton set out to do in writing *Paradise Lost*. To develop both these ideas we will now consider two features of the poem. The first has to do with an occasion in which Milton deliberately inserts himself into the narrative as a participating worshiper in a heavenly hymn. This is also a profession of faith. And the second follows from that as an extended consideration of what Milton, writing earlier about human love and needs, had called the "all-interpreting voice of charity" or love. Both may be

---

and the fulfillment of his promises to the elect. Hence for Lieb "the Son performs an extremely important function in *Paradise Lost*. He represents not only that which 'by Deitie' God 'is' but that which 'by Decree' He 'does.'" Lieb does not discuss, however, the sense of God's name associated with the word *all* nor that of the Son as identified with the word *love*. Our approaches are complementary rather than divergent; still there is every difference between them. An example is to be found in the contrasting use we make of the same text (*PL*, 3.412–15) in concluding our discussions. Lieb only intimates what may be developed from that text, without actually doing so. This is true as well of his revised version of his essay in his *Poetics of the Holy: A Reading of "Paradise Lost"* (Chapel Hill: University of North Carolina Press, 1981), chap. 9, "Name." My own use of this text becomes the programmatic basis for the rest of this essay as well as its final point.

summarized in that epitome of Christian doctrine by which Milton defined the end of education, namely, "to repair the ruins of our first parents by regaining to know God aright, and out of that knowledge to love him, to imitate him, to be like him, as we may the neerest, by possessing our souls of true vertue, which being united to the heavenly grace of faith, makes up the highest perfection."[8] But, as we shall see, knowledge of God is to love as faith is to the worship of God.

II

All of Christian doctrine, Milton tells us, consists of "FAITH, or KNOWLEDGE OF GOD, and LOVE, or THE WORSHIP OF GOD." Knowledge and love of God, then, are correlative and complementary, as are their variant terms, faith or belief, and worship. Faith in turn may be challenged by doubt or ignorance of God and his ways, to justify which is the avowed purpose of *Paradise Lost*. Thus it is not surprising that the poem has two ends, the one direct, to affirm faith and enhance the knowledge of God, the other oblique, to express the love of God devotionally, in a poetic act of worship. Faith is the substance of the poem's argument explicitly stated at the outset. Love is less evidently an attribute of its mode, which is oblique but unremittingly devotional.[9]

There is, however, a moment in the poem when Milton makes his devotional point explicit. But because of the modulating and reciprocal relationship of faith, knowledge, love, and worship, the point seems curious and emerges as an enigma, a play upon God's name. Its implications extend therefore to God's names as enigmas in Scripture and *Paradise Lost*. The enigma begins in book 3 with the poet's first account of that pattern of all human devotion, the angelic choral worship celebrating God's merciful

8. For "all-interpreting" love, see *The Doctrine and Discipline of Divorce*, in *CPW*, 2:309; then see *Of Education*, 2:366–67.

9. I have discussed the devotional aspects of the poem in other connections. See especially "Milton's Passionate Epic," in *Milton Studies I*, ed. James D. Simmonds (Pittsburgh: University of Pittsburgh Press, 1969), pp.167–92; "The Apocalypse within *Paradise Lost*," in *New Essays on "Paradise Lost*," ed. Thomas Kranidas (Berkeley: University of California Press, 1969), pp.131–178; and also "Ecclesiology," an entry in *A Milton Encyclopedia*, gen. ed. William B. Hunter, Jr., (Lewisburg, Pa.: Bucknell University Press, 1978–1980), 2:190–203.

judgment upon man's impending fall and the Son's intercession. There are two aspects to the enigma of God's name in this passage. The first is paradoxically transparent, relating to the use of the word *all* as delimiting the bounds between God's knowable attributes and power and their absoluteness, which is humanly unknowable. In this respect the word becomes a name whose bearing tends toward the fuller realization of faith as the knowledge of God. As such, in its absoluteness, it can serve as a term for the transcendent character of the Son of God, but most appropriately it is the absolute term for the Father.

The second aspect of God's name celebrated in this angelic hymn is the Son's identity as Love, which first makes itself known in his offered intercession for man's fall, but which becomes specifically a reciprocity of natures exchanged between man and God. Hence it takes the form not only of the Son's intercession, but also, as Milton defined it, of man's worship of God. Through these key terms, the inclusive *all* and the transitive *love*, the angelic hymn should be seen as both doctrine and devotion, and in that duality it can be taken as a microcosm of *Paradise Lost*. If we consider further how *All* and *Love* serve in this context as names, we may trace two of the brightest figurations interwoven within the complex fabric of the poem. For as we go on we will find that, as alternate aspects of faith and worship, the words or names that are their corollaries are everywhere inseparably conjoined, as indeed in the *Christian Doctrine* Milton tells us they must be.[10]

The great choral hymn of book 3 is presented as if it were sung, but in a kind of narrative accommodation, Milton himself becoming the oracular vehicle of revelation describing how God is first celebrated in his primal attributes:

> Thee Father, first they sung Omnipotent,
> Immutable, Immortal, Infinite
> Eternal King; thee Author of all being,
> Fountain of Light, thyself invisible
> Amidst the glorious brightness where thou sit'st
> Throned inaccessible. (3.372–77)

10. *CD*, 1.1, in *CPW*, 6:129.

The Father is specifically named according to those attributes pertaining to his nature and his efficacy or power.[11] As the Omnipotent and Author of all being, his efficacy is primary. But as Eternal King, his name reflexively enlarges our sense of both the divine and the human nature that in the immediately preceding commission God gave the Son as "Head of all mankind" and exemplar of "Heavenly love" (3.285, 298), in whom

> Love hath abounded more than Glory abounds,
> Therefore thy Humiliation shall exalt
> With thee thy Manhood also to this Throne. (3.312–14)

Looking forward, as the Son himself does before casting Satan out of Heaven, God proclaims the future victory and its consummation,

> With Joy and Love triumphing and fair Truth.
> Then thou thy regal Sceptre shalt lay by
> For regal Sceptre then no more shall need,
> God shall be All in All. (3.338–41)

At this point the enigma of God's name is transparent. God's nature and his efficacy both being absolute, every term for either his nature or powers must finally be absorbed by the word *all*.[12]

11. The order of the attributive divine names in *PL*, 3.372–77, reverses the order in which they are designated and discussed in *CD*, 1.2 (*CPW*, 6:139–52). Doctrinally, as things to understand and believe, the progression of nominative attributes is from the lesser to the greater. However, as attributes and names of God to be celebrated in worship, the progression is from the greater to the lesser.

12. The tradition within which *all* absorbs or comprehends subordinate elements in the universal chain of being, or signifies attributes and qualities absolute in God, all of which hence tend to invest the word with the sense of being a name of God, is extensive. I cite but a few of the more relevant instances.

Tertullian, writing of worship, explains that if Christians are to say "hallowed be Thy name," they are to know that the name of God is a secret revealed in his Son, who, "of Himself . . . sanctifies all others." Specifically, in saying "'Hallowed be Thy name,' we pray this, that it may be hallowed in us who are in Him, as well as in all others. . . , that we may obey this precept, too, in 'praying for all' . . . And Therefore with suspended utterance, not saying, 'Hallowed be it in us,' we say —'in all'" (*On Prayer* 3, in *The Ante-Nicene Fathers*, ed. Alexander Roberts and James Donaldson, rev. A. Cleveland Coxe [Grand Rapids, Mich.: Eerdman's, 1951–1953], 3:682). Augustine describes the beatific enjoyment of God's universal harmony as a promise awaiting the saints, when "all the numbers . . . of the corporal harmony shall not lie hid" (*The City of God*, 22.30, trans. John Healy and ed. Randolph Vincent Greenwood Tasker [London: J. M. Dent, 1945], 2:404).

Extended toward mankind, the same power and attributes must be mediated from absoluteness through the Son. Thus the hymn praises next the Son's intercession by naming first the quality he shares with "All" as the only accessible derivation from God's absoluteness. "Thee next they sang, of all Creation first" (3.383). There is a descending order in the attributive names that follow for the Son, mirroring the descent from absoluteness to human love. But this last term, *love*, is really the hinge on which the human-and-divine natures swing heavenward again, back toward God's absoluteness. It is here that Milton intervenes to become, with scarce any modulation, part of the angelic chorus, interjecting as the coda to their song of praise a specific offering on his part. The way his devotion is assimilated to the angelic praise anticipates Adam and Eve's assimilation of their morning devotion to the universal song of praise they sense all Creation sings to its maker. What is curious here is how, in taking his cue from the last words of the angelic chorus celebrating "unexampled Love, / Love nowhere to be found less than divine," Milton not only joins his voice unto the angel choir but, more specifically, in an oblique compact with the reader, also

---

Compare the unfallen Adam who comes into existence knowing that God is "through all numbers absolute, though One" (*PL*, 8.421).

Jacob Boehme calls God "the ONE, which is ALL," and "the same is ALL, and yet is only ONE" (*Mysterium Magnum*, trans. John Sparrow, ed. C. V. B[arker], [London: J. M. Watkins, 1965], 1:21, 25). The conceptions involved are elaborated at length by John Davies in *Summa Totalis, or, All in All*, and *The Same for Ever*, in *The Complete Works*, ed. Alexander Balloch Grosart (New York: AMS Press, 1967), vol. 1; see especially stanza 4 of the first section, p. 6, of facsimile of ed. of 1607. John Donne in *Metempsychosis* (stanza 8, line 74) calls Christ "That all which always was all everywhere," though the Milton of *Paradise Lost* would not have agreed with that. And Merritt Y. Hughes notes in *Complete Poems*, with respect to Milton's use of the phrase in *PL*, 3.378–82, its relationship to Sylvester's translation of Du Bartas's *Divine Weeks*: "Before all Time, all Matter, Form, and Place, / God all in all, and all in God it was: / . . . all spirit, all light, / All Majestie, all-self Omnipotent, / Invisible."

On Love as a name of God, there is an interesting discussion by Dionysius the Areopagite, in *The Divine Names*, 4.17, quoting first from a hymn to Love as a name of God, then glossing it as indicating the all-animating, all-moving universal power, the idea that finds its most memorable expression in the final lines of Dante's *Divine Comedy*. Dionysius thinks of it as a power moving "through all to the Good from Itself" (*Dionysius the Areopagite on the Divine Names and the Mystical Theology*, trans. Clarence Edwin Rolt [New York: Macmillan, 1920], p. 51).

professes a sacramental vow that fuses the didactic or narrative and the devotional aspects of *Paradise Lost*.[13]

> Hail Son of God, Savior of Men, thy Name
> Shall be the copious matter of my Song
> Henceforth, and never shall my Harp thy praise
> Forget, nor from thy Father's praise disjoin. (3.412–15)

Rhetorically this is the climax of the choral hymn, and its most fervent asseveration, "thy Name / Shall be the copious matter of my Song / Henceforth," can be taken with "name" functioning metonymically to signify the whole scope of the Son's redemptive function. The name, as the copious matter of Milton's song, would signify the complete theodicy of *Paradise Lost* or the fulfillment of the poem's didactic purpose, its function as an expression of faith. But insofar as "matter" here is joined to praise, the Son's name as Love is in some ulterior sense always the sustained devotional object of the poem, whatever else the poem may seem to be doing at any point.

The devotional thrust of Milton's poem may be left on one side so that we can focus on this striking use of the divine name to signify the extended matter or argument of *Paradise Lost*. Milton's apparent meaning would seem to relate to his exposition in the *Christian Doctrine* of the names of God and of the Son as the means by which to know them. But the Son's name, as the Word of God or Logos, is very particularly a specific attribute of God's creative power, insofar as the Son as the Word was the beginning of creation, as he is its end, the Alpha and Omega of Revelation. Thus he is in a special sense the efficacy of God manifest in the world of time and space, if not the very archetype of the created universe. In these respects Milton's equation of the Son's divine name with the copious matter of his song takes on a "mystic" (as Milton used that word) coloration, as if in

---

13. On the sacramental significance for Milton of a public religious or devotional commitment, a vow being an act of external worship, see *CD*, in *CPW*, 6:679–82, and Fixler, "Ecclesiology," p. 202. [Since, as Pecheux has shown (p. 101), Milton's narrator's close to the angelic hymn in *PL*., 3.412–15, identifies him with such prophets as Isaiah and Jeremiah, the passage combines in microcosm the didactic, devotional, and vatic functions of the epic voice. Editor's note.]

some sense the poem itself was but a figure for the divine creative nature and its Power.

Now this is not an idea that can be tested as a hypothesis, but it is, I think, useful for considering further, this time within one contextual pattern, the highly allusive interplay of divine name and meaning, where the name of God or that of the Son is either directly or indirectly evoked in forms that resonate with the complex overtones of passages in Scripture where the name of God figures enigmatically. What such consideration might suggest in the identity of the poetic matter (or argument) of *Paradise Lost* and of God's name is, ultimately, the metaphysical nature poetic form had for Milton, or his understanding of the function that a poem such as *Paradise Lost* might have in the hierarchy of knowledge wherein the knowledge of all things leads by stages to the knowledge of God. But so to know God, in terms either of his power or of human worship, is, in the first instance, always to know first the name and nature of the Son, for even as early as the Mosaic dispensation men are to learn, as Adam learns, "that to God is no access / Without Mediator" (12.239–40). How Adam learns to know God, and his Mediator as Love, is one of the more interesting things to emerge from this line of consideration.

The name of God is, in effect, Adam's first concern following his awakening moments of consciousness at his creation. Adam's account of these moments is a response to Raphael's larger account of the six days of Creation and its Sabbath, which in turn is part of his ministry to Adam and Eve, the object of which is to give them sufficient knowledge to stand or fall. If they stand, they will, with spiritual insight, rise in their apprehension of all things until they ascend fully in the scale of knowledge and being to achieve their highest potentiality as near-angelic creatures, with a commensurately angelic intuition of their own nature and of the divine nature. This is the prospect self-perfection in grace holds for them, as expressed by Raphael's figure of the plant rooted in nature but whose flowers and fruit "by gradual scale sublim'd" express at last a spirituality that suggests the flowering of an angelic intuition in human nature, beyond discourse of

reason. In this context Adam's first perceptions, instinctual ges-
tures, and fundamental questions are charged with a directed
significance, the end of which, no less than its beginning, is involved with God's name.

When Adam awakens it is as if in fulfillment of the divine
mandate of his creation on the sixth day as one

> who not prone
> And Brute as other Creatures, but endu'd
> With Sanctity of Reason, might erect
> His Stature, and upright with Front serene
> Govern the rest, self-knowing, and from thence
> Magnanimous to correspond with Heav'n,
> But grateful to acknowledge whence his good
> Descends, thither with heart and voice and eyes
> Directed in Devotion, to adore
> And worship God supreme. (7.506–15)

But both self-knowledge and the knowledge and love of God in
Adam's own account of his emergent consciousness take a cir-
cuitous route, however securely both are guided by the poem's
inevitable epistemological hierarchies. Thus Adam's first conscious experiences are appropriately physical, as instinctually he
revels in the spontaneous quickness of his body, its motions, sen-
sations, and perceptions. Then the first active quickening of the
spirit mediating between body and soul within him appears in
his instinct to *know* who he was "or where or from what cause" he
existed (8.270), things that (though he does not yet know it) are
not merely fundamental but also ultimate questions. But no
sooner does he wish to know his *fons et origo* than he can speak,
and the first things he utters are names.

He begins to name first the sun, the primal source of his
knowledge of the light by which he perceives things. Then he
names the earth of which he is made and the things between
Heaven and earth. To these he turns with the question now
shaping itself in his consciousness, "Tell, if ye saw, how came I
thus, how here?" (8.277). His first use of language is instinct with
an innate logic, and he knows intuitively that if he does not exist

of himself, "by some great Maker then." Further, Adam's state of grace is instinct with the desire to use his knowledge gratefully, "How may I know him, how adore, / From whom I have that thus I move and live?" (8.280–81). But it is as if Adam's instincts and reason had outstripped his natural capacities, which must begin in his physical nature. There, if knowledge is to go beyond sense perception, it is first evident in the generative processes of the unconscious mind, as in the fantasies of dreams. Hence he sinks in sleep again, only to find before him in his dream a figure he knows to be divine, who leads him to the heart of Eden. However, once there, his quest is shown to him to be manifestly directed by a remote appetite. This would seem to be the meaning of the forbidden tree he is brought to see in his dream and by the fruit of which he is first powerfully tempted. Only then does he awaken to find himself truly on Eden's mount, before God himself, who, raising him from his prostrate adoration, the unconscious physical expression of Adam's first instinct to love, speaks the words, "Whom thou soughts't I am" (8.316).

Of course we hear what Adam cannot, the meaning implicit in the nominal predicate *I am*. We hear at once the echo and foreshadowing of the scriptural divine revelation of self to Moses on Mount Sinai when the prophet asked for the name of the God who sent him to renew the Covenant with Israel and hears him call himself, "I am that I am," enjoining Moses to tell the Israelites, "say I am sent me." We hear also the foreshadowing of that revelation within the Temple's precincts by which in the Gospel of John Jesus identified himself to the Pharisees—"Before Abraham was I am" (8:58)—and so provoked their attempt to stone him for blaspheming God's name. But though what Adam hears is only the nominal predicate, even here the phrase reverberates, as it does in God's utterance at the beginning of creation in *Paradise Lost*, "I am who fill / Infinitude" (7.168–69). For in all these instances the predicate of divine identity, *I am*, is a name that points to the fact that in Scripture the formulaic name partly conceals and partly reveals itself to us as a word of extended power. We know (from the *Christian Doctrine*) that this word, the tetragrammaton YHWH, signifies God's nature, his promises, his truth, and his power as Spirit by whom all things are.[14] But what Adam hears remains at that point only a predicate of identity, not a word of power or the name of God. It would seem that this limitation is implicit not only in Adam's uninstructed condition but also in the as yet unordered priorities of his motivation.

Indeed Adam had not yet consciously asked to know God's name. He had been more indefinite, seeking to know his maker, whose wisdom in turn was first to show him what *need* or *appetite* really prompted his quest, inasmuch as it was to be by achieving the end of that quest that Adam might come to know his Maker. At the beginning of the quest, however, there is only an apparent disjunction. For God no sooner said, "Whom thou soughts't I am," and gave Adam dominion in Paradise, than he interdicted the forbidden fruits of the Tree of Knowledge. Significantly, only then did Adam go on to name all living things. And by this he was brought to the awareness of his singular deficiency, a man living alone, and thence somehow to couple his need for a wife with a need to know the name of God:

> O by what Name, for thou above all these
> Above mankind, or aught than mankind higher,
> Surpassest far my naming, how may I
> Adore thee, Author of this Universe,
> And all this good to man, for whose well being. . . .
> Thou hast provided all things: but with mee
> I see not who partakes. (8.357–61, 363–64)

Having pointedly asked God's name, it is to that question alone that Adam receives no direct answer, for God instead goes right on to the question of his need for a mate, apparently ignoring Adam's first question.

The reason is, I suggest, that the answer to the prior question of Adam's social and sexual insufficiency in some sense involves his ignorance of God's name and accounts for its incomprehensibility to him when he had heard it used allusively (forty-one lines earlier) as *I am*. For the name by which truly to know God,

14. *CD*, 1.1, in *CPW*, 6:138–40. See Socrates, in Plato's *Cratylus* (400–401): the only certainty we can have about God's name is that what he calls himself is true.

insofar as his power will be exerted through a Mediator, is Love, and Adam as yet consciously knows nothing of that force in itself save its working on him as his need or appetite. Yet as the peculiar function of Christianity was to reveal *Love* as God's hitherto secret name, the name that must succeed the Hebraic *Yahweh* or *I am*, that name *Love* is to Christians only shadowed forth in the Hebrew Bible, an adumbration apparently taken by Milton to be the reason for the recurrence in the Old Testament of questions as to the divine name, along with refusals to render it. In each such scriptural case, however, the disjunction of question and answer is only apparent, for each involves the renewal on God's part of his special grace in his covenant with the elect, that covenant first solemnized in its primordial form when newly created Adam was brought before the trees of Knowledge and Life and told to choose only Life. Put another way, in *Paradise Lost* and in the Old Testament God demonstrates himself as Love *without* identifying himself by this name.

In effect, then, God's silence as to his name at this juncture in *Paradise Lost* is tantamount to a specific refusal to answer, such as is recorded in Scripture in the case of Jacob and in another way of Samson's father, both of whom asked God's name. The former had met, wrestled, and prevailed with someone in the night who, before Jacob would let him go, gave him the name *Israel*, a name of divine power and one signifying also the blessings of the covenant between him and God. But when Jacob in turn asked his adversary's name, the answer was only, "Wherefore is it that thou dost ask my name?" (Gen. 32:29). Whereupon Jacob knew he had just seen God face-to-face. On the second occasion Manoah asked to know the name of the angel foretelling Samson's birth, again with a promise that is an implied covenant, and Manoah too was answered by a refusal: "Why askest thou thus after my name, seeing it is secret?" (Judges, 13:18). In the *Christian Doctrine* Milton cited this passage in the Latin of the Junius Tremellius Bible that related the name refused to God's identity. There, instead of the name's secrecy, what is emphasized is that it is "an object for wonder." The passage in Judges confirmed for Milton the incomprehensibility or the mystery of God's powers and of his ways, which included of course the mysteries of providence in the offers of his covenants.[15] It is through these covenants that God as Love is made manifest.

Turning back from Scripture to Adam's question in *Paradise Lost*, God's silence appears as deliberate and significant. Adam clearly was led to ask God's name by the process of naming all creatures, a process symbolically equivalent to knowing them, by virtue of being himself above them in the hierarchy of all created things in nature. This is no small power, since naming and such knowledge implied a metaphysical or Platonic correlative, a knowledge of the true and preexisting forms of things, their essence, within the hierarchical paradigm of being.[16] But true knowledge of things *higher* than himself, beyond the natural order, Adam could not yet expect to have, because his knowledge of even himself, a far lower creature in the scale of being than God and his angels, was imperfect. Nor could his self-knowledge be perfected until the appetite of his lower physical nature, which led him first to be brought in dream to the forbidden tree, and then led him to couple God's name to his need for a mate, found its object in Eve and learned through her to transcend itself in the discovery of higher kinds of love. First he was to learn that just love of self as an image of God in whose image he was made and with whom the magnanimous man corresponded. The implicit sense of God's tacit refusal to name himself when Adam first asks points, therefore, to the hierarchical and dialectic way Adam must go; from sexual desire to social love, to self-knowledge, and from that to the true knowledge and love of God.

This course in fact is spelled out within the context of Adam's account to Raphael of his own and Eve's creation, the passage indeed wherein he tells of asking God's name. But there, in short

15. *CD*, 1.1, in *CPW*, 6:152.
16. See *Cratylus* for Plato's discussion of names in relation to Ideas and compare this paraphrase of Proclus' commentary on the *Cratylus*: "In order for the human mind to name the various characteristics of the material world. . . . it must first know their true forms preexisting . . . in the Paradigm of Being. Then it must call upon the act of naming, which, however, the human soul possesses by its very nature. For naming is only that aspect of the general art of copying possessed by every soul in which the soul copies the eternal Ideas into the materials of words" (Laurence Jay Rosan, *The Philosophy of Proclus* [New York: Cosmos, 1949], p. 199).

order, Adam's digression on his erotic weakness, the ascendancy over his reason of his physical love—his need—for Eve, leads Raphael to rebuke him and to reaffirm even more specifically in relation to Eve the warning God directed to Adam in his first dream, the one wherein God brought him to look upon the forbidden fruit of knowledge for the first time. Adam's carnal knowledge of Eve, which crowds his imagination so soon after his concern for God's name, thus seems an ambiguous correlative of two aspects of knowledge: on the one hand the self-knowledge that could lead Adam to higher perfection and, on the other hand, the forbidden knowledge that is fatal in being identified with the forbidden fruit and fallen sexuality. In effect what Raphael says is that desire or sexual appetite is sanctified only when it leads higher, through the love of woman and the regard for self, to its end-all and be-all, the love of God. But such erotic desire is fatal when it disorders Adam's self-understanding by putting sensory ecstasy before reasonable control, which would then plunge him downward in a perversion of the true direction of his nature, his uprightness, by which he was created to know God.

The point may be made more explicit by another reference to Scripture significant to Milton. The relationship he saw between knowledge and love of God, on the one hand, and the hierarchical ascent or descent of man in nature, on the other, is exemplified by his critical use of Psalm 91 in *Paradise Regained*, when Jesus is set by Satan on the pinnacle of the Temple in Jerusalem and instead of falling stands, while Satan falls. That psalm begins by paralleling and equating divine love and the knowledge of God's name. "Because he hath set his love upon me, therefore will I deliver him: I will set him on high because he hath known my name." [17]

God's appearance to Adam in the Garden of Eden in this episode of man's first awakening is matched after the Fall by the descent of the Son, as the Word of God, to judge Adam and Eve:

17. See James H. Sims, "Psalm 90 [91 in Hebrew and Protestant versions] and the Pattern of Temptation in *A Dialogue of Comfort* and *Paradise Regained*," *Moreana* 19 (June 1982): 34–35.

"the voice of God they heard / Now walking in the Garden" (10.97–98). Here again the poetic and scriptural contexts both involve typologically God's mysterious name, inasmuch as this first divine judgment of Adam is the type of the last judgment of man. John in Revelation wrote that the last judgment is delivered by the mysterious Apocalyptic rider on the white horse, who was called Faithful and True, but who "had a name written that no man knew, but he himself. . . . and his name is called The Word of God" (Rev. 19:11–13). Milton had earlier written that this passage signified "the hidden might of Christ,"[18] and in *Paradise Lost* the Word of God indeed appears as Judge and Intercessor both, while the panoply of the Son's descent from Heaven, with thrones, dominions, and principalities, suggests the other names Revelation also gives him in the same passage wherein he is called "The Word of God," namely, "King of Kings and Lord of Lords."

Thus, God's judgment upon Adam's disobedience in the Fall was also a judgment upon his disordering of due hierarchy, a condemnation of his failure in self-knowledge and implicitly for his failure to know God or to believe in the justice of his ways. Overarching this judgment, the name of God (as it is suggestively withheld from Jacob and Manoah, yet revealed to Moses, equated with love by the Psalmist, identified with Jesus in John, and then referred to in Revelation) thus signifies within itself not only the divine creative power but also, as Love, specifically the mystery of the divine Covenant with Man, a mystery that is to unfold for Adam as the wisdom to recognize, in the alignment of his own self-knowledge and his self-love, the knowledge and love of God as well.

III

We return now to Milton's specific invocation in the angelic hymn of the *name* of the Son of God as the copious *matter* of his song, and in explicating this curious equation it is well to distinguish again the two main aspects of the Son, as Logos, or Word

18. *The Reason of Church Government*, in *CPW*, 1:85.

of God, here to be related to the name of God, and as Mediator or Intercessor-Redeemer, a role intrinsic to the action of *Paradise Lost*. In both capacities the Son functions within the great hierarchy of being, first as the downward expression of God's Wisdom and Love within the creative process as a whole, then as the upwardly mediating Intercessor through whom the human creature may come to know and love his forgiving Maker. To the extent that the Son's name is germinal in the creative process, the account of Creation at the center of Milton's poem in book 7 involves the expansion of God's name into those specific attributes, wisdom and love, as they work in the creative process. Thus the Muse that Milton invokes to inspire his account of Creation is Urania, whose name and meaning derive at least in part from Plato's *Symposium* where, as the "heavenly Muse" (187E) she is identified with Aphrodite/Urania, the higher or the more spiritual form of two kinds of generative love. Her lower, more physical personification is Aphrodite/Pandemus (180C–D), who, through Ficino's *Commentary* on the *Symposium*, became conventionally the lower Venus of Renaissance mythology, presiding over purely physical generation.[19]

Though Milton's Urania is the higher Venus, or Love, she has something of her lower sister's natural procreative force. In this, Milton's third invocation to the Muse of *Paradise Lost*, she is paired allusively with an even higher generative figure, God's Wisdom, called her sister, in a figure intimating God's generative pleasure in his creative nature (7.8–12). In the same book, Wisdom and Urania, as "Sapience and Love / Immense" (195–96), both invest the Son of God, who "Girt with omnipotence, with radiance crowned / Of majesty divine" (194–95), goes forth to create the universe with the Father's generative power. He is explicitly in name "The King of Glory in his powerful Word" (208), but spe-

19. Marsilio Ficino, *Opera Omnia* (Basil, 1576; facsimile reprint, Torino: Bottegha D'erasmo, 1959; reissued 1962), 2.1326 ff.; or see Sears Jayne's translation of Ficino's *Commentary on Plato's Symposium*, University of Missouri Studies 19, no. 1 (Columbia: University of Missouri Press, 1944), pp. 142, 151–52, 191–92. See also my discussion of Urania as a name of Love and as the structural thematic keynote of books 7 and 8 in "Plato's Four Furors and the Real Structure of *Paradise Lost*," *PMLA* 92 (1977): esp. 955–57.

cifically in meaning he is the expressive force of generative love and of life. It is here, in the Son's going forth as the Word, that the Father sends with him his "overshadowing Spirit" and speaks the words of power intrinsic in the tetragrammaton, his Yahwistic name, "I am who fill / Infinitude" (165, 168–69).

We should note that this moment in the great act of all-creating Love parallels by inversion that earlier moment in Heaven when the Son is sent forth, with the Father's power as "Virtue and Grace / Immense" (6.703–4), with all the panoply of divine powers, but destructively, in wrath, not love, to drive Satan and his followers down to Hell. Thus in the powers of God's name there must also be seen the correlative antithesis of Love and Wrath, or, with respect to the covenant with man, reward and punishment.[20] In *Paradise Lost* the antithetical correlation of love and wrath (or destruction) extends from the divinely creative to the humanly procreative process, from the powers of God to the meaning of love in human life.

In the account of Creation, as in the act itself, in which process God's love and wisdom are expressed, but which also involves the secret efficacy of the divine name, Satan and all evil are pointedly excluded lest God "incensed at such eruption bold, / Destruction with Creation might have mixed" (8.235–36). But God's destructive wrath, insofar as it threatens spiritual death to mankind, as well, figures in the extension of the Creation story that Adam takes up in book 8, when he tells Raphael what he knows of his own making, of his awakening, his desire to know God's name, and that need of his for woman which led to Eve's creation. I suggest that it is to this last need, the desire at once natural and carnal, that Milton's evocation of the Orphic terror

20. These projections of God's Justice may be the attributes involved in the Apocalyptic "two-handed engine at the door" in *Lycidas*. "In mystical divinity," wrote Edward Benlowes, Milton's contemporary, God's "two-handed sword is the Word and the Spirit, which wounds and heals; and what is shed in this holy war is not blood but love" (Introduction to *Theophilia*, in *Minor Poets of the Caroline Period*, ed. George B. Saintsbury [Oxford: Oxford University Press, 1905–1920], 1:321). See also my discussion of these themes in "'Unexpressive Song': Form and Enigma Variations in *Lycidas*, a New Reading," in *Milton Studies XV*, ed. James D. Simmonds (Pittsburgh: University of Pittsburgh Press, 1981), pp. 237–40, 246–48.

alludes precisely in his invocation to Urania governing this whole section of the poem (books 7 and 8), the sexual terror of woman symbolized by "that wild Rout" of Maenads "that tore the *Thracian* Bard / In *Rhodope*" (7.34–35). By the same token it is of the self-destructiveness inherent in the misprision of sexual need that Raphael warns Adam, the need that will lead him to mistake the meaning of the love he feels for Eve, and which he must transcend in a hierarchical spiritual movement rather than allow it to suborn both his reason and will (8.540–94).

Hence the capacity for love with which Adam is initially endowed is incomplete unless it is invested with wisdom as well. And for both love and wisdom to function in man he needs to know that the creative efficacy of God in the Son is particularly signified as "Sapience and Love Immense," the enormousness of love being only a partial power without wisdom. Such divine attributes are, as Milton affirms in the *Christian Doctrine*, what is signified by the names of God. The Father, then, is he who can say, "I am who fill / Infinitude," the Omnipotent who sets the original condition for all man's being and knowledge. Hence, all that Adam learns of his place in the universal hierarchy, his descent from "one first matter all," is implicit in the words *I am*, which is the predicate of all being as well as the rigor of that universal justice undergirding the cosmic order. But the Son, who is Love more mild, the Word and Voice of God, Mediator and agent of Creation, is, contrastively, "unexampled Love, / Love nowhere to be found less than Divine" (3.410–11). And as creative Love he is meant to stand as the model for Adam's procreative passion, a feeling nearly immense yet equally to be enlarged by wisdom.

The links between Adam's thoughts of God's adoration and name and his thoughts of his need to share his own life with a woman are now clear. It is his need to know and his need to love that bring into alignment his instinct for God's name and his instinct to experience—through the love of Eve—that wisely liberating transcendence of physical love itself, by which, in knowing himself, he may come to know God. Yet fully to understand what is implicit in this sequence of meaning, Adam must know, alternatively, what is possible through such willful disobedience and self-love as led to Satan's fall, the only type of his fall, if he is to fall. Nor is it less part of that sequence in knowing for Adam to grasp the providential cycle by which God's Love will restore all, then resolve beatifically into the All in All, the knowledge that will fit him to live with Paradise lost. As sense then expands from sense throughout the work, in very truth it is precision and not poetic license that Milton expresses when rhapsodically he exclaims with the choraling angels, "Hail, Son of God, Savior of Men, thy Name / Shall be the copious matter of my Song." The name of God is, in short, the argument of Milton's poem.

The Gospel of John and *Paradise Regained*: Jesus as "True Light"

Stella P. Revard

ilton's extensive use of the Gospel of John in *Christian Doctrine* and *Paradise Lost* is well documented, and in view of the transcendental concerns of these works it is hardly surprising that Milton depends so heavily in them on the gospel that most fully describes the relationship of the divine Son to the divine Father. Yet, as critics such as Ira Clark have recognized, we must not neglect the influence of John on *Paradise Regained* because this poem more directly concerns the Son preparing himself for an earthly ministry than it does the operations of the divine Logos.[1] Neither should we dismiss John's influence on *Paradise Regained* because it, alone of the gospels, does not recount the temptation in the wilderness that is the main subject of Milton's brief epic. Milton had to elaborate greatly on this biblical episode, and, as critics have pointed out, he uses language and allusions from other parts of the Bible to describe this episode as well as to create those sections of *Paradise Regained* that are without direct biblical authority: Jesus' soliloquies, his conversations with Satan, and his responses to the Satanic offers of Parthia, Rome, and Athens.[2] Throughout major portions of *Paradise Regained*, therefore, Milton had the opportunity to draw extensively from the Gospel of

1. For the citation of John in *Paradise Regained*, see Ira Clark, "*Paradise Regained* and the Gospel according to John," *Modern Philology* 71 (1973): 1–15; James H. Sims, *The Bible in Milton's Epics* (Gainesville: University of Florida Press, 1962), pp. 274–78; Louis L. Martz, "*Paradise Regained*: The Meditative Combat," *ELH* 27 (1960): 238.

2. James Sims has illustrated how Milton's phrasing in *Paradise Regained* often suggests sections of the Bible other than the one that appears to be his principal source. Sims cites the fact that the thief's words from the cross (Luke 23:39) underlie Satan's plea in the first temptation to "save thyself and us" (*The Bible in Milton's Epics*, pp. 154–55).

John, using the gospel not only to build his characterization of Jesus but also to support and amplify scenes where other biblical texts seem to be more directly invoked. Moreover, his treatment of two central themes of *Paradise Regained* could scarcely have been realized without the Gospel of John. As Milton's Jesus searches for his identity as eternal Son and as he confronts Satanic lies with the light of his truth, echoes and arguments from the last of the gospels everywhere underlie the text of Milton's poem.

At first glance it is not easy to detect Johannine influence when an episode seems obviously to be drawn from one or another synoptic gospel. For example, important concepts from John inform Jesus' first encounter with Satan at the end of book 1, even though the episode itself is based literally on Matthew 4:3–4 and Luke 4:3–4, where Jesus is tempted by Satan to turn stones to bread. Milton has taken care to quote Jesus' words from Matthew and Luke, as he shows Jesus rejecting Satan: "is it not written / . . . Man lives not by Bread only, but each Word / Proceeding from the mouth of God" (*PR*, 1.347–50).[3] The episode itself, however, is framed in a much larger context than those of Matthew and Luke, for Milton gives Jesus the opportunity not only to repulse Satan but also to uncover his falsehood, demonstrating himself at the end of this book, as at the end of each subsequent book, to be the truth of God. Satan comes to the Son in *Paradise Regained* disguised, and the Son immediately penetrates the disguise, affirming his own identity as he discloses Satan's: "Knowing who I am, as I know who thou art?" (*PR*, 1.356). Jesus has here used the formulaic *I am* (from Exod. 3:14) to declare his identity, and, as Ira Clark has pointed out, the usage throughout *Paradise Regained* is peculiarly Johannine.[4] It recalls the incident in the Gospel of John where Jesus, taunted by the Jews to tell who he is, tells them: "Before Abraham was, I am" (John

3. Citations of Milton's poetry are from *Complete Poems and Major Prose*, ed. Merritt Y. Hughes (New York: Odyssey Press, 1957). *The Greek New Testament* (New York: United Bible Societies, 1966) has been consulted at all points, although quotations are from the AV.
4. Clark, "*Paradise Regained*," pp. 14–15; see also Sims, *Bible in Milton's Epics*, pp. 194–95.

8:58). The Son's play on the word *bread* in this passage also suggests several incidents and some important key concepts from John. Milton begins the Son's reply to Satan with a query: "Think'st thou such force in Bread?" (*PR*, 1.347). In Matthew and in Luke, Jesus refuses to perform a miracle—to make bread at the devil's behest—that he later in his ministry willingly performs for the good of man. Throughout the gospels Jesus is depicted as the maker of earthly bread, but only in the Gospel of John does he discuss the difference between the earthly bread with which he fed men and the bread of God, the Word. In the sixth chapter of John, Jesus, having fed the five thousand the previous day, is besought by the multitude to repeat the miracle, whereupon he rebukes those who seek him because they ate of the loaves and were filled (John 6:26). He urges his followers to work not for the food that perishes but for that which remains for life eternal (John 6:27) and declares himself the "bread of God," come down from Heaven, which gives life to the world (John 6:33). Distinguishing between the bread of life and the manna that the fathers ate in the wilderness, Jesus demonstrates the difference between earthly and spiritual nourishment. In *Paradise Regained*, Milton has retained this distinction and uses it to make this passage far more than the Son's first repulse of Satanic temptation. The first query the Son makes about the force of bread implies the superiority of the spiritual bread, the Word, over the earthly. His recollection of the feeding of "Our Fathers here with Manna" (*PR*, 1.351) promises, as Jesus did in John 6:49–50, that as God cared for man physically in the past, he will now give the gift of spiritual bread, the Son, to sustain everlasting life.

The contrasts drawn in this passage between physical and spiritual hunger are later employed in *Paradise Regained* in another passage that also has precedent in John. In book 2 Milton's Jesus, reflecting on his bodily hunger, affirms his greater spiritual hunger: "Mee hung'ring more to do my Father's will" (*PR*, 2.259). Milton appears to be echoing the fourth chapter of John, in which Jesus, found alone by his disciples who urge him to eat, tells them that he has food to eat that they do not know of: "My meat is to do the will of him that sent me, and to finish his work"

(John 4:34).[5] Milton most likely knew not only these passages in the fourth and sixth chapters of John that connect spiritual and bodily nourishment but also the commentaries of Calvin and Luther on these chapters.[6] Luther pointed out how Jesus in the sixth chapter of John "places two types of food side by side: the perishable and the eternal" and urges men to labor for the second, which the "Son of man shall give unto you: for him hath God the Father sealed" (John 6:27). Luther comments that God's designation of Christ as the bread of life is the seal of authority that God has placed on the Son.[7] Calvin comments further:

> Christ's intention is to declare that his task was imposed upon him by the Father, and that the appointment of the Father is as a seal engraved upon him. In this way, he emphasizes that all he has is from the Father. In short, it is not for everybody to feed souls with incorruptible food, when Christ comes forth with the promise of so great a blessing. He adds that he has God's approval and has been sent to us with God's own seal as the mark of his mission.[8]

Calvin's and Luther's commentaries point out that John's use of the metaphor of "bread" designates Jesus not only as the nourishment and word of God but also as the instrument "sealed" by the Father for man's salvation. In making Jesus' first words to Satan a query about "bread," Milton informs us not only that Jesus knows he is the bread of life for man, but also that in going into the wilderness and trusting to the "Word / Proceeding from

5. See Lee S. Cox, "Food-Word Imagery in *Paradise Regained*," *ELH* 28 (1961): 225–43.
6. See Georgia B. Christopher, *Milton and the Science of the Saints* (Princeton: Princeton University Press, 1982), for Milton's use of the commentaries of Calvin and Luther. See also her discussion of these in connection with *Paradise Regained*, esp. pp. 199–224.
7. Martin Luther, *Sermons on the Gospel of St. John*, chaps. 6–8, in *Luther's Works*, ed. Jaroslav Pelikan (St. Louis: Concordia Publishing House, 1959), 23, 9, 14–16. On the seal of the Father, Luther further comments: "God has only one seal, and this He has set on Christ. On Him alone He has bestowed the Holy Spirit, so that all men should look only to him. All of Holy Writ points solely to Him, attesting that He alone possesses seal and letter; for He is the exemplar, made, given, and offered to be our sole help. Thus God Himself spoke from heaven (Matt. 17:5): 'This is My beloved Son, with whom I am well pleased; listen to Him'" (*Works*, 23, 16).
8. Calvin, *Commentaries*, trans. and ed. Joseph Harountunian and Louise Pettibone Smith (Philadelphia: Westminster Press, 1948), p. 159.

the mouth of God" he is displaying the seal of authority that God has given him as the mark of his mission.

As the use of John in this episode at the end of book 1 illustrates, the gospel is important for *Paradise Regained* because of its portrayal of Jesus as the Word, the "true Light" of God, the instrument of truth sealed by God to counter Satan's darkness and falsehood in the world. Throughout the Gospel of John the metaphors of Jesus as Word, Truth, and Light occur and recur, beginning with the first annunciation of Jesus as the Word (1:1), the light of men that shines in the darkness (1:4–5), and the "true Light" (1:9), whose glory is "full of grace and truth" (1:14). Moreover, as Jesus is identified with light and truth and names himself "the way, the truth, and the life" (John 14:6), all those who oppose him, whether they be the ignorant and worldly, the hypocritical Pharisees, or the Father of lies, Satan himself, are said to walk in darkness: "for every one that doeth evil hateth. the light, neither cometh to the light, lest his deeds be reproved" (John 3:20). Both Calvin and Luther comment upon the importance of the metaphor of Jesus as "true Light" (John 1:9–10), explaining how this text presents a figure both for the true man-god Jesus and for the truth that he brings into the world. Calvin explains that Jesus is the true light because his brightness is his own, not derived from others; Luther observes, "this Light, Christ, is not merely a light for itself; but with this light He illumines men, so that all reason, wisdom, and dexterity that are not false or devilish emanate from this Light, who is the Wisdom of the eternal Father."[9] For Milton the role of the Son as the "true Light" that contests with Satanic darkness is central to *Paradise Regained*, and the Gospel of John as the principal source

9. Calvin, *Commentaries*, p. 132. Calvin comments: "The Evangelist meant to distinguish Christ from all others, so that no one would think He has the light in common with men and angels. The distinction is made to point out that whatever is bright in heaven and on earth derives its splendor from another; Christ on the other hand is himself light, and his brightness is his own, filling the whole world with his radiance; and there is no other source or cause of light. He is called the true light becuse it is his nature to illumine." Luther, *Sermons on the Gospel of John*, chaps. 1–4, in *Works*, 22, 30. Ira Clark points out that both Giovanni Diodati in his annotations and the Westminster Assembly annotators stress the Gospel of John's witness to the Logos incarnate (Clark, "*Paradise Regained*," p. 2).

for the concept again and again influences Milton's presentation of scenes in his brief epic.

Consider, for example, the crucial scene of the baptism of Jesus, presented early in the first book of *Paradise Regained*. All four gospels relate the event, but the Gospel of John presents it as the occasion of John the Baptist's testimony to the sonship of Jesus. Therefore, in John the baptism marks not only the meeting of prophet and Christ and the beginning of Jesus' ministry but also John's public recognition of Jesus' divine nature. The prophet, as the Gospel of John recounts, has been divinely prepared for Jesus' coming: "but he that sent me to baptize with water, the same said unto me, Upon whom thou shalt see the Spirit descending, and remaining on him, the same is he which baptizeth with the Holy Ghost. And I saw, and bare record that this is the Son of God" (John 1:33–34). Milton takes his cue from John and presents the baptism as the public event of testimony.

> him the Baptist soon
> Descried, divinely warn'd, and witness bore
> As to his worthier, and would have resign'd
> To him his Heavenly Office, nor was long
> His witness unconfirm'd; on him baptiz'd
> Heaven open'd, and in likeness of a Dove
> The Spirit descended. (*PR*, 1.25–31)

In *Paradise Regained* John the Baptist is also "divinely warn'd," and Milton chooses to make his public testimony the beginning episode in the poem that will examine the effect of the "witness of sonship" both on Jesus and on Satan.[10]

In the long meditation in book 1, Milton shows us Jesus musing on John's testimony and other testimonies that have preceded it, both inner and outer, to his special identity as son and true light. Like the Jesus of the Gospel of John, Milton's Son affirms that his knowledge of who he is comes from self-testimony ("What from within I feel myself," 1.198), from experience ("What from without comes often to my ears," 1.199), and from

10. See Clark, "*Paradise Regained*," p. 1.

reading of Scripture. The first of these, his own inner prompt-
ings, led him to believe that his special goal was to promote
truth: "myself I thought / Born to that end, born to promote all
truth" (1.204–5). The mission that Milton's Jesus here defines is
basically the same as the one the gospel writer consistently sets
forth. From the first chapter (John 1:8), throughout the gospel
(John 8:12, 8:36, 13:35–36, 14:6), to the final scene before the
crucifixion, Jesus is described as the light of truth, a bringer of
truth, a liberator through truth. His response to Pilate defines at
the very end of his ministry the goal that has motivated it from
the beginning: "for this cause came I into the world that I should
bear witness to the truth" (John 18:37). It is hardly accidental
that Milton makes the Son's first private declaration of his purpose so close in phrasing to the last public declaration and makes
his Jesus articulate as he is about to undertake his trial against
Satan a goal to which the Johannine Jesus holds fast even in his
last trial in the world.

Important as inner testimony is for the Jesus of the gospel and
the Jesus of *Paradise Regained*, the Son does not speak from his
authority alone, but from the testimony of the Father, which in
the gospel and in Milton's epic comes both as the voice from
Heaven, affirming Jesus' words (John 12:28; *PR*, 1.31–32, 283–
85), and through the testimony of Scripture. In John 5:37, Jesus
tells the Jews who are clamoring for proof of his identity that the
Father bears witness to him and urges them to search the scriptures for the full testimony of who he is (John 5:39). In *Paradise
Regained* the Son not only speaks of his delight in Scripture early
in life (*PR*, 1.207–8) but also turns to the Bible for confirmation
of the special birth his mother has told him of:

> This having heard, straight I again revolv'd
> The Law and Prophets, searching what was writ
> Concerning the Messiah, to our Scribes
> Known partly, and soon found of whom they spake
> I am. (1.259–63)

The use of the formulaic *I am* here, as in the speech that follows
later (1.355), has direct precedence from John 8:58 ("Before
Abraham was, I am"), where Jesus adopted the name of God

in order to declare his oneness with the Father; used here by Milton it is the first of the repeated signals in *Paradise Regained* that the Son knows who he is and is ready to assume authority from God.[11]

At the conclusion of the Son's meditation, Milton once more draws on the Gospel of John to demonstrate the particular kind of dependence and interdependence that characterizes the relationship of Father and Son. It is a crucial moment for the Son. He declares himself ready to begin his ministry, stating that the time is "now full, that I no more should live obscure, / But openly begin, as best becomes / The Authority which I deriv'd from Heaven" (*PR*, 1.287–89). In the Gospel of John at the very start of his ministry, the Son explains that everything he does is prompted by the Father, that the Son "can do nothing of himself" (5 : 19), that the Father gives him life and authority and the Son performs those works the Father has given him to execute (5 : 26–27). The Son in *Paradise Regained* in accepting the authority from Heaven demonstrates similarly both the willingness to do God's will without question and an assurance that he has the right to the authority he wields.

In the drama of *Paradise Regained* that follows, the Son defines the nature of that heavenly authority he has assumed and rejects the worldly authority that Satan would urge upon him. This distinction is entirely Johannine and involves what may be Milton's closest link with the Gospel of John. From the beginning of John, the gospel writer shows Jesus in dialogue with the world, explaining who he is, what his mission is, and, to seekers like Nicodemus or the Samaritan Woman, to his disciples, to the doubting Pharisees, distinguishing the claims of the world from those of God. Jesus, as the gospel insists again and again, is of another world and speaks with otherworldly values, scorning the fame, riches, wisdom, and power of this world.[12] His insistence that the values of the other world transcend those of this one puzzles Nicodemus, who questions Jesus about the heavenly truth he has

11. See Ibid., pp. 14–15. Jesus uses the formulaic *I am* in *Paradise Regained*, 1.263, 355; 3.106–17; Satan employs it parodically in 4.518–20.
12. See esp. John 3 : 13, 31; 6 : 33, 38; 8 : 23, 42; 16 : 28; 17 : 16.

known firsthand, exasperates the Pharisees who find his other-worldliness blasphemous, baffles Pilate, and even eludes his own disciples. Indeed, this very dialogue that the Gospel of John presents to us, particularly when it is between Jesus and such adversarial forces as the Pharisees and Pilate, may serve as the model for the dialogue we find in *Paradise Regained* between the Son and Satan.

The contest that we see unfold in the Gospel of John between the Pharisees and Jesus, particularly in chapters 5–8, resembles the contest in *Paradise Regained*. Truth and falsehood face one another in the persons of the Son and Satan or Satanic adversaries, and the questions raised in these debates are remarkably alike. Both Satan and the Pharisees demand to know who Jesus is and where his authority comes from; both urge him to prove himself, tempting him in order to discredit him utterly. The beginning point of this "dialogue" in the Gospel of John is, so to speak, at verses 17–18 of chapter 5, where the Jews have begun to murmur against Jesus and seek to kill him because he has worked miracles on the sabbath day and because he said "that God was his Father, making himself equal with God" (5:18). In the long speech at the end of Chapter 5, Jesus answers the objections of the Jews, characterizing himself as the Son and "truth" of God, testified of by the Father and promoting through his work the Father's truth. In chapter 7, after Jesus has gone up to the feast of the tabernacles, the "dialogue" continues, with Jesus once more affirming who he is and whence he is: "Ye both know me, and ye know whence I am: and I am not come of myself, but he that sent me is true, whom ye know not. But I know him: for I am from him, and he hath sent me" (John 7:28–29). The dialogue reaches a kind of climax at chapter 8, where Jesus, speaking to the Pharisees, proclaims: "I am the light of the world" and promises that whoever walks with him "shall not walk in darkness" (John 8:12). When the Pharisees counter that his record "is not true" (John 8:13), Jesus not only insists that his record is true (8:14) but also adds that those who abide with him shall know the truth and be set free by it (8:32). He and his truth come from God the Father; if, as Jesus states, the Jewish leaders knew God as Father, they would also know the truth. But, rather

than being the children of God, these Pharisees are the children
of Satan, the father of lies:

> Ye are of your father the devil, and the lusts of your father ye will
> do. He was a murderer from the beginning, and abode not in the
> truth, because there is no truth in him. When he speaketh a lie,
> he speaketh of his own: for he is a liar and the father of it. (John
> 8:44)

Although Milton had in Judeo-Christian and classical literature many models for verbal contests, the most prominent ones
being, as critics of *Paradise Regained* have long recognized, those
between Job and his persecutors in the Old Testament and those
between Socrates and his opponents in Plato's dialogues, none of
these is closer to *Paradise Regained* in the persons and issues involved than the contest in the Gospel of John.[13] For in the Gospel
of John, as in *Paradise Regained*, it is Jesus who speaks, affirms
who he is and where he has come from, and defends himself as
the "truth" of God. The Pharisees, like Satan in *Paradise Regained*,
represent the "world" and its measures of success and failure.
Full of hypocritical concern, defenders of self, self-interest, and
their "good" in the world, they profess to admire virtue and
righteousness while they scheme to have Jesus murdered. In the
dialogues between Jesus and the Pharisees in chapters 5–8, and
continuing into chapters 9–10, the gospel writer identifies Jesus
with truth and the Pharisees with lying, creating a kind of drama
in which Jesus as the Word confronts his enemies in the world.
Thus, though the writer of the Gospel of John has not provided
an account of Jesus' dialogue with Satan in the wilderness, he has
given a vivid account of Jesus' confrontations with the children
of Satan, the Pharisees, in the streets and porches and before the
temple in Jerusalem.

The first extended interview between Jesus and Satan at the
conclusion of book 1 of *Paradise Regained* shows clearly the influence of the dialogue in John, for in it the Son sharply indicts
Satan for his hypocrisy, self-interest, and lying, just as Jesus in

13. See Barbara K. Lewalski, *Milton's Brief Epic: The Genre, Meaning, and Art of
Paradise Regained* (Providence: Brown University Press, 1966), pp. 3–129; Irene
Samuel, *Plato and Milton* (Ithaca: Cornell University Press, 1947).

the gospel indicts the Pharisees. Milton's Satan, pretending piety
and concern, attempts, after the Son has uncovered his identity
and repulsed his first temptation, to persuade Jesus that he
bears malice neither toward him nor toward man and actually
promotes "truth" and good in the world. But Jesus denies that
"truth" and Satan can be paired, asserting, in words that echo
John 8:44, that Satan is "composed of lies / From the beginning,
and in lies [will] end" (*PR*, 1.406–7). Contrasting his own nourishment from the word of God with Satan's from lies, he further
tells Satan, "lying is thy sustenance, thy food" (1.429). Of Satan's
boast that through "oracles, portents, and dreams" (1.395) he
conveys God's truth to man, the Son affirms that Satan mixes
truth in the oracles "to vent more lies" (1.433). But now, says
Jesus, Satan's oracles shall cease, for

> God hath now sent his living Oracle
> Into the World to teach his final will,
> And sends his Spirit of Truth henceforth to dwell
> In pious Hearts, an inward Oracle
> To all truth requisite for men to know. (1.460–64)

It is significant that Milton concludes book 1 of *Paradise Regained* with the definition of Satan as the lie, of the Son as the
truth and living oracle of God, and with the promise that the
Holy Ghost, the Spirit of Truth, will be sent into the world. In so
doing, Milton evokes a passage from the Gospel of John, echoing now not Jesus' words of denunciation to the Pharisees but his
words of assurance to his disciples, immediately before his betrayal and death. Reassuring them of the promise that by truth
they may come to the Father (John 14:6), he tells them that after
he has gone the Father will send another Comforter, even the
Spirit of Truth (John 14:16–17), who will guide them to all truth
(John 16:13). Praying that God will sanctify them through his
truth (John 17:17), Jesus tells them to rejoice, for he has overcome the world (John 16:33). By placing at this point in the
poem, just as Jesus has concluded his first round of argument
with Satan, an allusion to the climactic passage of prophecy in
the Gospel of John, Milton sets the tone for the coming contest
and subtly forecasts its parallelism with Jesus' final contest in the

world. The words he speaks to Satan, promising the advent of the Spirit of Truth, seem almost words of comfort to those disciples, Andrew and Simon, who, at the beginning of book 2, lament the absence of the one whose words were "full of grace and truth" (*PR* 2.34), promising some deliverance now at hand. For Jesus now seems to tell them, though absent from them, that he will "overcome the world" in this contest as in the ultimate one and that, though he must leave them finally, as he does now, his triumph will make possible the coming of the Spirit of Truth.

Whatever other issues are raised in the debates between the Son and Satan in books 2, 3, and 4, the basic opposition of truth and falsehood established in book 1 remains constant. Satan disappears at the end of book 1, his "gray dissimulation" fading into thin air, but reappears in the final books to cast new spells and vent more lies. Jesus stands unmoved by Satan's new assaults, again and again uncovering his deceptions, rejecting his authority, and defining the kind of honor, virtue, merit, and praise that belong properly to a king, not of this world, but of another. In these last books more than a few of the themes pursued in the debates between the Son and Satan have their source in the Gospel of John.[14] Like the Pharisees in John, Satan continues to question who Jesus is and where he has come from, seeking to discredit his claim that he is from the Father and one with the Father. Jesus maintains throughout his insistence on otherworldly values, speaking to Satan, as he did to Nicodemus in John 3:11 of "that we do know and testify[ing] that we have seen," and rejecting the fame, riches, power, and kingship of a merely earthly kind. Like the Johannine Jesus, Milton's Son has come "unto his own, and his own received him not" (John 1:11); through the whole course of the epic, he endures the ignominy and insult of being offered "by gift what is [his] own" (*PR*, 2.381) by the very one who has usurped the honors and powers that rightfully belong to him (*PR*, 4.183–84). When in book 4 Satan

14. The debate on glory at the beginning of book 3 of *Paradise Regained* seems to echo, for example, Jesus' quarrel with the Pharisees in John 7 and 8, particularly his words of defense: "He that speaketh of himself seeketh his own glory: but he that seeketh his glory that sent him, the same is true, and no unrighteousness is in him" (John 7:18). Compare *PR*, 3.106–7.

promises the kingdoms of the world to Jesus on condition that Jesus fall down and worship him, Jesus not only spurns the blasphemous offer but also rebukes Satan for having the effrontery to "offer them to me the Son of God, / To me my own" (4.190–91).

The debate between the Son and Satan in *Paradise Regained* on the nature of the Son's kingship, which forms so important a part of books 2, 3, and 4 and is, of course, the basis of Satan's offers of Parthia, Rome, and Athens, also has precedence in the Gospel of John in the last climactic dialogue that Jesus holds with Pilate. In all four gospels, Pilate questions Jesus about the nature of his kingship, but only in the Gospel of John does Jesus give more than a perfunctory reply to Pilate's demands. In the other gospels, in reply to Pilate's question whether he is king of the Jews, Jesus says only "Εὺ λέγεις" (you say so) and refuses to respond further or defend himself. In John, however, Jesus answers Pilate as he had answered the Pharisees, and what follows is an extended, if brief, dialogue, like those that have preceded in the gospel, on the subject of Jesus' identity, now as king rather than son, and his goal in the world. When Pilate asks him directly, "Art thou the King of the Jews?" (John 18:33), Jesus replies, turning about Pilate's query by posing a question of his own: "Sayest thou this thing of thyself, or did others tell it thee of me?" (18:34). Pilate's interjection, "Am I a Jew?" and his response that Jesus' nation and priests have delivered him up reveal the source of his first question. Jesus then repudiates his kingship over the Jews and their betrayal of him to the Romans by his next response:

> My kingdom is not of this world: if my kingdom were of this world, then would my servants fight, that I should not be delivered to the Jews: but now is my kingdom not from hence. (John 18:36)

This repudiation of the earthly kingdom is an important part of the dialogue in *Paradise Regained* between the Son and Satan, for, as Milton shows us in Jesus' meditation in book 1, he had early in his life reflected that he might "rescue *Israel* from the *Roman* yoke" (*PR*, 1.217), asserting a kind of earthly leadership over the Jews. It is to such impulses that Satan appeals at the end of book 2 and again in book 3, when he offers first riches and then military power to Jesus in order that he might establish his throne in Israel. But Jesus has already determined that his is not a kingdom of might and fleshly power and that to free truth and restore equity, one must first "by winning words . . . conquer willing hearts" (*PR*, 1.222). He sees true kingship in terms of guiding "Nations in the way of truth" (2.472). He has come to distrust "the people's praise" (3.48), and his resounding denunciation of the Jews who have abandoned their "ancient Patrimony" and are "unhumbl'd, unrepentant, unreform'd" (3.428–29) resembles his outcry against the Pharisees who have forsaken the ways of their father Abraham (John 8:39–41). It is "some wond'rous call" to true repentance that must bring the Jews back to God, and this call to truth is, Milton's Jesus here suggests, the basis of his ministry and his kingship: "So spake Israel's true King, and to the Fiend / Made answer meet. . . / So fares it when with truth falsehood contends" (*PR*, 3.441–43).

In the dialogue with Pilate in the Gospel of John, Jesus strongly affirms his kingship over truth at the very moment that he denies his kingship of the world. Replying to Pilate's repeated demand whether he is a king, Jesus says first, you say that I am, then adds immediately that he was born to witness to the truth and that everyone that is of the truth hears his voice (John 18:37). Pilate, ending this first of his two dialogues with Jesus, asks, "What is truth?" (John 18:38). The scriptural tradition of Milton's own time, as witnessed by the marginal commentary of the Geneva Bible, asserts that Pilate's final question is "mocking and disdainful." [15] Whether or not Milton would have agreed with that view, we cannot know. Pilate is not an adversary to Jesus as the Pharisees and the high priests are, but he is, nonetheless, the one to whom Jesus is delivered and by whose authority Jesus ultimately is crucified; therefore, as worldly judge, questioner,

15. The commentary to the Geneva Bible indicates that, throughout his dealings with Jesus, Pilate takes a mocking attitude. Not only is his question, "What is truth?" a disdainful one, but his later words (John 19:5), after Jesus is delivered to him wearing a crown of thorns and a purple garment, "Beholde the man," are spoken "in mockerie, because Christ called him self King," *The Geneva Bible: A Facsimile of the 1560 Edition* (Madison: University of Wisconsin Press, 1969).

and tester of Jesus, he serves as another surrogate for Satan. As Jesus in *Paradise Regained* is delivered into the power of Satan to be tried, so Jesus in the gospel is delivered to Pilate, who likewise urges his worldly authority over Jesus and threatens him with his power over life and death. Milton's Son tells Satan at the outset of his trial, "Do as thou find'st / Permission from above; thou canst not more" (*PR*, 1.495–96), determining until the end, even in the face of the terrors of the storm in book 4, to "endure the time, till which expir'd, / Thou has permission on me" (4.174–75). This attitude is much like that which Jesus assumes toward Pilate in the Gospel of John, even when Pilate threatens him with his authority: "Knowest thou not that I have power to crucify thee, and have power to release thee?" (John 19:10). Jesus, however, regards Pilate as merely the instrument of the Almighty to work out his will and replies, "Thou couldest have no power at all against me, except it were given thee from above" (John 19:11). From the beginning of his ministry in John, Jesus shows, first to his mother at Cana (John 2:4), then to his brothers before the feast of the tabernacles (John 7:6), that he is aware that God is ordering the events of his life according to his own plan. When he tells his mother or his brothers, "My time is not yet come," he is refusing to anticipate that time, and when, before his betrayal, he refuses to ask God to save him from this hour, he is accepting the fact that "for this cause I came to this hour" (John 12:27). Before Pilate, he exhibits the same timely patience that is also seen in Milton's Jesus when he tells Satan: "All things are best fulfill'd in thir due time, / And time there is for all things, Truth hath said" (*PR*, 3.182–83).[16] To the goal of truth the Johannine Jesus and Milton's Jesus are constant, and, by echoing Jesus' trial before Pilate in the Son's trial by Satan, Milton takes the opportunity to emphasize this constancy. Though each trial leads inexorably to the death on the cross, Jesus shrinks from neither but holds fast to truth in the face of Pilate's or Satan's threats and questionings.

16. On the question of timely patience in *Paradise Regained*, see Laurie Zwicky, "Kairos in *Paradise Regained*: The Divine Plan," *ELH* 31 (1964): 271–77, and Edward W. Tayler, *Milton's Poetry: Its Development in Time* (Pittsburgh: Duquesne University Press, 1979).

Throughout the Gospel of John, whether the questioner is Pharisee, disciple, or final judge, Pilate, one question is persistently repeated: "Who or whence art thou?" It is one of Pilate's last exasperated demands to Jesus in his final interview (John 19:9), to which Jesus gives no answer. Throughout the gospel, moreover, it is one of Jesus' tactics, which Milton carefully adapts to *Paradise Regained*, to answer all queries about his person and kingdom indirectly or with another question. Hence, when the Pharisees demand to know who he is, Jesus tells them, "Even the same that I said unto you from the beginning" (John 8:25), or when they ask where he comes from and where he is going, he answers, "Ye are from beneath; I am from above: ye are of this world; I am not of this world" (John 8:23). When Pilate wants to know if Jesus is a king, Jesus neither affirms nor denies; moreover, he tells Pilate what his kingdom is *not*, rather than what it is.

Milton's Jesus adopts a stance toward Satan similar to that adopted by the Johannine Jesus toward his different questioners. Satan in *Paradise Regained* desperately wants to know two things: who Jesus is and what kind of kingdom he is to establish. From the time he hears the words of John the Baptist and sees the dove descend over Jesus' head, he is intent on discovering who this "son" Jesus is and when his kingdom is to come.[17] As in the Gospel of John, Jesus in *Paradise Regained* never says directly who he is, neither affirms nor denies that he is a king, and, though he says much indirectly about kingdoms and kingship, showing the deficiencies of earthly rulers such as the Emperor Tiberius or earthly kingdoms such as Parthia, Rome, and Athens, he never tells Satan when or how his kingdom is to come or what it will be like. Rather, he enigmatically describes it as a "tree / Spreading and overshadowing all the Earth" or as a "stone that

17. The quibble over the meaning of the term *Son of God*, which reaches a climax in book 4 of *Paradise Regained* when Satan declares, "All men are Sons of God; yet thee I thought / In some respect far higher so declar'd" (4.519–20), may find its source in Jesus' declaration, "Is it not written in your law, I said, Ye are gods? If he called them gods, unto whom the word of God came, and the scripture cannot be broken; Say ye of him, whom the Father hath sanctified, and sent into the world, Thou blasphemest: because I said, I am the Son of God?" (John 10:34–36).

shall to pieces dash / All Monarchies besides" (*PR*, 4.147–50). Further he refuses to disclose his means, telling Satan, "Means there shall be to this, but what the means, / Is not for thee to know, nor me to tell" (*PR*, 4.152–53).[18] Yet, like Jesus in the Gospel of John, the Son in *Paradise Regained* makes clear that his kingdom is a moral, not a physical, realm, a kingdom of truth proclaimed by the one who said that he came into the world to witness to the truth.

In this light, it is no accident that Milton reserves Athens, the moral and intellectual center of the western world, as the last of the kingdoms offered to the Son by Satan and that the Son, in rejecting Athens, takes the opportunity to tell Satan what a real kingdom of truth is like. True learning, says the Son, comes from God: "he who receives / Light from above, from the fountain of light, / No other doctrine needs" (*PR*, 4.288–90). The gospel that told Milton that Jesus was the "true light" of God (John 1:9) also describes the Jews marveling at Jesus' learning: "How knoweth this man letters, having never learned?" (John 7:15). Here and throughout the gospel Jesus ascribes his knowledge to God, "My doctrine is not mine, but his that sent me" (John 7:16), and refers to Scripture as providing all-sufficient guidance for man. Milton's Jesus in the very first book of *Paradise Regained* had told Satan that God had sent "his living Oracle / Into the World to teach his final will" and henceforth will send "his Spirit of Truth" as "inward Oracle / To all truth requisite for men to know" (1.460–64). As though to confirm the power of divine teaching, the Son here repudiates the so-called wisdom of Athens, commending in its place the "better teaching" of "men divinely taught" (4.357). Truth, learned from Scripture, is "what makes a Nation happy, and keeps it so" and is also with the Law what "best form[s] a King" (4.362–64).

In the Gospel of John, Pilate questions hollowly, "What is truth?"; Jesus does not reply, nor does Pilate wait for his answer. In the last of the Son's extended debates with Satan in *Paradise Regained*, Milton seems to provide the answer to that question.

18. Possibly an echo of Jesus' words to his apostles before his ascension, when asked about the coming of the kingdom: "It is not for you to know the time or the seasons, which the Father hath put in his own power" (Acts 1:7).

The Son's rejection of the "falsehood" of Athens not only lays the foundation for his kingdom of truth but also permits him, as Satan tempts him on the final pinnacle, to stand upon that truth, the truth of Scripture, as his only resource: "Also it is written, / Tempt not the Lord thy God" (4.560—61). Having proved himself through God's truth and as God's truth, the Son can now be hailed by the angels in the closing hymn of *Paradise Regained* as "True Image of the Father" (4.596). Milton's brief epic has affirmed the description in the Gospel of John of Jesus as "true Light."

Milton and Covenant: The Christian View of Old Testament Theology

John T. Shawcross

ovenant implies three concepts: unilateral covenant (God toward man), mutual covenant (God and man), and federal covenant (the group in allegiance to God). Extending these concepts, the metaphor of covenant is employed for human relationships; for example, political covenant (a fusion of mutual and federal), which describes compacts of men and men, generally of groups for mutual protection or achievement. Another metaphor of mutual covenant (man and woman) was marriage, as in John Milton's divorce tracts and especially in *The Doctrine and Discipline of Divorce*. "The Covenant" and "Covenanters," during the middle seventeenth century, however, always meant the political covenant of the National Covenant of Scotland, concluded at Greyfriars Kirkyard, Edinburgh, on 28 February 1638 and developed by the Presbyterian General Assembly in Glasgow in November 1638. The Covenant was an outgrowth of reactions against the Service Book of 1637 as Popish and of English compilation, leading to the Confession of Faith after the English Westminster movement joined with the Scots.[1] The Solemn League and Covenant between the Covenanters and the English Parliamentarians, 17 August 1643, was an extension of the National Covenant, more strongly in the sphere of politics and referenced frequently by Milton in prose and poetry. Milton, it would seem, took the Covenant—that is, he subscribed to the Solemn League and Covenant—but he came to repudiate Presbyterian coercive policy.[2]

1. For a general discussion of the matter, see Jane Lane [Elaine Kidner Dakers], *The Reign of King Covenant* (London: Hale, 1956).
2. So noted by A. H. Drysdale, *History of the Presbyterians in England: Their Rise, Decline, and Revival* (London, 1889), p. 314. In *Tetrachordon* (1645) Milton wrote

I am here concerned not with the extension of the concepts of covenant into human relationships but with Milton's attitudes toward the Old Covenant, that of the Old Testament as cited between God and Moses on Mount Sinai, and the New Covenant, that of the New Testament as exemplified through the Son. An understanding of theological covenant for Milton will, of course, inform an understanding of his use of the concept in temporal spheres. One view of Milton and covenant has been that expressed by B. Eugene McCarthy, referring to a statement in *De doctrina christiana* (1.12):[3] "Such a covenant was to Milton not Old Testament in nature, for there God imposed his will on people, but distinctly Christian, a new covenant of grace, a true covenant that allowed voluntary acceptance by man."[4] Working out of the metaphor of mutual covenant applied to men and men, as in *The Tenure of Kings and Magistrates* (1649)[5] or *A Treatise of Civil Power* (1659),[6] Milton scholars have talked of the need for faith on both sides of covenant and of benefit for both parties, but they have little examined the concept in Milton's theology.[7] A most impor-

---

"*I saw, and was partaker, of your Vows and Cov'nants, Parlament of England*" (p. A2r), and see "*On the new forcers of Conscience.*"

3. "For if our personal religion were not in some degree dependent on ourselves, and in our own power, God could not properly enter into a covenant with us," trans. Charles R. Sumner, in *Works*, 15:215. John Carey's more exacting translation in *CPW*, 6:398, reads: "Obviously if religious matters were not under our control, or to some extent within our power and choice, God could not enter into a covenant with us."

4. See his entry on "Covenant Religion," *A Milton Encyclopedia*, gen. ed. William B. Hunter (Lewisburg, Pa.: Bucknell University Press, 1978), 2:91. My differences with what may be inferred from this statement will become clear.

5. "No understanding man can bee ignorant that Covnants are ever made according to the present state of persons and of things; and have ever the more general laws of nature and of reason included in them, though not express'd. If I make a voluntary Covnant as with a man, to doe him good, and he prove afterward a monster to me, I should conceave a disoblegement" (*CPW*, 3:231–32).

6. "Let who so will interpret or determine, so it be according to true church-discipline; which is exercis'd on them only who have willingly joind themselves in that covnant of union" (*CPW*, 7:245).

7. For example, it is not pursued by C. A. Patrides in *Milton and the Christian Tradition* (Oxford: Clarendon Press, 1966), despite an extensive discussion of grace, or by Maurice Kelley in *This Great Argument* (Princeton: Princeton University Press, 1941), despite a summary of 1.26–28 of *De doctrina christiana* on the covenant of grace (pp. 172–78). Kelley does cite parallels in *Paradise Lost*, book 12.

tant and most illuminating exception is Joseph E. Duncan in *Milton's Earthly Paradise*.[8] Before looking at Milton and covenant, we should review covenant theology, for it is not a clearcut philosophy, nor a simple set of scriptural readings.

Two covenants are involved: that of works and that of grace. John Cocceius (1603–1669) is often credited with the division of the covenant of works as existent before the Fall and of the covenant of grace as existent thereafter, and in this latter concept he is considered a founder of federal theology and soteriology. This kind of division posited a first covenant of works between God and man (unilateral covenant), broken as Adam and Eve abrogated natural law within themselves. However, the ideas and divisions lay in numerous writings prior to the seventeenth century. In contrast, William Perkins (1558–1602) talked of a covenant of grace for the elect before Creation, because of God's prescience, and of a covenant of works only after the Fall.[9] Obedience can be related to a covenant of works, and thus Mosaic law has been seen as part of that covenant. Such a view posited a second covenant of works in reaffirming natural law in the Ten Commandments (the Law) and led to assignment of Old Testament covenant as an imposition of God's will on the people, such as that to which McCarthy refers. Implied in the Law is God's healing of man's depravity and man's trust in a future Messiah.[10] *The Dutch Annotations upon the Whole Bible* contrasted a Covenant of the Law with a Covenant of Grace.[11] But since perfect obedience for man after the Fall is impossible, further thinking concluded, the covenant of grace came to subsume works. For the

8. (Minneapolis: University of Minnesota Press, 1972), esp. pp. 132–47.

9. William Perkins, *A Golden Chaine* (London, 1591), chap. 19.

10. This is basically Jewish rather than Christian. C. A. Patrides notes in *The Grand Design of God: The Literary Form of the Christian View of History* (London: Routledge and Kegan Paul, 1972), pp. 4–5: "Jewish writers chose invariably as their theme God's covenant with Israel. That covenant is an explanation—'the shadow of the future thrown back on the past'—of God's constant efforts to safeguard Israel." The quotation comes from Alfred North Whitehead in *Adventures in Ideas* (New York: Macmillan, 1933), p. 82.

11. Translated by Theodore Haak (London, 1657), note to Deut. 18:15: "*Mosçh* stood between God and the people in the Covenant of the Law, Gal. 3.19, so is Christ the onely Mediator between God and his people in the Covenant of Grace."

strict Calvinist the covenant meant an absolute grace for the elect, but for other believers, the Arminian, for example, it was a conditional grace for the faithful and repentant. Previously Heinrich Bullinger (1504–1575) had argued that the Mosaic law was not part of the covenant of works and that only a covenant of grace existed for man. Zacharias Ursinus (1534–1583) viewed the covenant of grace as informing both the Old and the New testaments, and it was out of Ursinus' arguments that covenant theology arose. Thus, the protevangelium is the first statement of the covenant of grace, which is seen as mutual covenant, man's action being true faith and true obedience. The Confession of Faith, deriving from the mainstream of beliefs in the sixteenth and seventeenth centuries, assigned Adam as federal head, acknowledged both covenants, but saw the covenant of grace as that of the Law and the gospel.[12]

Ideological problems exist in the treatment of the Tree of Knowledge and the Tree of Life. The Tree of Knowledge represented the covenant of works, and it thus, for some, came to represent the Law. The sun in the Heavens represented Justice, and shadow the dispensation of mercy or God's grace. While Adam and Eve were able to partake freely of the Tree of Life, the Tree of Knowledge after the Fall became the source of the material of the Cross, the Crucifixion occurring upon the same spot as the disobedience. Through Christ's mediation, the Tree of Knowledge was abrogated for man, who through his acceptance and maintenance of the covenant of grace could hope for a future

12. Comparison with chap. 3, "Concerning God's Eternal Decrees," of the contemporary *Confession of Faith* of the Westminster Assembly (first published as *The Humble Advice of the Assembly of Divines . . . Concerning a Confession of Faith* in 1646) is instructive for various issues regarding covenant mentioned here. For example, section 5 reads: "Before the creation of the world, according to His eternal, unchangeable plan and the hidden purpose and good pleasure of His will, God has chosen in Christ those of mankind who are predestined to life and to everlasting glory. He has done this solely out of His own mercy and love and completely to the praise of His wonderful grace. This choice was completely independent of His foreknowledge of how His created beings would be or act. Neither their faith nor good works had any part in influencing His selection" (*The Westminster Confession of Faith*, ed. Douglas Kelly, Hugh McClure, and Philip B. Rollinson [Greenwood, S.C.: Attic Press, 1979], p. 7). Compare also questions 22 and 32 of the "Larger [or Longer] Catechism."

partaking of the Tree of Life. It was a rather easy equation for some to see the Tree of Knowledge as the covenant of works and the Tree of Life as the covenant of grace. To William Ames (1576–1633), the Tree of Knowledge was a sacrament of death; the Tree of Life, a sacrament of life.[13] Was therefore the covenant of grace existent before the Fall? and was there then no true covenant of works?

While the Old and the New covenants were repeatedly contrasted—one written on stone, the other on human hearts; one a written code, the other the spirit of the living God; one condemnatory, transient, and veiling glory, the other righteous, permanent, and directly manifesting God's glory[14]—Christian concepts of the sixteenth and seventeenth centuries saw both as covenants of grace, although as Delbert R. Hillers remarks, "the Christian had something new, but it was not a covenant."[15] Covenant, of course, implies something agreed upon whereby one party does this if and when the other party does that. Covenant required parties to the agreement, stipulations, and ritual enactments (for which an exchange of commodity, a handshake, and the like could replace blood sacrifice). The Hebrew word for covenant, *b'rît* (from Akkadian *brt*, to bind), was used in the Old Testament to express federal covenant, which could be achieved metaphorically through stones (Job 5:23), eyes (Job 31:1: "I made a covenant with mine eyes"), death (Isa. 28:15), and day and night (Jer. 33:20–21: "Thus saith the Lord; If ye can break my covenant of the day, and my covenant of the night, . . . then may also my covenant be broken with David my servant, that he should not have a son to reign upon his throne"). It was related frequently to marriage (see Prov. 2:17), and it became equivalent with the Law (see 1 Kings 8:21) and true religion (see Jer. 9:13). The Christian theologians satisfied the terminology of *covenant* and *binding* by making man's faith and obedience his part of the agreement, although they split on man's ability to fulfill his con-

13. William Ames, *The Marrow of Sacred Divinity* (London, 1642), p. 55 (chap. 10, item 33).
14. See 2 Cor. 3:6–18 and Heb. 8.
15. *Covenant: The History of a Biblical Idea* (Baltimore: Johns Hopkins University Press, 1969), p. 188.

ditions and thus elicited postulations of absolute or of conditional grace. Accordingly, the Ten Commandments of Moses were read in terms of the "new commandment" of Jesus (John 13:34), "That ye love one another; as I have loved you, that ye also love one another." "The person of Jesus has, so to speak, taken over the original notion: the saving event is *his* death, the new commandment is to love in imitation of *his* example, the guilt of abusing communion is that one has profaned *his* body and blood."[16] Blood sacrifice, Mosaic or Christological, transfers guilt to the people who will suffer the fate of the sacrificed, should they fall into disobedience and a lack of faith. Blood sacrifice always invokes curse. The blood of Christ is seen as inaugurating the New Covenant.[17]

Christian thinking on covenant of grace thus retained certain conceptions of *b'rît*, namely, its connotation of the mysteries of God's salvific acts, its divinely guaranteed promise, and its expectation of man's obedience. It implied promises for obedience and penalties for disobedience. Covenant is likewise perpetual (see Gen. 17:13). Among the ritual enactments is circumcision (see Gen. 17:10–11 and Acts 3:25, 7:8); among the signs of the covenant is the rainbow (see Gen. 9:13 and Isa. 54:9–10 where it is called the *b'rît* of peace). While the God of the Old Testament had been viewed by some theologians as a man of war and a taskmaster and the God of the New Testament as a god of love, others, like William Ames, a student of Perkins, saw the Old and New covenants somewhat reversed: "1. In the kind, for that [the Old] was as it were a covenant of friendship betweene the Creator and the creature: but this [the New] is a covenant of reconciliation between enemies. / 14.2. In the efficient: for in that [the Old] there was an agreement of two parties, namely God and man: but in this [the New] God onely doth covenant."[18]

Milton's position can be outlined as follows:

1. The prohibition of eating of the Tree of Knowledge does not constitute a covenant of works: it is not a covenant and it does not involve works (*CD*, 1.10; *Works*, 15:113).

16. Ibid.
17. Compare Heb. 9:11–22.
18. Ames, *Marrow of Sacred Divinity*, p. 114 (chap. 24, items 13–14).

Mosaic law is a covenant of grace

2. No command is properly a covenant (*CD*, 1.10; *Works*, 15:115). The Tree of Knowledge does not, therefore, represent a covenant of works, and Mosaic law, though it involves works, is not a covenant of works since it involves commandments. It is, rather, a covenant of grace (*CD* 1.26; *Works*, 16:99).

3. The Tree of Knowledge does not constitute a sacrament. The Tree of Life should probably not be considered a sacrament but a symbol (or the nutriment) of eternal life (*CD*, 1.10; *Works*, 15:115).

4. "Every covenant, when originally concluded, is intended to be perpetual and indissoluble, however soon it may be broken by the bad faith of one of the parties" (*CD*, 1.10; *Works*, 15:173, 175).[19]

5. Covenant requires mutual action and independence (*CD*, 1.12; *Works*, 15:215, quoted in part in n. 3).[20]

6. Covenant implies certain conditions to be performed by both parties (*CD*, 1.25; *Works*, 16:79).

7. The covenant of grace always implies the stipulation that man follow God's commandments and seek Him in faith (*CD*, 1.14; *Works*, 14:113, 115). Therefore, there could be no covenant of grace existent before the Fall because Adam was filled with natural law.

8. Predestinated mankind are those who maintain the covenant of grace (ibid.). Likewise God extends sufficient grace for salvation to all; he "excludes no one from the pale of repentance and eternal salvation, till he has despised and rejected the propositions of sufficient grace, offered even to a late hour" (*CD*, 1.4; *Works*, 14:153).[21]

9. The covenant of grace is first declared in Genesis 3:15 in God's prophecy of the efficacy of Eve's seed, the protevangelium. Its manifestation consists in its exhibition and ratification,

---

19. While the Sumner translation is often inexact, Carey's translation is, as here, often insufficiently literal for critical use. Milton specifically used "foedus," that is, covenant, here.

20. Milton thus rejects unilateral covenant and in so doing reinforces his rejection of the prohibition as a covenant.

21. The implications here led Duncan, in *Milton's Earthly Paradise*, to talk of a covenant of redemption.

and both existed under the Law and continue under the gospel (*CD*, 1.26; *Works*, 16:99).[22]

10. The covenant of grace gave promise of Messiah, and thus the law's imperfection was manifested in the person of Moses himself (*CD*, 1.26; *Works*, 16:109, 111). "But what neither the law itself nor the observers of the law could attain, faith in God through Christ has attained, and that even to eternal life" (*CD*, 1.26; *Works*, 16:111).

11. "The gospel is the new dispensation of the covenant of grace, far more excellent and perfect than the law" (*CD*, 1.27; *Works*, 16:113). The gospel (the New Covenant) abolished Mosaic law (the Old Covenant) (*CD*, 1.27; *Works*, 16:125).

12. The representation of the covenant of grace was circumcision and the passover under the Old Covenant and baptism and the Lord's supper (which is metaphoric) under the New; these latter two are sacraments (*CD*, 1.28; *Works*, 16:165, 193).

13. Church-discipline implies federal covenant (*CD*, 1.32; *Works*, 16:321, 323).[23]

Clearly Milton is not in agreement with William Perkins, Johann Wollebius (d. 1629),[24] or William Ames on many of these issues. But aside from item 8 above alongside item 10, his views are not exceptional: he sees the Old Covenant fully supplanted by the New Covenant, although its signs (such as circumcision and the rainbow) are still significant as signs; he understands the Law both as a representation of the covenant of grace and as works by which man can manifest his obedience to God; he views the covenant of grace as being made in the protevangelium and continuing to the present time; the covenant is prophetic,[25]

22. See also C. A. Patrides, "The 'Protevangelium' in Renaissance Theology and *Paradise Lost*," *Studies in English Literature* 3 (1963): 19–30.
23. William Riley Parker, *Milton: A Biography* (Oxford: Clarendon Press, 1968), 1:487–91, reviewed some of Milton's ideas in *De doctrina christiana*.
24. For example, Wollebius talks of a covenant of works (*The Abridgment of Christian Divinitie* [London, 1650], 1.8.55), and he calls the Trees a double sacrament (1.7.55).
25. The Old Testament prophetic covenant offers promise through Nathan to David (2 Sam. 7:5–17), through David's continuing dynastic reign (2 Sam. 23:5, Ps. 89:28–29), through the prophetic-messianic expectation of Isa. 11:1, 10, and through the New Covenant of Hos. 2:18–23 and the renewal of the Old in Ezek. 20:34–38. David as true shepherd is the burden of, for example, Jer.

promising Messiah and salvation in return for faith and obedience, that is, in return for love.

Milton's passage in *De doctrina christiana* on free will and divine decrees has been badly translated by Sumner, leading to confusion of what he asserts later in the treatise and what Adam says in *Paradise Lost*. Milton wrote (*CD*, 1.3; *Works*, 14:80): "Qualis itaque materia sive obiectum divini consilii erat, nempe angelus vel homo libera voluntate impertiendus, qui posset labi, vel non labi, tale procul dubio decretum ipsum erat, ut omnia quae exinde consecuta sunt mala, potuissent sequi, vel non sequi: si steteris, manebis; non steteris, eiiciere: si non comederis, vives; comederis, moriere." Sumner's translation is: "Seeing, therefore, that in assigning the gift of free will God suffered both men and angels to stand or fall at their own uncontrolled choice, there can be no doubt that the decree itself bore a strict analogy to the object which the divine counsel regarded, not necessitating the evil consequences which ensued, but leaving them contingent; hence the covenant was of this kind: If thou stand, thou shalt abide in Paradise: if thou fall, thou shalt be cast out; if thou eat not the forbidden fruit, thou shalt live: if thou eat, thou shalt die." There is no mention of covenant in the original, nor could there be in Milton's way of thinking; the other extrapolations may be excused because they are implied in the relationship here between free will and the event that *comederis* particularly alludes to. Carey's translation is a great improvement, though not without fault: "The matter or object of the divine plan was that angels and men alike should be endowed with free will, so that they could either fall or not fall. Doubtless God's actual decree bore a close resemblance to this, so that all the evils which have since happened as a result of the fall could either happen or not: if you stand firm, you still stay; if you do not, you will be thrown out; if you do not eat it, you will live; if you do, you will die."[26] What Milton presents in the last part of this passage is a paraphrase of Genesis 2:16−17, 3:2−3. Not to eat the fruit of the

---

23:4−5 and Ezek. 37:24, and the covenant in the heart is the message of Jer. 32:39−41.

26. *CPW*, 6:163.

Tree is a prohibition, involving commandment, but therefore no covenant is made. The exercise of free will in connection with this prohibition will bring a corresponding enactment of God's decree, which is that through exercise of free will angels and men may fall or not fall. The eating of the fruit is clearly symbolic; it symbolizes whether Adam and Eve will *stand firm* (*steteris*), that is, show faith, by not eating, or will not stand firm, that is, show a lack of faith, by eating. The significance is not in the eating or not eating except as it evinces faith or nonfaith. One eats to live, but this eating brings death; not to eat can lead to death, but this not eating brings life. The prohibition has *not* involved a contractual arrangement, although there is a reward or a punishment attached to the observance of that prohibition.

Michael Lieb has shown that Milton's view of the first prohibition is not only extralegal but also dispensational; it is reflective of ceremonial law and harkens back to the concept of taboo. Accordingly, the first prohibition is associated culturally, not doctrinally, with ceremonial law and has no basis in reason, which is the foundation of moral and natural law.[27]

The confusion comes from an equation of prohibition with covenant and of both with decree. Each is a separate concept, however interrelated they may be. Prohibition exists for specific acts (or nonacts), though it may be symbolic of many, and is expressed by a superior or authority figure (parent, teacher, law enforcer) only; clearly reward or punishment is implied. Covenant may exist for specific acts or for a range of acts and entails acceptance from both parties to the contract; clearly forfeiture for *either party* is implied should covenant be broken. In the matter of God, it is rejection of that God who does not uphold his part in the covenant; Milton's concern in *Paradise Lost* is to explain God's actions to men and thus to argue against man's interpretation that God has not upheld his part in the covenant, a concept one finds at the base of modern revisionist theology. De-

27. Michael Lieb, "*Paradise Lost* and the Myth of Prohibition," in *Eyes Fast Fixt*, ed. Albert C. Labriola and Michael Lieb, special issue of *Milton Studies* 7 (1975): 233–65. For further discussion of prohibition and other concerns of this essay, see also Lieb's *Poetics of the Holy: A Reading of "Paradise Lost"* (Chapel Hill: University of North Carolina Press, 1981).

cree may apply to a specific act or a range of acts whereby a superior or authority figure has declared future action that he has power to enforce; whether that future action takes place and the nature of that future action may involve prohibition, but the action *never* involves covenant. Compare the Father's remarks on prohibition in *Paradise Lost* 3.94–99, on decree in 3.100–128 and 10.43–47, and on covenant (which word appears in *Paradise Lost* only in books 11 and 12 after the Fall and the annunciation of the protevangelium) in 11.113–16, in comparison with the Judgment, not yet covenant, of 10.179–81, and Eve and Adam's acceptance in 10.930–36, 952–65, and 1086–92, repeated as 1098–1104. Immediately thereafter, as book 11 begins and Prevenient Grace descends, it has become covenant.

Adam's words in *Paradise Lost* 10.752–59, in the midst of his soliloquy which, as often observed, reflects a human wallowing in blame-placing and ego-aggrandizement, indicate a lack of understanding of prohibition and a kind of equation with covenant, an equation that has persisted in the minds of commentators on the Bible and on Milton:

> To the loss of that,
> Sufficient penaltie, why hast thou added
> The sense of endless woes? inexplicable
> Thy Justice seems; yet to say truth, too late,
> I thus contest; then should have been refus'd
> Those terms whatever, when they were propos'd:
> Thou didst accept them; wilt thou enjoy the good,
> Then cavil the conditions?[28]

Adam talks of "terms," of their being "propos'd," and of his acceptance of them; but the prohibition has not involved and does not involve "terms" (only reward or punishment), was not "propos'd" to him, but imposed (as he himself has just argued, his will did not concur to his being), and has not therefore brought in any question of acceptance or nonacceptance. When the teacher says to the student, "You will not cheat," there are no

28. Quotations of the poetry throughout the essay come from my edition of *The Complete Poetry of John Milton* (Garden City: Doubleday, 1971).

terms, no proposal for the student to accept or not accept. Adam's reading of the prohibition, *now, after the Fall*, as covenant is in a way, Milton implies, at the base of Satan's and man's lack of understanding of God's ways: certainly no one thinks that God made a covenant with the angels, including Satan. He has made a decree, that is all: through the exercise of free will angels may "fall" or not "fall." No prohibition was expounded for the angels, because none was deemed necessary; for man, prohibition as symbolic of faith or nonfaith was deemed necessary. Since prohibition was broken through the external influence of guile rather than through *totally free* will, mercy is granted by means of covenant. The teacher says to the cheating student who admits his act, If you in all further tests and papers do not cheat, you will receive a passing grade and your first infraction will be ignored; if you do cheat in any way, you will be immediately failed without further recourse.

Another case of inaccurate translation that causes major difficulty on this issue is found in *Christian Doctrine* 1.11, "On the Fall of Our First Parents, and Of Sin": "Adamus enim communis omnium parens et caput sicut in foedere, sive mandata accipiendo, ita etiam in defectione pro universa gente humana stetit aut lapsus est" (*Works*, 15:182). Sumner has: "For Adam being the common parent and head of all, it follows that, as in the covenant, that is, in receiving the commandment of God, so also in the defection from God, he either stood or fell for the whole human race" (*Works*, 15:183). Carey reads: "For Adam, the parent and head of all men, either stood or fell as a representative of the whole human race: this was true both when the covenant was made, that is, when he received God's commands, and also when he sinned" (*CPW*, 6:384–85). Kelley adds a note for *covenant*: "'foedere.' For Milton's earlier denial of any covenant on this matter, see above, p. 351." Neither translator has rendered *accipiendo* or the words around it correctly: it is a gerund in the ablative case and means "in receiving" (which Sumner does give). But the phrase is parallel with *in foedere*, and the two parts are separated by *sive*, "or," thus removing them from apposition. The fairly literal translation should be: "Indeed, Adam, the universal parent and head of all, just as in the covenant, or in receiving commands, so likewise in his defection stood or fell for the whole human race." Milton's concern in this passage is to explain "AND IN THEM ALL THEIR POSTERITY." Milton says that all Adam's posterity partake of all his actions: just as in Adam's covenant with God (described at the end of *Paradise Lost*, book 10 and beginning of book 11, as we have seen) and in the *commands* he received (it is plural, not simply the singular prohibition against eating of the Tree of Knowledge), so in his rebellion.

Thus, for the Milton of *De doctrina christiana*, a covenant between God and man did not exist until the Fall. Indeed, there was no need, Adam and Eve being filled with natural law.[29] Covenant is a covenant of grace, first stated in the protevangelium and continued in perpetuity despite some men's failures; it is the Old Covenant when it posits a future Messiah and it is the New Covenant when the Son of God has been incarnated as Jesus to become the Christ. The Old Covenant of grace is dispensed through God's promise of Messiah and salvation in return for faith and obedience, which are within man's control as one gifted with free will. The mediatorial office of the prophet (such as Moses) is to instruct the people in profitable things; this is seen in the Law. Such instruction will help man achieve works by which he will manifest his obedience to God. The New Covenant of grace is dispensed through the example of the Son's humiliation and exaltation (as shown in the gospel). The meditorial office of the Son as prophet "IS TO INSTRUCT HIS CHURCH IN HEAVENLY TRUTH, AND TO DECLARE THE WHOLE WILL OF HIS FATHER" (*Works*, 15:287, 289). Providence includes the begetting of the Son before man's time began because God's prescience foresaw the need for the atonement and the example of the Son,

29. Compare the discussions cited in Heinrich Heppe, *Reformed Dogmatics Set Out and Illustrated from the Sources*, rev. and ed. Ernst Bizer, trans. G. T. Thomson (London: George Allen and Unwin, 1950), pp. 291–94. Theorists cited, unlike Milton, accept covenant prior to the Fall. The basic definition of Johannes Henricus Heideggerus (*Corpus Theologiae* [Zurich, 1700], 9.29) fits Milton's view: "The law of nature is defined as the divine law by which God first imbued Adam, and in him the common nature of rationally endowed men, with the knowledge of what is honourable and base," but the remainder of the definition, which alleges that man is "bound" to pursue or avoid, Milton does not accept.

whose "prophetical function began with the creation of the world" (*Works*, 15:291).[30]

The mediatorial office of the priest (such as Melchizedek) was to act between God and man, to perform sacrifice, and to enact sacred rites in order to aid in the salvation of man. The Son's priestly role is as redeemer of sinners through his sacrifice and as intercessor with the Father (*Works*, 15:291). Again God has provided for man "from the foundation of the world" (*Works*, 15:293).

The mediatorial office of the king (such as David) is to unite and lead his people, protecting them and subduing their enemies. A federal covenant is involved. The Son's kingly function is to govern and preserve the Church by an inward law and spiritual power, having purchased it, and to conquer and subdue its enemies (*Works*, 15:297). The inward law, the gift of the Spirit, is the covenant written on men's hearts, "given at Jerusalem on the fiftieth day from the crucifixion, as the Mosaic law was given on the fiftieth day from the passover in Mount Sinai" (*Works*, 15:299), that is, on Pentecost, the feast of the descent of the Holy Spirit. The Church, of course, is "THE ASSEMBLY OF THOSE WHO ARE CALLED . . . whether actually regenerate or otherwise" (*Works*, 15:219).[31]

In all, Christ's mediatorial office is "that whereby . . . HE VOLUNTARILY PERFORMED, AND CONTINUES TO PERFORM, ON BEHALF OF MAN, WHATEVER IS REQUISITE FOR OBTAINING RECONCILIATION WITH GOD, AND ETERNAL SALVATION" (*CD*, 1.15; *Works*, 15:285).

The covenant of grace is a mutual covenant between God and man: God will shine his grace—his free and unmerited favor—on that man (potentially a sinner) who follows the stipulation of God's commandment and who thereby seeks Him in faith. He who by an act of will breaks obedience and thus implies a lack of faith in God's covenant causes God to withdraw his grace. God's grace withdrawn, man falls into sin, having given vent to so-

---

30. Compare my discussion in *With Mortal Voice: The Creation of "Paradise Lost"* (Lexington: University Press of Kentucky, 1982), pp. 21–28.

31. Christ's offices in *Paradise Regain'd* are discussed by Barbara K. Lewalski in *Milton's Brief Epic: The Genre, Meaning, and Art of "Paradise Regained"* (Providence: Brown University Press, 1966), pp. 182–92.

called original sin, that is, the innate propensity to sin (evil concupiscence), as well as to personal sin. While man can never rid himself of "the sin which is common to all men," as Milton calls it (*Works*, 15:181), he can reject the act of sin, and thereby he will be rejecting personal sin, both its evil concupiscence and its act. However, though the covenant has been abrogated by the man who sins, the covenant continues in perpetuity, and God will shine his grace on him who abides by his part in the covenant thereafter. For the sinner may be renovated. The covenant is sealed by sacraments, but for Milton and Protestantism in general these include only baptism and the Lord's supper.[32] Man as part of Christ's church, the invisible church, is engaged in federal covenant as well as mutual covenant. Christ's kingdom governs not only the bodies of men and man but also their and his minds and consciences. Governance is achieved through inward law and spiritual power, not through external force.

It should be clear, I think, that Milton did not consider Old Testament theology one in which God imposed His will on the people, that he looked upon the Old Covenant as one of grace, not one involving a reconciliation between enemies, and that the difference of Old and New was the difference between following a set of rules and being of such inward spirit (essence) that righteousness (insofar as humankind is capable) would lead inevitably to obedience.[33] The Old Testament was looked upon typo-

32. Milton (*Works*, 16:165) and Heppe (*Reformed Dogmatics*, pp. 609–10) note that baptism answers to circumcision and the Lord's supper to the Passover under the Mosaic dispensation. Milton states his concept of sacrament definitively: "a sacrament is a thing to be used, not abstained from . . . a pledge, as it were, and memorial of obedience" (*Works*, 15:115). Clearly it is a sign of faith by man toward God under the covenant of grace (*Works*, 16:165). Milton would agree with Heppe (p. 591) that a sacrament is not a *res sacra* (a sacred thing) but a *res sacrans* (a thing that consecrates).

33. As I have shown elsewhere, this concept underlies the message of *The Tenure of Kings and Magistrates*: "Milton's contribution to political theory appears in points of counsel . . . 1. educate man to judge more objectively, without the false thinking of custom or self-interest, . . . 4. develop a proper regard of each man for every other. . . . Milton's contribution is fundamental to an improved political world rather than tangible structures, laws, and principles" ("The Higher Wisdom of *The Tenure of Kings and Magistrates*," in *Achievements of the Left Hand: Essays on the Prose of John Milton*, ed. Michael Lieb and John T. Shawcross [Amherst: University of Massachusetts Press, 1974], pp. 155–56).

logically, even in such matters as covenant; the fulfillment came with the antitype of the New Testament. The nonexistence of covenant prior to the protevangelium (for Milton and others) obviates any typological dimension before that time. Its creation at the protevangelium, which points to Christ for the Christian, brings into being the antitype and thence types that preceded the antitype. The new commandment was not, indeed, a commandment at all, but a sure sign of the shift from law to spirit. It is also clear, I think, that Milton's attitude toward predestinated mankind has tendencies toward that which is called Arminianism, but it has only tendencies. It is not the same thing, although most have used the term *Arminian* as if all Reformed Protestants of the early seventeenth century were to be categorized as Calvinist or Arminian only.[34] That is, there seems to be an attitude that if one is not a strict Calvinist, he is an Arminian, and further that no other Protestant group could carry the label *reformed*. While some Calvinists seem to have believed in a strict doctrine of election and thus of absolute grace, others in varying ways and degrees held that grace was not confined to the elect and that election included both those elect from the beginning of time and those who gained salvation through obedience and faith. Milton specifically dissociates God's prescience from predestination as meaningless of concern. The problem basically lay in Calvin's division of all men into the elect or the reprobate, which leads to supralapsarianism, the belief that God decreed the fall of man.[35] The Calvinist emphasized the covenant of grace[36] for an elect and was also concerned with freedom of

34. William B. Hunter, "John Milton: Autobiographer," *Milton Quarterly* 8 (1974): 100–104, seems to divide religion at the time into the purely Calvinistic and the Arminian.

35. See Kelley, *CPW*, 6:77–79.

36. "Upon the eternal testament of the Father, upon the likewise eternal vow of surety by the Son and upon the pact between Father and Son rests God's covenant of grace with the elect. . . . 'The covenant of grace is a gratuitous agreement between an offended God and certain offending men, in which of His grace and sheer good pleasure and to the same sobered believers God has assigned righteousness and life in the same Christ the Mediator, and these in turn, by promising to produce faith and sobriety to God through the grace of Christ, obtain from Him righteousness and the right to expect life'" (Heppe, *Reformed Dogmatics*, p. 382, quoting Heidegger 11.8).

will.[37] The Church of England and others emphasized man's freedom of will by which he could satisfy or not satisfy his part in the mutual pact. While Arminian views had their effect upon the Church of England during the 1620s and 1630s, Church of England dogma is not coincident with Arminianism. The umbrella of a basic Reformed dogma covers both: "The elect are introduced into the covenant of grace by two means:—(1) by the *meritum Christi*, since Christ merits for believers not merely righteousness and eternal life, but has also secured that they should be reborn to faith; and (2) by the 'effectual regeneration of the Spirit of life in Christ, which is also called conversion.'"[38]

The standard interpretation of Milton's theology seems to be that he was opposed to Arminianism at least through the 1640s (see remarks in *The Doctrine and Discipline of Divorce*, *CPW*, 2.293, and *Areopagitica*, *CPW*, 2:519–20). Kelley writes, "Just when Milton took his leave of Calvin and orthodoxy is not certain" (*CPW*, 6:82). But the discussion in *Areopagitica* of purifying by trial suggests to him that "if Milton had not consciously and openly accepted Remonstrant doctrines by the time of *Areopagitica*, he had at least taken a position that would logically develop into the Arminianism advanced in the *Christian Doctrine*" (ibid.). Milton's Arminianism rests for Kelley in Milton's belief in man's freedom of choice and denial that predestination was an absolute decree.[39] Yet he notes differences from Arminian dogma: predestination "not *to* belief, but *on condition of* belief and continuation in faith"; and Milton's rejection of reprobation.

The point is, Milton's thinking agreed with certain ideas set forth by Arminius and accepted by others, but it did not agree

37. Calvin wrote, "God equipped man's soul with a mind, with which to discern good from evil, righteous from unrighteous, and to see by the previous light of reason what must be followed or fled from. . . . To this He joined the will, with which lies choice" (*Institutio Christianae Religionis* [Berlin, 1834], 1.15.8). Choice is to direct appetite and control all organic movements, will thus assenting to the control of reason. Therefore, freedom of will is seen as willing good. See Heppe, *Reformed Dogmatics*, p. 242.

38. Heppe, *Reformed Dogmatics*, p. 388, citing Cocceius, *Summa Doctrinae de Foedere et Testamento Dei*, in *Opera. Tom. VI* (Amsterdam, 1673), 7:215, 223.

39. Unjustifiedly, he says this differently, creating a false impression: "his belief that from eternity God bestowed on man a freedom of choice, and that consequently not all divine decrees are absolute" (*PW*, 6:83).

with other ideas. To call Milton an Arminian is thus invalid, de- ✓
spite agreement with certain ideas. Further, there is no evidence
that Milton changed his ideas on the matters raised in this paper,
whether around 1644 or during the late 1650s. This all leads
Kelley into two objectionable statements: first, "Milton's second
doctrinal errancy is Arminianism" (CPW, 6:74; the first for Kelley is antitrinitarianism, which issue I shall not engage), and second, "For his beliefs on decrees and predestination Milton's
sources have yet to be determined" (CPW, 6:85). Surely antitrinitarianism is of a totally different realm of "errancy," since it
goes to the heart of Christian theology, from that of Arminianism, since that differs only with (basically) one theologian's concepts. Certainly Arminianism is not doctrinally errant, except to
him who advances Calvinist thought as doctrine, a position Milton would never allow. Further, of course, Arminius staunchly
argued his Calvinist orthodoxy. The second misleading statement implies that Milton, of necessity, must have derived his
ideas from some source, not allowing for the possibility that the
ideas are independent and resultant from thinking about such
issues, provoked by the writings of various people—Perkins,
Wollebius, Ames, Episcopius, and others. It is, I think, time we
stop calling Milton an Arminian and acknowledge instead his
agreement with certain Arminian ideas only.[40] And it should

40. Dennis Danielson in "Milton's Arminianism and *Paradise Lost*," *Milton
Studies* 12 (1978): 47–73, comments, "Although it would not be right to claim that
Milton was in any sense a 'card-carrying' Arminian, there is no doubt that the
term can be applied meaningfully, especially to his later writings" (p. 47). While I
commend Danielson's discussion of ideas in the poem, I cannot agree that Milton
reversed his theological position and "was himself arguing an Arminian position
against what he had previously accepted as the truth. This truth had been set
down in 1647 in the Westminster Confession" (p. 61). This attitude is based on
seeing Milton's earlier critical remarks on Arminians as espousing "the truth"
and his later statements in *De doctrina christiana* as espousing Arminianism,
rather than viewing his position as basically consistent and independent. (See
also a revision of this article in Danielson's *Milton's Good God: A Study in Literary
Theodicy* [Cambridge: Cambridge University Press, 1982]). In a recent unpub-
lished paper in which he argues that "Calvinism and Arminianism . . . came to
mean something different in Milton's later years," Danielson suggests that Milton's views did not change so much as expand "and that the theological opinions
Milton set forth in *Christian Doctrine* and in *Paradise Lost* concerning election,
predestination, grace, and free will are Arminian in the doctrinal sense of that
term." With this position I have no disagreement.

be pointed out that this in no way means that he took those ideas from Arminius, though I would not deny the possibility of influence.

James Dale, in the entry on "Arminianism" in *A Milton Encyclopedia* (1:83–84), remarks, "*CD* and *PL* are both Arminian," and after *Areopagitica* "he never attacked the Remonstrants in any way. Rather, it is clear that he turned again to their position, sympathizing with them in *Way* (6:366; 1st ed. only) and expressly defending their position as scriptural in *TR* (6:168)." In *The Ready and Easy Way* Milton wrote: "in summ, I verily suppose ther would be then no more pretending to a fifth monarchie of the saints: but much peace and tranquillitie would follow; as the United Netherlands have found by experience: who while they persecuted the *Arminians*, were in much disquiet among themselves, and in danger to have broke asunder into a civil war; since they have left off persecuting, they have livd in much more concord and prosperitie" (Ed. 1; *CPW*, 7:380–82). In no way is this a positive statement or a negative statement toward the Arminians: it is an example of the good results of toleration. In *Of True Religion, Haeresie, Schism, Toleration* Milton wrote: "But here the Papist will angrily demand, what! Are Lutherans, Calvinists, Anabaptists, Socinians, Arminians, no Hereticks? I answer, all these may have some errors, but are no Hereticks" (*CPW*, 8:423); and "The *Arminian* lastly is condemn'd for setting up free will against free grace; but that Imputation he disclaims in all his writings, and grounds himself largely upon Scripture only" (*CPW*, 8:425–26). Milton is concerned with the accurate use of the word *heresy*, as his discussion following indicates, and with an accurate understanding of what Arminians have written. It is not a

---

Mary Ann Radzinowicz in *Toward "Samson Agonistes": The Growth of Milton's Mind* (Princeton: Princeton University Press, 1978) engages in a lengthy discussion of "Arminianism and *Samson Agonistes*," pp. 339–47, posited on the "heresy" of contingent predestination. She speaks of "Milton's 'heretical' Arianism or subordinationism" (p. 340), which she links with his "'heretical' Arminianism," accompanied by the usual repetition of his alleged change in belief. Her argument appears to be dependent on an inadequate understanding of free will in Calvin, Arminius, and Milton, inexactness in discussing election in Arminius and Milton, and the weighted and inaccurate use of the word *heresy*.

defense of Arminian position, by any means. His words *cannot* be interpreted to mean that he was an Arminian.

De doctrina christiana is not Arminian: its theological position agrees in some points with that of Arminianism—that is all. Had commentators addressed themselves to the audience of Milton's work they would not have been led into such unfounded categorizing.[41] The audience for the work, as William B. Hunter has shown, is three groups: "the Reformed scholastics on the continent, with their unmentionable brethren in Scotland and England, the school of Saumur, and the Arminians. Representative opinions from all three are cited, and authorities from the former two are named. Milton, however, does not commit himself to identification with any single point of view."[42]

Milton says of predestination (by which he refers to only election, not reprobation) that "GOD IN PITY TO MANKIND, THOUGH FORESEEING THAT THEY WOULD FALL OF THEIR OWN ACCORD, PREDESTINATED TO ETERNAL SALVATION BEFORE THE FOUNDATION OF THE WORLD THOSE WHO SHOULD BELIEVE AND CONTINUE IN THE FAITH" (*Works*, 14:91). "Election . . . is not a part of predestination. . . . For, speaking accurately, the ultimate purpose of predestination is salvation of believers" (*Works*, 14:99); "predestination was not an absolute decree before the fall of man" (*Works*, 14:103). That is, God elected before time began those who were to be saved, but he predestinated those who would be saved through Christ. The Father says in *Paradise Lost*, 3.183–97:

> Some I have chosen of peculiar grace
> Elect above the rest; so is my will:
> The rest shall hear me call, and oft be warnd

41. Another category that Milton has been recently assigned to, the Antinomian, also should be voided. Milton at no point argues the nullification of the Law; Law is, rather, replaced as representative of the covenant of grace by a new covenant of grace, one working through spirit rather than through commandment. Certainly there are affinities in Milton's position with antinomian emphasis on the higher status of devotion of heart over compulsion of law, but never does he proceed to a doctrine of exemption from moral law.

42. "The Theological Context of Milton's *Christian Doctrine*," in *Achievements of the Left Hand*, p. 273. Hunter also evidences the disagreements of Milton's systematic theology with that of the Arminians.

> Thir sinful state, and to appease betimes
> Th'incensed Deitie, while offerd grace
> Invites; for I will cleer thir senses dark,
> What may suffice, and soft'n stonie hearts
> To pray, repent, and bring obedience due . . .
> And I will place within them as a guide
> My Umpire *Conscience*, whom if they will hear,
> Light after light well us'd they shall attain,
> And to the end persisting, safe arrive.

While election "is nearly synonymous with eternal predestination," they are not the same: predestination purposes the salvation of believers; election elects those who are saved. Prescience, in the sense of foreknowledge of who would and who would not be saved, is inapplicable both to predestination, which did not exist until after the Fall, and to election, which is the act of saving, through Christ, those who believe and continue in the faith (*Works*, 14.125).

In what ways do these beliefs in covenant inform the poetry? To that I shall now turn. *Upon the Circumcision* talks of "that great Cov'nant which we still transgress" and its full satisfaction by Christ. The reference is to Genesis 17:7, 10, the everlasting covenant made with Abraham that every manchild be circumcised as a sign of the covenant. While the poem is dedicated to the Feast of the Circumcision of Jesus, 1 January, eight days after his birth, Milton's double vision superimposes the rite on the passion of Christ, whereby Jesus as man has given example of the entire satisfaction of God's covenant of salvation for man's faith and obedience, that is, love. The circumcision becomes a seal of obedience (just as the sacraments are seals of obedience), intended as a constant reminder to man of the covenant. Jesus has united the Old and New covenants through his following of the Law and his love: "O more exceeding love or law more just? / Just law indeed, but more exceeding love!" That man is potentially sinful and needs the example of Christ to fulfill his part in the covenant is clear throughout the poem. The blood sacrifices of circumcision and of crucifixion are detailed: as the "wounding smart" moves to become "Huge pangs and strong" that "Will peirce more neer his heart," the bodily has proceeded to the spiritual. Without the incarnation of the Son "we by right-ful doom remediles / Were lost in death" because of "our excess." This poem, written sometime in the 1630s, illustrates well the at-titudes toward covenant that underlie *De doctrina christiana*.

Sometime earlier, perhaps in December 1631, Milton had talked of his lot in life, whether mean or low: "All is, if I have grace to use it so, / As ever in my great task-maisters eye" (Son-net 7, lines 13–14). Read against the covenant of grace, the lines indicate the prescience of God, but not any ordination from Him; the expectation of predestination; and the grace extended to man through the inward law (his "inward ripenes"). The in-ward ripeness is, first, a maturity of mind and self (as opposed to external physicality); second, in context of covenant, it implies that he has not been faced with circumstances demanding his obedience in such theological terms: his virtue has been, so to speak, cloistered, it has not been sufficiently exercised and breathed, it has not sallied out to see the adversary (see *Areopagi-tica, CPW*, 2:514–15). His inward ripeness much less appears, but the gift of the spirit differs for men, "according as God hath dealt to every man the measure of faith" (Romans 12:3).

The rainbow as sign of God's covenant has significance for *On the Morning of Christs Nativity, Comus,* and *Epitaphium Damonis.* In stanza 15 of the "Nativity Ode," Truth, Justice, and Mercy, the collocation drawn from Psalm 85, are viewed as "Orb'd in a Rain-bow." These are the three daughters of God representing the three persons of the Trinity, the Father, the Holy Spirit, and the Son, and who, combined as indivisible, are Peace, the fourth daughter. The stanza comments upon the immediately preced-ing stanza, the central stanza of "The Hymne," which contem-plates salvation for him who is "long" enwrapped in "holy Song." Then "speckl'd vanity / Will sicken soon and die, / And leprous sin will melt from earthly mould," and "Heav'n . . . Will open wide the Gates of her high Palace Hall." "Long" implies one's lifetime of "holy Song" rather than only spasmodic singing, and the "holy Song" implies praise of God through the only real means of praise, emulation of the Christ whose birth is being cel-ebrated in the poem. Again Milton presents a double vision, one the start of man's redemption and the other the result of his maintenance of his part in the covenant of grace. The rainbow that descends reminds man of his sinfulness, of the punishment that such truth demands, but of the mercy that will intercede ("Mercy will sit between") for the singer enwrapped in holy song.

Milton's reference to Christ's College in *Elegia prima* is interesting in this connection: "Its bare fields are unwelcome, so unyielding are they of mild shadows; / how improperly that place assembles the followers of Phoebus!" (lines 13–14). While the landscape reflects the fen country of Cambridge and while the reference to Phoebus puns on the students' being at *Christ*'s College (as well perhaps on the lack of receptivity of poetry), Milton has engaged the Tree-Sun-Shadow (Truth-Justice-Mercy) image cited before. There is no Law (the Tree) in the Christian sense here (no covenant of grace), only "the threats of a stern tutor"; and ironically, at Christ's, there is no mercy (the shadow) for infractions of or disagreements with those threats. Suggested is rigidity in idea and conduct (apparently devolving from William Chappell), allowing the presence only of the Sun ("justice"), not of the Son. Here is unilateral covenant descending from authority only, a concept consistently rejected by Milton. It does not involve prohibition.

As *Comus* begins, the Attendant Spirit, whose world lies "Before the starry threshold of *Joves* court," is garbed in "sky robes spun out of *Iris* woof." As it ends he returns to his "Ocean" where "*Iris* . . . with humid bow / Waters the odorous banks that blow." The sign of the covenant frames this poem/drama of the need for chastity, which may be bodily assailed without spiritually succumbing. The sign reminds the auditors and readers that man, whose virtue may be feeble in countering force, will still be saved when he upholds his part of the covenant. Heaven itself will stoop by sending a redeemer, a Sabrina, for those who have successfully resisted the temptations of the wilderness of the dark forest of life. The scriptural content of lines 1003–11— for example, out of Matthew 25:1–13, Luke 15:3–7, Matthew 19:28–29—should be manifest: the Son, Celestial Cupid, will be the bridegroom of the unspotted soul, Psyche, the soul that has wandered in labors long, and the result of the union will be eternal life and bliss. It is an intricate passage of classical and Chris-

tian imagery, but one turning on the covenant of grace. Man—
the Lady or Psyche—after "wandring labours long" which leave
him "unspotted" (man's part in the covenant as faithful and
obedient) will be rewarded "so *Jove* hath sworn," through the
doctrine of predestination. Comus's use of "rainbow" in his de-
ceptive and false account of the passage of the Lady's two brothers only emphasizes its significance in covenantal terms for the
poem. He says,

> I took it for a faery vision
> Of som gay creatures of the element
> That in the colours of the rainbow live
> And play i'th plighted clouds. I was aw-strook,
> And as I past, I worshipt; if those you seek
> It were a journey like the path to Heav'n,
> To help you find them. (298–304)

The virtuous, though untried, brothers do live in the rainbow of
the covenant of grace; seeking and indeed finding them will,
metaphorically, lead to the path to heaven. To find such a path
takes "the best land-pilot's art," Christ's art.

As Milton completes *Epitaphium Damonis* with Damon's apotheosis, he records that "Damon lives in the pure air, / the air he
so pure possesses: he rejected the rainbow with his foot" (lines
203–4). The Latin is "purum colit aethera Damon, / AEthera
purus habet, pluvium pede reppulit arcum." That is, Damon
saved, as befits one of "blushing modesty and youth without
blemish," one unmarried and deserving the "rewards of virgin-
ity," has ascended above the middle air of the heavens into the
pure air of heaven. His foot, as it were, treads the rainbow lying
beneath him in that middle air; for Damon the covenant has
been satisfied, its signs are no longer viable for him. We have
here, of course, another example of Milton's earlier orthodox
belief that the soul did not die and descend into the grave with
the body (as also in *Lycidas*, written some few years before). Later
Milton espouses mortalism, specifically psychopannychism. Damon or rather Damon's soul has joined in the immortal marriage
in heaven.

Paradise Regain'd is a concentrated study of the means by which

man can experience faith and obedience, fulfilling his covenant
with God, who will save man as he has the Son as man in the
literal removal of the Son by "a fiery Globe / Of Angels" "From
his uneasie station." Psalm 91:11–12 reads, "For he shall give his
angels charge over thee, to keep thee in all thy ways. / They shall
bear thee up in their hands, lest thou dash thy foot against a
stone." This covenant, incompletely recited by Satan in Matthew
4:6–7 and thus in *Paradise Regain'd*, 4.556–59, has been fulfilled by the Son's faith in standing on the tower and not being
tempted to force God to prove His word, despite the potential
danger of falling, and by God's salvation. Metaphorically, man is
always in danger of destruction when Satan tempts, whether he
resists or not; but the faithful will learn that destruction will not
come to pass, for God's power is limitless and his covenant will be
fulfilled. The point that Man as Son will always defeat Satan is
reinforced by the simile of Satan's fall and the Sphinx's suicide
when the answer to her riddle, "Man," was pronounced.

The Son likens his reign on David's throne to

> a tree
> Spreading and over-shadowing all the Earth,
> Or as a stone that shall to pieces dash
> All Monarchies besides throughout the world,
> And of my Kingdom there shall be no end. (4.147–51)

This tree is the Law (Truth); yet because of it there will be shadow
(Mercy). The stone meting Justice is that in Jesus' parable to the
Temple priests (Matthew 21:42–44): "Did ye never read in the
Scriptures, the stone which the builders rejected, the same is become the head of the corner: this is the Lord's doing, and it is
marvelous in our eyes? Therefore say I unto you, the kingdom
of God shall be taken from you, and given to a nation bringing
forth the fruits thereof. And whosoever shall fall on this stone
shall be broken: but on whomsoever it shall fall, it will grind him
to powder." And it is "Jesus Christ himself [who is] the chief corner stone" (Eph. 2:20). The Son's words particularly recall the
vision in Daniel of the great image of gold, silver, brass, iron,
and clay, which the "stone . . . cut out without hands . . . smote
. . . upon his feet that were of iron and clay, and brake them to

pieces" (Dan. 3:31–34). The stone "became a great mountain, and filled the whole earth" (3:35).

But the covenant of grace existent during the time period of the poem is undergoing change into the New Covenant: the tension of the poem is that between the Old Covenant, which was represented by the Law and gave promise of Messiah, and the New Covenant, which is represented by inward law and is in the process of being created by the Messiah who has come. Milton's poetic character is the Son, Jesus, the Savior, or the Messiah. The poem does not depict the literal blood sacrifice of the Christ, but it is with the blood of Christ that the New Covenant is inaugurated for mankind. His sacrifice transfers guilt to the people who will suffer death, should they fall into a lack of faith and disobedience. But this is futural. Satan, of course, cannot know of or understand the New Covenant being formed; his temptations try to get the Son to abrogate the Law; he tries to ascertain whether this is indeed the Messiah prophesied. But he is not capable of discerning how the Messiah's acts will come to free the people from his bondage. The Son is aware of being Messiah, as his first soliloquy makes clear, although he does not presume upon that knowledge, drawn from his mother's words, John the Baptist's address, and the Spirit descended. The assertion of his Messianic acts is the burden of the poem, only after which is he ready to "Now enter, and begin to save mankind." His Messianic acts all rest upon an inward law, asserted and reasserted as its maintenance becomes increasingly difficult. His glorious work in life will be to instruct mankind in heavenly truth and to declare the will of his Father, the mediatorial office of prophet. Such glorious work will instill an inward law in the faithful who follow him, confirmed by his death and resurrection, from which time the New Covenant will exist, engraved on their hearts with the descent of the Holy Spirit. The poem, however, is concerned with the development of that New Covenant of grace and with cogent example of the means to salvation.

Samson Agonistes is likewise a concentrated study, but of the man who through pride (and uxoriousness) has not held faith and obedience and who through humiliation has been renovated. The prophecy of the Great Deliverer, like all covenants, has not been voided by God, only by Samson, who must regain his inward spirit (the "inward eyes" by which the blind man is illuminated), for God extends "sufficient grace, offered even to a late hour." The delivery from bondage does not mean, Samson must learn, by force and by works. His recapitulation of the temptations conquered by the Son allows him to reject ease, worldly position, and pride, through the development of inward being. Although he is an Old Testament figure, Samson develops under a New Testament concept of grace. The presentation, however, has not created an anachronistic text. The changes within him have been seen as regeneration, although renovation might be more accurate. Objections to Samson's "regeneration" may have some foundation; instead of this term with its questionable connotations for the dramatic poem, we should probably view the changes of his inner self as a development of the effect of God's grace upon him. One problem for Samson in the past, one that finds negative and positive reprises in the interviews with Manoa, Dalila, and Harapha, is that works were conceived as covenant. Samson consistently argues for his fulfilling God's purposes by works—the slaying of the men at Ashkelon, the hundred foxes, the ass's jawbone—but it is not until inward spirit has wiped away pride that he can achieve one great act of deliverance (line 1389), which represents faith and obedience. He is not constrained to the Temple of Dagon (line 1370); he goes in some important cause, he knows not what (line 1379); and he concludes:

> Happ'n what may, of me expect to hear
> Nothing dishonourable, impure, unworthy
> Our God, our Law, my Nation, or my self,
> The last of me or no I cannot warrant. (1423–26)

In complement to *Paradise Regain'd*, where the New Covenant is developed and contrasted with the Old, *Samson Agonistes* shows how the covenant of grace was operative in Old Testament history and how the concept of the covenant as one of works is false.

It is *Paradise Lost* that most reflects covenant theology, particularly in book 12 as Adam learns "a better Cov'nant, disciplin'd / From shadowie Types to Truth, from Flesh to Spirit, / From imposition of strict Laws, to free / Acceptance of large Grace, from servil fear / To filial, works of Law to works of Faith" (302–6). Kelley presents extensive parallels between the epic and *De doctrina christiana* in the notes to his edition of the treatise. Duncan specifically relates the ideas we have looked at to the epic, pointing out Adam's erroneous view of his relation to God as covenant of works (10.754–59) and explaining the dialogue between the Father and Son in book 3 as the basis for the covenant of grace. The first use of "Mediator" in the poem, in conjunction with "Redeemer voluntarie," occurs in 10.60–61, just before the statement of the protevangelium in 10.179–81. Repentance and prayer end this book of the epic, dramatizing, as has been remarked, the change from Adam and Eve at the beginning of the book to their selves as they leave Paradise and the epic ends. "Prevenient grace" has descended simultaneously with this repentance and prayer (10.1086–92, which, because of its monumental importance, is repeated in lines 1098–1104, the final lines of the book). Its descent is stated in the third line of book 11, confirming the Covenant that now exists. It has removed "The stonie from thir hearts" and made them "new flesh," detailed in line four, perhaps with a glance to the mysticism of numbers. The rainbow as sign ends book 11 and will have such force "till fire purge all things new, / Both Heav'n and Earth, wherein the just shall dwell," referring to 2 Peter 3:12–13 ("Looking for and hasting unto the coming of the day of God, wherein the heavens being on fire shall be dissolved, and the elements shall melt with fervent heat? Nevertheless we, according to his promise, look for new heavens and a new earth, wherein dwelleth righteousness").

As book 12 and the poem draw to a close, Michael reprises the protevangelium and the conclusion of the world in a great conflagration, out of which will come

> New Heav'ns, new Earth, Ages of endless date
> Founded in righteousness and peace and love,
> To bring forth fruits Joy and Eternal Bliss. (12.549–51)

The parallel with the ending of *Comus* should be noted, and the further source in Revelation 21:1. Adam accepts this covenant of grace, having learned "that to Obey is best, / And love with fear the onely God" (561–62), for himself and his posterity. The poem will end with allusion to the further lines of Revelation 21:4: "And God shall wipe away all tears from their eyes; and there shall be no more death, neither sorrow, nor crying, neither shall there be any more pain: for the former things are passed away." The covenant of grace has clearly had its efficient beginning in the brief "now" of the narrative related from the end of book 10 to the end of the poem, and its actual beginning for mankind as Adam and Eve proceed "down the Cliff as fast / To the subjected Plain." The Plain of earth is, of course, to be contrasted with the Plain of Heaven at the center of the poem, above which only the Son acting for the Father has "Ascended" (6.762). Movement in life will be from one plain to the other (Eden having existed in some middle realm, appropriately), depending on where one chooses his place of rest. The covenant of grace that informs the total poem is the absolute assertion of Eternal Providence and the absolute means whereby, thus, the ways of God are justified to men (1.25–26).

Perhaps insufficiently remarked, however, is the importance of recognizing that, up to the Fall, God has not covenanted with Adam and Eve, in Milton's way of thinking.[43] They are filled with

43. A 1980 meeting of the New York Milton Seminar made clear to me the altered reading of *Paradise Lost* that an understanding of Milton's conception of covenant demands. Two revisions of what seem to be "standard" views arise: First, covenant does not operate in *Paradise Lost* until the protevangelium is stated in book 10 and is accepted by Adam and Eve as the book ends. The Father's pertinent discussion in book 3 is futural; its actualization is seen in books 11 and 12 as some keep the covenant and some do not, and as some attest to their inelectability and others act through inward grace to achieve hope of election— the predestinated like Noah and Elijah. The Father's words are *not* a gloss on Adam and Eve and the ensuing action of book 9. The subject of the poem— man's disobedience—is reemphasized as a test of man's commitment to God's command, as a demonstration of man's free will, and as the aberration of the natural law within him, which aberration accounts for the depravity of man after the Fall. The subject of the poem does not involve covenant as mutual act. Rather the basic truth is advanced that command ultimately achieves less than mutual agreement. It is a lesson for all men in their lives, especially Milton would say in their political and their married lives. God, of course, has foreknown this truth.

Further, typological reasoning and expression cannot exist in books 1–9, except as God the Father foresees. While Mary is referred to as the second Eve in 5.385–87, this is so only "Long after." Eve is not yet a type, but the narrator

natural law and have freedom of will. While the Old Testament saw, for instance, covenant in night and day, Adam and Eve's apostrophes (4.724–29; 5.160–79) praise what is simply nature. The promise that "from us two a Race / To fill the Earth, who shall with us extoll / Thy goodness infinite" (4.732–34) is one only of natural begetting, as the things of Eden reproduce and grow. It is not covenant. This progeny has no commitment, yet, to "Light after light well us'd." No human progeny is produced in Eden,[44] and the telescoped time would not so allow, but Milton does not have to face that issue of what might have been had Adam not been "fondly overcome with Femal charm" (9.999), since such matters are not biblical. What we have in books 4, 5, 7, 8, and the first part of 9, the prelapsarian books, is a view of man in whom "the whole law of nature [has been] so implanted and innate . . . that he needed no precept to enforce its observance" (*Works*, 15:115). The prohibition against the doing of one act does not establish covenant, is not involved in precept. "Man being formed after the image of God, it followed as a necessary consequence that he should be endued with natural wisdom, holiness, and righteousness" (*Works*, 15:53). One aspect of that natural wisdom permits Eve to counsel division of their labors, Adam tending the woodbine (with its connotations of symbiotic nature) and ivy (with its connotations of immortality) and Eve tending the roses (with their symbolic associations of beauty) and

---

makes certain for the reader, here and there, the significance of personages and events within Man's time frame (which does not begin until Adam and Eve leave Paradise). This realization is validated, I believe, by the statement made immediately upon pronouncement of the protevangelium (10.179–81) as the narrator establishes the antitypes of the Son and Mary as he remarks, "So spake this Oracle [the Son acting for the Father], then verifi'd / When *Jesus* son of *Mary* second *Eve*, / Saw Satan fall" (10.182–84), followed by a restatement of the protevangelium: "Whom he shall tread at last under our feet; / Eevn hee who now foretold his fatal bruise, / And to the Woman thus his Sentence turn'd" (10.190–92). The types of the Old Testament appear in books 11 and 12, which proceed up to the mortal existence of the antitype, after which the poem rapidly ends. (My disagreement with a major thrust of William Madsen's *From Shadowy Types to Truth* [New Haven: Yale University Press, 1968] is evident.)

44. Remark Eve's "but till more hands / Aid us, the work under our Labour grows, / Luxurious by restraint" (9.207–9), spoken not long before Satan's assault.

myrtle (with its connotations of immortality) *till Noon* (9.214–19); Adam says she has "well . . . motion'd, well [her] thoughts imployd" (9.229). Freedom of will enters to weigh warning, not covenant, when Adam considers that "harm / [may] Befall thee sever'd from me" (9.251–52). Another aspect of that natural wisdom concludes that her firmness to God and Adam should not be in doubt, though she is seducced (9.279–81). There is no breaking of covenant, no loss of grace, no defiance to God, no bad faith, and no disobedience.

With Eve's seduction and the partaking of the fruit of the Tree of Knowledge, there still is no breaking of covenant, no loss of grace, or even defiance to God, but there is disobedience that at least unconsciously exacts a lack of faith. Eve's argument that they are forbidden good and thus wisdom turns on the difference between knowing good by its being total (a seeming impossibility) and knowing it through contrast with that which is its opposite, and on the difference between innate wisdom and acquired wisdom through experience. There is only prohibition to be broached, and "Such prohibitions bind not" (9.760). After the Fall, man cannot in this life experience total good or achieve wisdom except through experience.

The grievous fall for mankind is Adam's fall, for he is not seduced directly by Satan but by a narcissistic view of Eve as "Flesh of Flesh, / Bone of my Bone": "Our State cannot be severd, we are one, / One Flesh; to loose thee were to loose my self" (9.914–15, 958–59). "Against his better knowledge, not deceav'd" he ate of the fruit, "fondly overcome with Femal charm" (9.998–99). (Perhaps we should remark that Adam by his action keeps what we would consider his marriage covenant with Eve.) Eve's is an act of disobedience and lack of faith through seduction; Adam's is an act of disobedience and a lack of consideration of faith. Milton is clear to state this: "Man falls deceiv'd / By the other *first*" (3.130–31, my emphasis), where *first* may relate to mankind's continued fall in the mortal world but also may stress that the first stage of the Fall is by deception (and thus it is through Eve that redemption must come) but implies that the second stage, which is continued through mankind's life, will be "Against man's better knowledge, not deceived." The reversal of the Fall must therefore be through obedience and faith potentially perverted by will.

Satan and his cohorts fell "by thir own suggestion . . . Self-tempted, self-deprav'd" (3.129–30). Again there is no covenant involved, and there is not even prohibition, but there is obedience, and thus ultimately faith. The Father at the begetting of the Son says,

> him who disobeys
> Mee disobeys, breaks union, and that day
> Cast out from God and blessed vision, falls
> Into utter darkness, deep ingulft, his place
> Ordaind without redemption, without end. (5.611–15)

Satan, through pride, "Thought himself impaird" (5.665). and moves to disobedience, largely because of a lack of faith in God, who sees all his angels as "United as one individual Soul" (5.610). (After the defeat of the rebellious angels, Michael, it will be remembered, reduces his army "Under thir Head imbodied all in one.") Satan's sense of individuation has set him apart from the Son, but also, it should be recognized, from the other angels, a more clearly observed fact after their fall at the beginning of the great consult in book 2. But that individuation has begun before the begetting of the Son; it does not scrutinize and grasp the distinct *essentiae* that are all of one *substantia*. It does not allow for the acceptance of subordination that underlies both *Paradise Lost* and *De doctrina christiana*. It has caused hierarchy in Heaven, even among the angels, to become levels of superiority rather than of administration. Perhaps what Milton is paralleling here is need for mutual covenant for all beings—human and otherwise, since only God is capable of understanding natural law, oneness, oneness that has many parts, and existence that unrelentingly manifests love.

The Miltonic Narrator and Scriptural Tradition: An Afterword

James H. Sims

central problem Milton faced in writing *De doctrina christiana* was how to adhere to the authority of the Bible alone when some of the "arbiters of or . . . supreme authorities for Christian belief" whom he claimed not to recognize were so well known to him that they were sometimes useful, both negatively and positively, in defending his interpretations.[1] He had found in reading some of the "more diffuse volumes of divinity" that the authors "sometimes violently attacked the truth as error and heresy, while calling error and heresy truth and upholding them not upon the authority of the Bible but as a result of habit and partisanship."[2] Yet on page after page of *De doctrina* he appeals to the authority of human interpreters by name (for example, Ambrose and Erasmus, *CPW*, 6:244–45) and uses traditional Protestant interpretations of texts without identifying his sources. As C. A. Patrides has said, Milton "unhesitatingly rejected human traditions if they happened to conflict with what he considered to be the sense of the Scriptures, yet readily invoked the Fathers if he found them supporting his individual—Protestant—interpretation of a particular idea."[3]

And the tension is not merely that between Scripture and external tradition; even within the canonical tradition that has preserved the Bible as one book, for example, divorce is condoned by Moses in Deuteronomy and condemned by Jesus in the Gospels. Milton's mighty efforts to reconcile the Old and New testaments on this subject gave the world his four tracts on this aspect

1. The quotation is from *CD*, in *CPW*, 6:124.
2. *CD*, *CPW*, 6:120.
3. *Milton and the Christian Tradition* (London: Oxford University Press, 1966), p. 3; compare n. 4.

of what he called "domestic liberty." But regardless of how difficult the task, the individual Christian, Milton believed, must depend on the indwelling Spirit, the internal Scripture, to interpret the text, the external Scripture.[4] Milton's solution was to
adhere to Scripture *as interpreted by the Spirit within him guiding his
reason*, even though this solution entailed rejecting as "tradition"
the readings of some other Christians who believed themselves
to be guided by the same divine interpreter within. John Shawcross has clearly demonstrated that Milton conceived of "covenant" differently from both Calvin and Arminius and sought to
present this fundamental doctrine in scriptural purity. Shawcross establishes as Milton's view in *De doctrina* that all covenants
with God are covenants of grace and that Milton exemplified in
his poetry his purely scriptural idea of covenant, departing in
important respects from both Calvinism and Arminianism.

As voluminously documented by Patrides in *Milton and the
Christian Tradition*, Milton's doctrines were not unique, though
his so clothing them in the singing robes of epic that they continue to be of interest even in a nontheological age is a unique
achievement. Indeed, as Patrides says, "Milton's peculiar power
consists precisely in this, that he used traditional ideas in such a
way that they were transformed into seeming novelties."[5] Yet he
found, in common with most disputatious Protestant writers of
his day, some traditional ideas more acceptable than others. Not
all that may be called scriptural tradition was acceptable to Milton, but within the wide range of belief and opinion that falls
under that rubric there was much with which he could agree.
The phrase *scriptural tradition* as used in this essay and in the title
of this book describes something like what Milton and his con-
temporaries called the analogy of faith: the comparison of text
with text within the one inspired Bible to ascertain that one's interpretation of a particular text did not violate the general tenor
of Scripture as a whole. The phrase may be further expanded to
include commonly held interpretations based on proper hermeneutical principles, even beliefs not literally stated in particular

4. *CPW*, 6:587.
5. Patrides, *Milton and Christian Tradition*, p. 5.

texts but reasonably inferrable from the scriptural words when the passage is compared with others on the same subject. For instace, Saint Paul says, "It is better to marry than to burn" (1 Cor. 7:9). Although many commentators read this to mean "burn in lust" and the text within its immediate context would seem to support that interpretation, Milton brings to bear on the passage both Genesis and the Song of Solomon. God saw that it was not good for man to be alone (Gen. 2:18) before the fall and he provided woman so that the "cheerfull society of wedlock" would ease the "intelligible flame" of burning in "an unkindly solitarines"; "this pure and . . . inbred desire of . . . conjugal fellowship . . . is that rational burning that marriage is to remedy," a desire that is really love, not to be quenched, "the spouse of Christ thought," by many waters nor to be drowned by floods.[6] Here Milton has not only used the analogy of faith by comparing the Pauline text with Old Testament verses on love and marriage, but he has also inferred that physical lust is not what Paul meant in Corinthians because the Genesis passage occurs before the Fall and the Song of Solomon text relates typologically to the love of Christ and his Church for each other. So labyrinthine can be the paths by which scriptural tradition leads to truth.

On the other hand, there are traditional beliefs that have no basis in canonical Scripture, that purport to fill in gaps in Scripture or to provide parallel material such as events, characters, and explanations neither included in nor suggested by the text of the Bible. This tradition may be called *parascriptural tradition*; it is roughly what lies behind what Milton calls "implicit faith," or belief based on the authority of a church or council but not individually and independently arrived at through study of the Scripture. All apocryphal books Milton would place in such a category and reject as unworthy of credence; though such traditions may be useful in providing illustrative anecdotes and sup-

---

6. *The Doctrine and Discipline of Divorce*, *CPW*, 2:251; Song of Solomon 8:7. Hebrew versions of the Bible add to the description of love in 8:6 as "a vehement flame" the source of the fire of love: Yahweh. (See the English translation of the Jewish Publication Society.)

porting moral instruction, Christian doctrine cannot be based on apocryphal texts unconfirmed by canonical texts.[7] Likewise, at least as substitutes for scriptural doctrine, "human traditions, written or unwritten, are expressly forbidden."[8]

Yet toleration of difference of opinion is essential to Christian fellowship and to progress toward the fullness of truth. In *Areopagitica* Milton argues that one reason licensing is wrong is that it hinders the movement of English Protestantism "toward the true knowledge of what we seem to know."[9] Since "opinion in good men is but knowledge in the making" (554), nothing can be more important than the free interplay of opinions of Spirit-led men who assiduously study the Bible. Opinion may evolve into knowledge and knowledge into faith for individual seekers; but others must not be forced against their consciences to accept such conclusions—one should "withold [*sic*] his consent from those opinions about which he does not feel fully convinced, unless the evidence of the Bible convinces him and induces his reason to assent and to believe."[10] An example of Milton's opinion becoming knowledge is his conviction that divorce on grounds of mental or emotional incompatibility is biblical; referring to his earlier tracts on the subject, he prefaced *The Judgement of Martin Bucer* with a defense to Parliament of his position, saying, "*what I wrote was not my opinion but my knowledge.*"[11] By the time of his completion of *De doctrina christiana*, his knowledge had apparently become a matter of firm belief, not only on the scriptural lawfulness of divorce and remarriage but also on the permissibility of polygamous marriage.[12] His prefatory epistle to *De doctrina* asserts his ability "to distinguish correctly in religion between matters of faith and matters of opinion,"[13] and the fer-

7. An example of Milton's use of the Apocrypha in an allusion is the story of Asmodeus and the wife of Tobias from Tobit 8:3, compared to Satan's approach to Eden and Eve, *Paradise Lost*, 4.166–71.

8. *CPW*, 6:591.

9. *Areopagitica*, *CPW*, 2:548.

10. *CPW*, 6:122.

11. *CPW*, 2:439.

12. Book 1, chap. 10.

13. *CPW*, 6:121.

vor with which he presents most of his ideas implies that study and prayer for guidance moved Milton from opinion through knowledge to faith.

Yet there are still areas in which his progress is not so advanced; he is noticeably reticent to interpret texts on the Holy Spirit, contenting himself with much more quotation than explication and recognizing that "it cannot be decided, from biblical evidence," how the Holy Spirit came to exist; "So we must leave the point open, since the sacred writers are so non-commital about it."[14] Again, the "possible spuriousness" of a famous proof-text used to support the doctrine of the Trinity (1 John 5:7) is said to be "a matter which does not involve the reader's faith but only his opinion" (298).

Milton's epic voice in *Paradise Lost* and *Paradise Regained* faces a problem similar to one of the most crucial his creator, the poet Milton, had dealt with as a systematic theologian: how to distinguish what can be presented as truth from falsehood or from mere matter of opinion. How, for instance, can one tell of the war in Heaven and the fall of angels and man with fidelity to Scripture as opposed to echoing what had come to be widely accepted as "truth" through centuries of accumulated pagan, Christian, and parascriptural tradition? It may be said that the Miltonic narrator has the double task of presenting the truth and composing his own *pseudodoxia epidemica* as he proceeds. But he is not left alone to perform the task; as the Holy Spirit guided Milton in distinguishing scriptural tradition from unscriptural in writing *De doctrina christiana*, the Heavenly Muse teaches the narrator the true story, the account consistent with Scripture, and also guides him in revealing the falsehood of spurious versions. To be sure that one is listening to the inner Spirit or to the Muse rather than to one's own proud ego is, however, difficult; as William Riggs has demonstrated, there is a Satanic potential in the poetic act of producing a *Paradise Lost* (or a *De doctrina*), a potential that Milton objectifies in analogies so as to keep clearly in sight the differences between "satanic self-sufficiency" and de-

14. *CPW*, 6:281–82.

pendence on God's Spirit.[15] The struggle of the narrator to tell the true story and not a false version is everywhere apparent, and the reader is thus made aware of his own danger. As the epic voice successfully controls his widely ranging mind and subdues pagan and parascriptural tradition to scriptural, he encourages the reader in the belief that he, too, can overcome the charm of influences that would lead to error as the voice guiding him affirms, rejects, or leaves open to choice the alternatives described. The Miltonic narrator firmly rejects traditions, no matter how revered their sources, that contradict the meaning of scriptural texts. As was mentioned in the Preface, the narrator of *Paradise Lost* briefly describes the tradition that the Garden of Eden was located in Ethiopia only to deny it and to affirm Eden's Assyrian location (*PL*, 4.281–82). When his account of Raphael's sharing a meal with Adam and Eve (*PL*, 5.440–43) alludes to Abraham's feasting the heavenly messengers in the Bible (Gen. 18:1–21), the narrator calls attention to the commonly accepted tradition that angels only appear to eat (based on Tobit 12:19) in order to strengthen and confirm the truth of an angel's ability to eat and digest human food. Thus the materiality of the angels is supported by Genesis 18, and, though no New Testament allusions are included, the fit reader may remember that Jesus ate fish and honey in his resurrected, and therefore spiritual, body (Luke 24:42; 1 Cor. 15:44), a body that passed through closed doors (John 20:19) and disappeared at will (Luke 24:31). Often the narrator need not remind his "fit audience" of the texts upon which his true account is based, since a brief reference to a story as erroneous or fabled is sufficient to cause recall of scriptural truth on the subject. Thus to state that pagans have "fabl'd, . . . Erring," a myth of Vulcan's fall from the courts of Zeus (*PL*, 1:741, 747), is to recall the biblical war in Heaven when Satan "was cast out into the earth, and his angels were cast out with him" (Rev. 12:9); and to deny that Urania was ever one of the nine muses or dwelt on Mount Olympus (*PL*, 7:5–7) while cou-

---

15. *The Christian Poet in "Paradise Lost"* (Berkeley: University of California Press, 1972), p. 45.

pling the denial with a reference to her playing in the presence of God with her sister, Wisdom, is to allude to Proverbs 8 : 30 and to connect the heavenly Muse with the Spirit of God.

Truth, Milton says in *Areopagitica*, "may have more shapes than one." "What else is all that rank of things indifferent, wherein Truth may be on this side, or on the other, without being unlike her self[?]"[16] He goes on to speak of "those neighboring differences, or rather indifferences [which] need not interrupt the *unity of the Spirit*, if we could but find among us *the bond of peace*."[17] It should not be surprising, therefore, that Milton's epic voice provides the reader with many more alternatives that allow for the free play of opinion than with alternatives that force a choice between truth and falsehood. Without the knowledge provided by clear revelation, one is not expected to make a commitment of faith but is free to consider several equally possible hypotheses. The reader of Milton's epics, like the seventeenth-century reader of theological tracts, can choose any one of many opinions about "things indifferent," when revelation is obscure or nonexistent: that one's curiosity desires a definitive answer does not obligate God or the epic voice to provide one. Where did Adam and Eve obtain tools with which to cultivate the Garden? They used "such Gardening Tools as Art yet rude, / Guiltless of fire had formed, or Angels brought" (*PL*, 9.391–92). When he clothed Adam and Eve after the Fall, how did God remove their skins from the animals? The reader has a choice:

> he clad
> Thir nakedness with Skins of Beasts, or slain,
> Or as the Snake with youthful Coate repaid. (*PL*, 10.216–18)

When God's angel blows his trumpet to herald divine judgment on man after the Fall, are the angel and the trumpet the same as those that centuries later will announce the giving of the Law on

16. *CPW*, 2:563. The phrase *things indifferent* comes from a marginal translation of Eccles. 27:1—"Many have sinned for a *small matter* [a thing indifferent]." For a discussion of the controversies over defining "things indifferent," and the complex and bitter struggles the concept gave rise to, see Ernest Sirluck, "Introduction," *CPW*, 2:68–69, and notes.

17. *CPW*, 2:565.

Sinai and, still later, will signal the final Judgment? One is free to suppose so—or not:

> hee blew
> His Trumpet, heard in *Oreb* since perhaps
> When God descended, and perhaps once more
> To sound at general Doom. (*PL*, 11.73–75)

When Jesus fasted forty days in the wilderness after his baptism, how did he shelter himself? Since the Bible does not say, one may speculate.

> Full forty days he pass'd, whether on hill
> Sometimes, anon in shady vale, each night
> Under the covert of some ancient Oak,
> Or Cedar, to defend him from the dew,
> Or harbour'd in one Cave, is not reveal'd. (*PR*, 1.303–7)

Brought down from the mountain when he viewed the kingdoms of the world, where did Jesus rest before the final temptation on the pinnacle of the temple?

> Our Savior meek and with untroubl'd mind
> After his aerie jaunt, though hurried sore,
> Hungry and cold betook him to his rest,
> Wherever, under some concourse of shades
> Whose branching arms thick intertwined might shield
> From dews and damps of night his shelter'd head. (*PR*, 4.401–6)

When the angels came to minister to Jesus after the Tempter left him, was it because he was suffering the ill effects of hunger and thirst?

> [The angels] soon refresh'd him wearied, and repair'd
> What hunger, if aught hunger had impair'd,
> Or thirst. (*PR*, 4.591–93)

In *Paradise Lost* the angelic secondary narrators, Raphael and Michael, present unresolved choices to Adam. Too well known to describe here is Raphael's suggestion that the Ptolemaic and the Copernican systems are equally valid from man's limited point of view (*PL*, 8.122–68); he echoes the epic voice's earlier mention of the same question:

> whither the prime Orb,
> Incredible how swift, had thither rowl'd
> Diurnal, or this less volubil Earth
> By shorter flight to th' East, had left him there (*PL*, 4.592–95)

The answer would, of course, be obvious to Uriel, seeing Earth from the vantage point of the sun and the vast reaches of outer space; but to man, whose point of view the epic voice reflects, the essential observation is that "Twilight gray / Had in her sober Liverie all things clad" (598–99), whatever the cosmic movements that caused that phenomenon. Similarly, fallen man observes that the Earth undergoes seasons of cold and heat; whether the alignment of Earth and the sun that causes those seasons was itself caused by the Earth's shifting off the center of its axis or by the sun's deviation from "the Equinoctial Road" is a "thing indifferent" to Adam—and to the reader who wishes to know "That which before us lies in daily life" (*PL*, 8.193). Jesus is in this as in all things the perfect example, when, in *Paradise Regained*, he recognizes that he may trust his Father to provide the knowledge he needs when he needs it: Why I am in this wilderness, he says,

> I learn not yet, perhaps I need not know;
> For what concerns my knowledge God reveals. (*PR*, 1.292–93)

Adam, in *Paradise Lost*, will at the needful time recall the curse on the serpent, especially that his head, and therefore Satan's power, shall be bruised by Eve's seed, and the timely memory saves the pair from despair and suicide and leads them to repentance and restoration to God's favor (*PL*, 10.1013–1104). Yet when the serpent is judged, Adam is aware only of the literal punishment meted out to the beast. At that time

> more to know
> Concern'd not Man (since he no further knew). (*PL*, 10.170–71)

Only later, when he needs to know further, he understands more fully what he has heard—to paraphrase Milton in *Areopagitica*, he has moved on to the true knowledge of what he had seemed to know.

It is natural to man, however, to be curious, to wish to know,

James H. Sims

and to be sure of what he knows. Even as the epic voice in *Paradise Regained* seems to reprimand us for wishing to know exactly how Satan was able to show Jesus the grandeur of Rome from a mountaintop in the Holy Land when both the curvature of the earth and intervening higher mountains would make such a sight physically impossible, we realize that he is himself "curious to inquire" into the problem: has Satan accomplished it by

> strange Parallax or Optic skill
> Of vision multiplyed through air, or glass
> Of Telescope [?] (*PR*, 4.40–43)

Knowing has its limits: in the capacity of the knower to understand and to use knowledge in appropriate timeliness, in relevance to the situation at hand. Yet curiosity persists, and Milton is careful to include it as an important characteristic of unfallen Adam and Eve. Adam, having heard of the war in Heaven and the fall of Satan, is by his curiosity "Led on, yet sinless, with desire to know / . . . how this World / . . . first began" (*PL*, 7.61–63), and even when he wishes to inquire more closely into planetary motions, Raphael assures him: "To ask or search I blame thee not, for Heav'n / Is as the Book of God before thee set" (*PL*, 8.66–67). Eve, even as she lends a credulous ear to the serpent's marvelous tale of a wisdom-giving fruit, follows him, and stands at the foot of the Tree of Knowledge of Good and Evil, is "yet sinless" as she discusses God's prohibition with the tempter. Her disobedience, not her curiosity, brings about her fall. (As Shawcross shows, there was no covenant of works here; abstinence from an act was commanded, not actions.) Jesus is led by curiosity to make his way to the "pleasant Grove" and to inspect the "woody Scene" in which Satan spreads a sumptuous banquet (*PR*, 2.289–365), but discerning Satan for who he is, he rejects the "Pompous Delicacies" (390). He overcomes temptation where Adam and Eve succumb to it, because, although his curiosity is no less keen than theirs, his determination to remember his Father's will and to obey it is always kept in the forefront of his consciousness. And the epic voice sings an "advent'rous Song," desiring to soar "Above th' *Aonian* Mount" with a "more Heroic" argument than earlier epic singers; not his curiosity to "see and

201

tell / of things invisible" can cause him to fail but loss of the inspiration of the Muse who knows and instructs him.

As Milton strove to do in *De doctrina christiana*, the epic voice in
Milton's epics strives to ward off the errors of pagan and parascriptural tradition and to follow scriptural tradition; the victory is not a prior one so that the Muse inspires his song with
scriptural truth alone. The struggle is in the poems; thus the
reader sees together the difficulty and necessity of winning such
a struggle, of distinguishing from among the rich storehouse of
his memory those features that are worthy of knowing and believing. To do so necessitates setting such truth in contrast with
the false and the doubtful; at the same time it involves providing
a constant reminder that between truth and falsehood there is a
vast area sown thick with "things indifferent," with entertaining
speculative hypotheses that can help allay curiosity without putting in jeopardy one's loyalty to God's revealed truth. There is a
tension created by the narrator's effort to separate that which is
plainly scriptural, and therefore true, tradition from that which
is apocryphal or antiscriptural; yet that tension is eased by the
opportunity for fascinating flights of imagination concerning
matters upon which one's eternal destiny does not depend.[18]

The essays that precede the present one, and thus make up
the main body of this book, show that Milton, the author, and his
persona, the Miltonic narrator, whether in his major or minor
poetry, are identical in their concern for separating truth from
falsehood. But, perhaps even more important because less frequently perceived by those who interpret Milton's works, Milton
and his speaking voice are also identical in their wondering ad-
miration for and their constant invitation to the reader to share
in the rich and satisfying realm open to free inquiry and inno-
cent speculation. God has set boundaries to human knowledge,
as Raphael tells Adam, and man should not invent dogmatic answers to questions concerning matters God has not chosen to re-

18. I cannot agree, however, with Robert Crosman (*Reading "Paradise Lost"*
[Bloomington: Indiana University Press, 1980], p. 207) that Milton's narrator's
treatment of Gen. 3:22 in *PL*, 11.93–98, is intended to leave it to the reader "to
choose between . . . a God of Wrath or a God of Love." One's conception of God
is hardly a "thing indifferent."

veal but has instead "supprest in Night, / To none communicable in Earth or Heaven" (*PL*, 7.123–34). However, the questions themselves are blameless (*PL*, 8.66), and there is certainly God's plenty that human intelligence can and will come to a knowledge of. Some matters cannot be known apart from divine revelation, but "Anough is left besides to search and know" (*PL*, 7.125).

That Milton was centrally concerned with the believer's freedom to inquire into God's truth according to sound hermeneutical principles and with his reason guided by the Spirit is the underlying assumption of all the essays in this book. The foregoing discussions of scriptural influence on Milton's literary art skillfully trace some of the ramifications of Milton's convictions and exegetical methods. Michael Lieb describes Milton's brilliant amalgamation in *Lycidas* of a convention of classical pastoral elegy with a formulaic, prophetic utterance, resulting in the apotheosis of the elegy as well as of Lycidas himself: impermanent meanings of immortality for both men and poems are shaken off, and the permanent meaning is clarified. Leland Ryken demonstrates that central features of Milton's epic form result from prototypical models in Genesis, Exodus, and Revelation. Sister Christopher Pecheux identifies the Canaanite and Hebrew traditions that converge in Scripture to shape, ultimately, the council scenes, both infernal and heavenly, in *Paradise Lost*, while Harold Fisch reveals the relevance of the Book of Job and rabbinical tradition to the ironic relationships developed between the creation of an animate universe of life and the dark universe of death with which the epic opens. Michael Fixler follows Adam's movement upward toward God as an ascent moving on the twin scriptural tracks of knowledge and love, both of which culminate in the name of God. Stella Revard turns to *Paradise Regained* for evidence from the brief epic that the Johannine tradition of the manifest Son of God pervades Milton's characterization of Jesus and provides the framework for his dialectic with Satan. Finally, John Shawcross's investigation of Milton's individualistic doctrine of covenant, a doctrine neither neatly Calvinist nor wholly Arminian, illuminates important aspects of Milton's poetry.

In each of these analyses what stands out is Milton's freedom to experiment, to invent, to create; yet it is a freedom always extrapolated on a trajectory established by Scripture and scriptural tradition. The shift from lament to triumph in *Lycidas* reaches back to classical and scriptural formulaic utterance and points to future salvation. The classical ideal of heroism is stood on its head, and for the celebration of human achievement we find substituted the denigration of man's efforts and the exaltation of God. The epic poet does not merely narrate events on Olympus, he places himself in the council of the gods in the tradition of Micaiah and Jeremiah, adding to his poetic powers a prophetic stance. Hell becomes the opposite, a reversed mirror-image, of God's world of life and light. Adam ascends a Platonic ladder of love simultaneously with his growth in and transcendence of self-knowledge. Jesus constantly discerns his own identity and mission as well as his adversary's and personifies the complete Otherness of truth from falsehood; yet he allows Satan access to him and enjoys large leeway in his own trial-and-error approach to the discovery of truth. In *Paradise Lost* the first man and woman are filled with natural law and are free to experiment, to speculate, to acquire wisdom, unbound by covenant commitments until after the Fall. And, throughout these studies, we see that Scripture suggests what art creates, guides what imagination supplies, and makes aesthetically satisfying what structure concludes.

Such paradoxical firm anchoring in the text of Scripture and free sailing before the breath of the Spirit-Muse is only possible for a writer with convictions like Milton's. A magnificent creator of oxymorons, Milton never created a more breathtaking one than that in his lines epitomizing at once his conservative doctrinal position and his radically unique creativity within that conservative framework:

> the truth . . .
> Left only in those written Records pure,
> Though not but by the Spirit understood. (*PL*, 12.511, 513–14)

The truth is preserved in an external, objective text, but its meaning can only be known by the aid of an invisible, internal, and necessarily subjective Spirit! Once the individual has moved from opinion through knowledge to faith according to the dictates of his own conscience,

> on Earth
> Who against Faith and Conscience can be heard
> Infallible? (*PL*, 7.528–30)

About the Contributors

Harold Fisch is Professor of English and Comparative Literature at Bar-Ilan University, Ramat-Gan, Israel. Among his published works are: *Jerusalem and Albion: The Hebraic Factor in Seventeenth Century Literature* (1964), *Hamlet and the Word: The Covenant Pattern in Shakespeare* (1971), and an edition of Richard Overton, *Mans Mortalitie* (1968). He has written on Blake and Milton (in *William Blake: Essays for S. Foster Damon*, ed. A. H. Rosenfeld, 1969) and on Hebraic style in *Paradise Lost* (in *Language and Style in Milton*, ed. R. D. Emma and John T. Shawcross, 1967). He contributed the article on Hebraism for *A Milton Encyclopedia*. He has recently completed a book on archetypes to be entitled *A Remembered Future: A Study in Literary Mythology*. He is active in the field of Bible studies and has also written on several modern Hebrew writers.

Michael Fixler is Fletcher Professor of Rhetoric at Tufts University in Medford, Massachusetts. His published works include *Milton and the Kingdoms of God* (1964), and, as major articles in *Milton Studies*, *PMLA*, and elsewhere, the essential substance of a projected book to be called *The Cryptic Muse: Symbolic Form and Allusive Meaning in Milton's Poetry*. He contributed two major and several minor entries to the *Milton Encyclopedia* and has written on Yeats, Orwell, Berenson, and others. In 1973 he brought out the *Mentor Bible* and currently is revising for a new edition by Houghton Mifflin, the *Dartmouth Bible*. He has served on the editorial board of *Milton Studies* since its inception.

Michael Lieb is Professor of English at The University of Illinois, Chicago. His published works include *The Dialectics of Creation: Patterns of Birth and Regeneration in "Paradise Lost"* (1970) and *Poetics of the Holy: A Reading of "Paradise Lost"* (1981), as well as articles in *Milton Quarterly*, *Milton Studies*, *Studies in English Literature*, *ELH*, *Studies in Philology*, and *Harvard Theological Review*. His *Poetics of the Holy* received the James Holly Hanford Award of the Milton Society of America in 1982. Having

206

served as Treasurer of the Milton Society from 1973 to 1977, he was President of that organization in 1981. He is currently writing a book on the traditions of biblical prophecy.

Sister M. Christopher Pecheux, O.S.U. (familiar to Miltonists by her former title of Mother) was a member of the Ursuline Community in New Rochelle, New York, for many years and Professor of English at the College of New Rochelle from 1943 to 1981. Her writings include a book, *Milton: A Topographical Guide* (1981), and many articles in such journals as *Studies in Philology, Huntington Library Quarterly, Shakespeare Quarterly, Milton Quarterly, Milton Studies*, and *Contemporary Literature*. In addition, she contributed to *A Milton Encyclopedia* and to *Calm of Mind: Tercentenary Studies in "Paradise Regained" and "Samson Agonistes"* (1971). She served as a member of the executive committee of the Milton Society of America from 1970 to 1973. She died on 1 September 1982.

Stella P. Revard is Professor of English at Southern Illinois University, Edwardsville, where she teaches courses in both English Literature and Greek. Her book, *The War in Heaven: "Paradise Lost" and the Tradition of Satan's Rebellion* (1980), received the James Holly Hanford Award of the Milton Society of America in 1981. She has contributed articles on Milton and seventeenth-century literature comparative studies on Yeats and French Literature, Shelley, and Greek Literature to such journals as *PMLA, Modern Philology, Journal of English and Germanic Philology, Studies in English Literature, English Literary Renaissance, Papers on Literature and Language*, and *English Language Notes*. Currently at work on a book on the influence of Pindar on sixteenth- and seventeenth-century English poetry, she is serving as President of the Milton Society of America.

Leland Ryken is Professor of English at Wheaton College in Illinois. His books include *The Apocalyptic Vision in "Paradise Lost"* (1970), *The Literature of the Bible* (1974), *Triumphs of the Imagination: Literature in Christian Perspective* (1979), *The Christian Imagination* (1981), and *The New Testament in Literary Criticism* (1984). His scholarly articles have been published in *The Explicator, Huntington Library Quarterly, Tennessee Studies in Literature, Journal of English and Germanic Philology, Milton Quarterly, Christianity and Literature*, and *Christian Scholar's Review*. .

John T. Shawcross is Professor of English at the University of Kentucky. He is editor of *The Complete Poetry of John Milton* (rev. ed., 1971),

Language and Style in Milton (1967, with Ronald D. Emma), *Milton: The Critical Heritage* (2 vols., 1970, 1972), *Achievements of the Left Hand: Essays on Milton's Prose* (1974, with Michael Lieb), *A Milton Encyclopedia* (9 vols., 1978–1984, with William B. Hunter and John M. Steadman); compiler of *A Milton Bibliography, 1624–1700* (1984); and author of *With Mortal Voice: The Creation of "Paradise Lost"* (1982). In 1981 the Milton Society of America named him Honored Scholar in recognition of his distinguished contribution to Milton studies. He is completing a study called *The Self and the World: A Different Biography of John Milton.*

James H. Sims is Professor of English and Vice-President for Academic Affairs at The University of Southern Mississippi, Hattiesburg. His published works include *The Bible in Milton's Epics* (1962), *Dramatic Uses of Biblical Allusions in Marlowe and Shakespeare* (1966), and contributions to such journals as *Revue de Littérature Comparée, Comparative Literature, Shakespeare Quarterly, Milton Quarterly, Orbis Litterarum, Renaissance Papers*, and *Études Anglaises*. He wrote the article on the Bible for *A Milton Encyclopedia*, served as President of the Milton Society of America in 1976, and is an associate editor of *Seventeenth-Century News*. He is currently completing a book on the literature of the Old Testament entitled *The Shape of Scripture.*

Index

Index

Divine councils in *Paradise Lost*,
91–103
Dobbins, Austin C., 72*n*, 73
Doctrine and Discipline of Divorce, 160,.
163
Donne, John, 128*n*
Du Bartas, 48
Duncan, Joseph E., 162, 187

Eden, vii, 120, 132, 136, 188, 189,
197. *See also* Paradise
Elegia prima, 182
Elledge, Scott, 8
Emerson, Ralph Waldo, 30
Empson, William, 117, 118
Ephesians, Epistle to, 13, 119*n*, 162*n*,
184
Epitaphium Damonis, 181, 183
Epithets, 8
Erasmus, 192
Eve: mentioned, 7, 17, 88, 105, 113,
122, 123, 124, 128, 135, 136, 187–
90 *passim*, 197, 198, 200, 201; as
domestic heroine, 48–59, 69, 70;
and covenant, 162, 163, 169, 170,
188
Exodus: mentioned, 10, 47, 104,
119*n*, 143; as epic, 62–68, 79, 203
Ezekiel, 40, 82*n*, 167*n*, 168*n*

Ficino, Marsilio, 138
Fire imagery, 109–10
Fisch, Harold, 10, 27, 43*n*, 44, 54–55,
58*n*, 62*n*, 63, 203
Fish, Stanley, 67–68
Fixler, Michael, 6, 10, 12, 72–73, 203
Formulas: biblical, 12–13, 32–42; in
Milton's poetry, 13, 32–42; epic
formulas, 43–84 *passim*
Frye, Northrop, 12*n*, 14, 21, 22, 23,
50, 56, 57*n*, 73, 74
Frye, Roland M., 63

Genesis: mentioned, vii, 5, 7, 10, 47,
55, 56, 82, 105, 106, 108, 109, 110,
115, 165, 166, 168, 180, 194, 197,
202*n*; as epic, 53–59, 79, 203
Glass, Salomon, 34
Glatzer, Nahum N., 105

Gordon, Cyrus H., 53–54, 63
Gousset, Jacques, 34
Greene, Thomas, 58
Gregory, E. R., 45*n*
Gunkel, Hermann, 56

Habel, Norman, 58*n*
Haggai, biblical book of, 31, 32, 35,
39
Hagin, Peter, 44, 62, 169*n*
Haller, William, 52*n*, 53
Hart, Roy L., 5*n*
Heaven: mentioned, 8, 27, 75, 76,
121, 189, 191; council in, 87,
91–103; war in, 60, 65–66, 69–70,
71, 118, 196, 197, 201
Hebrews, Epistle to, 15, 17, 31, 32,
35, 39, 40, 41, 95, 164*n*, 165
Hell: mentioned, 75, 109, 110, 112,
113, 139, 204; council in, 87–90,
92, 93
Heresy, 178, 192
Herman, William R., 71
Hillers, Delbert R., 164
Hobsbaum, Philip, 5, 6
Homer, 26, 43, 48, 49, 51, 53, 54, 57,
59, 61–62, 77, 101, 102
Horace, 70
Hosea, biblical book of, 36*n*, 167*n*
Hughes, Merritt Y., 23
Hunter, G. K., 7
Hunter, William B., 179

Imagination: and the Bible, 3,
22–27; Milton's, 5–6, 12, 23–27,
116; and Milton's reader, 5–6; influenced by a poet's reading, 20
Ingalls, Jeremy, 53–54
Intertextual criticism, 20, 21, 45, 80
Isaac, 54, 55
Isaiah, biblical book of, 32, 36*n*, 41,
99–100, 101, 102, 103, 164, 165,
167*n*

Jacob, 54, 55, 56, 134
James, Epistle to, 8, 114
Jeremiah, biblical book of, 36*n*, 98,
99, 103, 164, 168*n*
Job, biblical book of: mentioned, 10,

Index

Radzinowicz, Mary Ann, 12, 44, 178*n*
Raleigh, Walter, 5
Raphael, viii, 13, 51, 58–59, 122, 130, 135–36, 139–40, 197, 199, 201–2
Rauber, D. F., 64
Ready and Easy Way, 178
Reason of Church Government, 11, 46, 47, 72, 75, 80, 137
Repetition: in the Bible, 6–7; in Milton's poetry, 6–7, 31–42 *passim*
Revard, Stella, 10, 17, 22, 72*n*, 203
Revelation, biblical book of: mentioned, 10, 32, 33*n*, 39, 40, 41, 46, 47, 137, 187, 188, 197; as epic, 72–79, 203
Richmond, Hugh M., 54, 61
Ricouer, Paul, 29
Ridenour, George M., 44
Riggs, William, 196–97
Robinson, H. Wheeler, 82*n*, 99, 102–3
Romans, Epistle to, 16–17, 181
Rosenblatt, Jason P, 58*n*, 59, 62*n*
Ross, James, 99
Ryken, Leland, vii, 71*n*, 203

Samson Agonistes, 9, 12, 15, 75, 104, 185–86
Samuel, First Book of, 33*n*
Samuel, Second Book of, 167*n*
Samuel, Irene, 50
Satan: in *Paradise Lost*, 16, 27, 51, 66, 87–94 *passim*, 113, 117–22 *passim*, 127, 139, 141, 171, 190, 191, 200; in the Bible, 78; in *Paradise Regained*, 136, 142–59 *passim*, 184, 185, 201, 203, 204
Schenck, Ferdinand S., 63
Schneidau, Herbert, 62
Schokel, Luis Alonso, 63
Scriptural tradition, definition of, vii, 18, 81, 193–94
Seaman, John E., 50
Shawcross, John, 10, 19, 21, 60*n*, 62*n*, 193, 201, 203
Simon, Ulrich, 57*n*
Sims, James H., 18, 21, 32, 43*n*, 46*n*, 58*n*, 66*n*, 101*n*, 107–8, 111*n*, 136, 142*n*

Sirluck, Ernest, 73, 198
Snow imagery, 110–12
Song of Solomon, 46, 53*n*, 194
Sonnets of Milton, 7, 9, 18, 26, 181
Spencer, T. J. B., 44, 51*n*
Spenser, Edmund, 20, 46, 61, 114
Steadman, John M., 44, 45, 47, 49, 61, 63, 67–68, 80, 114*n*
Style: biblical, 4–9, 25–26; Miltonic, 4–9, 25–26
Summers, Joseph, 51–52, 63, 68

Talbert, Charles H., 24
Tenure of Kings and Magistrates, 161, 174*n*
Tertullian, 127*n*
Theocritus, 32
Things indifferent, 198, 200, 202
Thompson, Elbert N. S., 44
Thompson, Francis, 26
Tillyard, E. M. W., 50, 59
Timothy, First Epistle to, 16
Tobit, 197
Toliver, Harold E., 49
Tolstoy, Leo, 53
Treatise of Civil Power, 161
Tur-Sinai, N. H., 105, 109

Upon the Circumcision, 180
Ursinus, Zacharias,163

Virgil, 26, 43, 48, 51, 54, 59, 61, 62, 63, 77, 102
Visionary literature as biblical genre, 13, 74

Watkins, W. B. C., 5*n*
Watt, Ian, 52
Webber, Joan, 47, 48*n*, 57, 61
Westermann, Claus, 38
Weiss, Johannes, 25
Wilder, Amos, 14, 47
Wilding, Michael, 45*n*, 51
Wilkie, Brian, 47
Wilson, Thomas, 34
Wittreich, Joseph A., Jr., 13, 32, 43–44, 72*n*, 73–74, 75, 77, 80
Wollebius, Johann, 167, 177
Woodhouse, A. S. P., 44, 71*n*

212